THE

EVERYTHING®
EASY FRENCH
COOKBOOK

Dear Reader,

If there's one thing I would like you to understand with this book, it's that French cuisine is easy. Since I moved to the United States, I have been amazed at how my native cuisine is too often seen as overly elaborate.

I was raised by women who were all very busy working, and still had time to prepare meals for their family to share and enjoy together. And guess what: They were not superwomen! They just inherited a great tradition that I'm happy to pass along to you now.

Now, before you start cooking, let me give you the best advice I was given, by my uncle Bernard, a great chef (and a great teacher!): Let the good ingredients do the job, and always take your time. *"Mijote, mijote, mijote."* Simmer, simmer, simmer. Just prepare it a day ahead and enjoy.

These 300 recipes are the ones every French family cooks at home on a regular basis. I hope you find as much pleasure in making them as I found in writing them. I was thinking of you trying to make them at home, miles and miles away from the small strange country where they were invented.

Bon appétit!

Cécile

Welcome to the EVERYTHING. Series!

These handy, accessible books give you all you need to tackle a difficult project, gain a new hobby, comprehend a fascinating topic, prepare for an exam, or even brush up on something you learned back in school but have since forgotten.

You can choose to read an Everything® book from cover to cover or just pick out the information you want from our four useful boxes: e-questions, e-facts, e-alerts, and e-ssentials.

We give you everything you need to know on the subject, but throw in a lot of fun stuff along the way, too.

We now have more than 400 Everything® books in print, spanning such wide-ranging categories as weddings, pregnancy, cooking, music instruction, foreign language, crafts, pets, New Age, and so much more. When you're done reading them all, you can finally say you know Everything®!

QUESTION

Answers to common questions

FACT

Important snippets of information

ALERT

Urgent warnings

ESSENTIAL

Quick handy tips

PUBLISHER Karen Cooper

MANAGING EDITOR, EVERYTHING® SERIES Lisa Laing

COPY CHIEF Casey Ebert

ASSISTANT PRODUCTION EDITOR Alex Guarco

ACQUISITIONS EDITOR Eileen Mullan

ASSOCIATE DEVELOPMENT EDITOR Eileen Mullan

EVERYTHING® SERIES COVER DESIGNER Erin Alexander

Visit the entire Everything® series at *www.everything.com*

THE
EVERYTHING®
EASY FRENCH
COOKBOOK

Cécile Delarue

Adams Media

New York London Toronto Sydney New Delhi

This book is dedicated to the women who first cooked for me and showed me the way: my grandmothers, Laurence and Georgine, and my mother, Danielle; to my Uncle Bernard, who taught me how to cook and how to love food; and to the two men I cook for every day: my husband, Olivier, and the little bun that patiently waited in my oven while I was writing this book.

Adams Media
An Imprint of Simon & Schuster, Inc.
57 Littlefield Street
Avon, Massachusetts 02322
Copyright © 2015 by Simon & Schuster, Inc.

An Everything® Series Book.
Everything® and everything.com® are registered trademarks of Simon & Schuster, Inc.

ADAMS MEDIA and colophon are trademarks of Simon and Schuster.

For information about special discounts for bulk purchases, please contact Simon & Schuster Special Sales at 1-866-506-1949 or business@simonandschuster.com.

The Simon & Schuster Speakers Bureau can bring authors to your live event. For more information or to book an event contact the Simon & Schuster Speakers Bureau at 1-866-248-3049 or visit our website at www.simonspeakers.com.

Cover and interior photos by Kelly Jaggers

Manufactured in the United States of America

10 9 8 7 6 5 4 3

Library of Congress Cataloging-in-Publication Data has been applied for.

ISBN 978-1-4405-8396-4
ISBN 978-1-4405-8397-1 (ebook)

Contents

Acknowledgments

Thank you to Adrien Sarre, from the French Consulate of Los Angeles, and his mom's great advice, and *merci beaucoup* to my two favorite readers, Olivier Bonnard and Denis Rossano, who were kind enough to read and proof this manuscript without even asking to taste all the 300 recipes, as they would have loved to (Denis, I know it was hard, and you know you can come anytime to have *cochonneries* at our table).

This book would not have been possible without the help all of my friends and family, who have patiently tried my cooking since my very first attempt at *Caramel* and *Chantilly* with my friend Melanie (sorry, *Papa,* for the burned pans) and my *Gâteau au Chocolat* experimentations with my brother Louis-Marie.

Merci aussi to the Adams Media team, who was crazy enough to trust me for this job, particularly Eileen Mullan.

Introduction

JUST SAY THE TWO words "French cuisine" and you probably instantly think of fine dining, wonderful meals, amazing chefs, and fabulous restaurants! Food lovers all over the world dream of going to *la belle France*, and the best cooks all try to spend some time learning the basics of the art of cooking in this beautiful country. For decades now, dozens of French chefs and French food enthusiasts have managed to convince the American people that there's a trick to the way the French cook and eat. But does it mean you have to be Julia Child to master it? Not at all!

Cooking in France is part of life, and as any good part of life, it has to be enjoyable and easy, from the beginning to the end. It's all about simplicity, authenticity, and *la gourmandise*, the love of good food.

Bien manger, eating well, is key to the way the French approach their daily life. Eating should never be thought of as a dull part of the day you have to get through quickly so you can go back to serious things like work. Breakfast, lunch, and supper are the three times in the day when you pay attention to yourself, and give your body and soul some time and energy.

There's no real "fast" food in the traditional French spirit, but that doesn't mean French cooking isn't efficient. Even with their endless *pause déjeuner* (lunch break) and five weeks a year of vacation time, the French still have one of the best productivity rates in the world! The same goes for cooking. Taking some time to make your dinner from scratch will allow you to unwind from the day, and feed yourself and your loved ones with more than just a sum of calories. *Bien manger* means eating something that tastes good, but that is also good for you, well balanced. *Bien cuisiner*, cooking well, follows the same rules: It means cooking well, not necessarily spending years in the kitchen.

If some French women seem to "have it all," it's not because they have good genes! It's because they have great food education. They were raised in a culture where you learn to make the best out of what you have, and try to enjoy it in moderation (no bingeing!). The average French home cook does not strive to be perfect, making complicated dishes while running a marathon on a treadmill! She (or he!) takes twenty minutes to prepare something wholesome that will be tasty and healthy for the family or the friends who are sharing the table, a meal you can finish without feeling bloated or stuffed.

What the French cook always tries to find is the now famous *petit je ne sais quoi*: the little thing that will suddenly change everything. It's a touch of spice, a dash of orange-blossom water, or just the best meat in town. And it makes all the difference.

Balance is key, as is using good ingredients. You will discover through this book that, as the French say, "Paris wasn't built in a day." French cuisine didn't emerge as the best in the world at the wave of a (hungry) magic wand. It was built through centuries of history, thanks mainly to its rich soils and good climate. That's how good wines, good meat, good vegetables, and therefore good meals are made, and that's how the French cuisine should be understood: trying to make the best out of what you have around you. It means cooking with fresh and in-season produce, and trying to find the best ingredients you can. *C'est tout!*

The 300 recipes of this book will show you how to create traditional French cuisine at home. You're about to discover that it's not that difficult, and always rewarding.

CHAPTER 1

Parlez-Vous French Cuisine?

France has been a symbol of great cooking for centuries now, and that is no different today. Some of the best chefs in the world are from, or live, in France, taking advantage of the country's fresh ingredients, classic cooking techniques, and an attitude of *Bien manger*, or eating well. But if the best chefs were born in France, it's because they had the best moms! Many French cooks learned at an early age to enjoy good food and company. In fact, the French are obsessed with eating, and they are proud of it. They can spend hours at the table, enjoying a great dish while talking about what they are going to eat the next day, or their latest cooking adventure. For French cooks, the love of food makes the meal.

History of French Cuisine

Gastronomy is so important to the French culture that it has recently been inscribed by UNESCO on its list of Intangible Cultural Heritages of Humanity! When did it all start? Was it in ancient Gaul, a few years before Christ, where Romans were said to love to come and taste the local "barbaric" cooking of what would later become France? In the Renaissance, when cooks would compete for the best use of strange spices coming from India? Or with Louis XIV, the Sun King, who loved to show off in his new Versailles Palace, and would throw epic dinners to impress people of the court or visiting royals from other countries? No one really knows. But one thing is certain: Good food has always been part of the French identity and DNA.

Evolution of French Food

In France, the past centuries have been spent turning a common need—you cook to eat, and you eat to live—into a complex and sophisticated art. Contemporary French cuisine started in the seventeenth century, when French chefs started to show their differences by refusing to cook like other chefs in Europe. They invented a technique for cooking that was as close to nature possible, with fewer spices and plainer, genuine flavors. That's also when they started inventing techniques that are still now part of the French cooking culture: broths, *roux*, hollandaise sauce, etc. Famous chefs wrote cookbooks so they could share their creations, some of which are still part of the daily cooking life in France: In *Le Cuisinier Français* (the French cook), published in 1651, François Pierre La Varenne explained how to make *feuilleté*, or puff pastry, for the first time, and in *Le Cuisinier* (The Cook) in 1656, Pierre de Lune shared his perfect herb mix, the *bouquet garni*, which is still mandatory in many good savory French recipes. That's also when the normal course of a dinner was defined: no more sweet and savory dishes served at the same time, as used to be the case.

ESSENTIAL

Most of the international words associated with eating actually come from the French language. You can go anywhere in the world, say "restaurant," "chef," or "croissant," and everyone knows what you mean.

Seventeenth-century French diners then started to develop an eating etiquette, which stated that you should never eat a savory dish and a sweet dish at the same time, as was the case at banquets during the Middle Ages. The new rule also stated that you should always start your meal with soup or an appetizer, followed by meat or fish, then dessert. This order is still followed religiously to this day!

New ingredients, vegetables and fruits, were shipped from America, and these new foods inspired chefs to invent new dishes with the very exotic potato, tomato, or pineapple.

The French art of cooking and eating flourished even more in the nineteenth century, which has been described as *le siècle d'or de la gastronomie*, or "the golden century of gastronomy."

Great French men like Jean Anthelme Brillat-Savarin and Georges Auguste Escoffier started writing about taste, recipes, and how to cook elaborate meals with the strangest elements, while great French women like *la mère Brazier* and *la mère Blanc* became famous chefs as they developed recipes and attracted people from all over the world to their small restaurants in Lyon, now considered the capital of gastronomy. La mere Brazier's *Poularde Demi Deuil* (a fat chicken cooked with black truffles) recipe is still a gastronomic legend.

French chefs began traveling all over the world, especially to the United States, where they invented new dishes, as Louis Diat did, one of the first celebrity chefs. Diat created his famous dish *Vichyssoise* not in Vichy, France, but at the Ritz-Carlton in New York.

Then came what was called *nouvelle cuisine*. In May 1968, when French youths invaded the streets of Paris for a month to protest against the government and a too conservative French society, throwing rocks at policemen and proclaiming "Be realistic, ask the impossible," another revolution was beginning in the best restaurants of the country.

Chefs were fed up with complicated, heavy sauces that used too much butter. They started to cook with reduced stocks in place of flour-thickened sauces, and tried to emphasize the flavor and pleasure of a fresh ingredient. Paul Bocuse, Alain Chapel, Michel Guérard, and Jean and Pierre Troisgros developed the idea that a good meal didn't mean an overflowing plate, and that you could find satisfaction in elaborate, tasty dishes that would rock your palate more than they would make your waistline explode.

French Cuisine Now

So what is the French cuisine like now? There's always someone saying that innovation in French cuisine is over. But French chefs like Joël Robuchon, Michel Bras, Alain Ducasse, Anne-Sophie Pic, or Iñaki Aizpitarte show their clients every day that they are still on top of the eating world.

Does it mean that French cuisine is a high-end luxury that most common people cannot afford, or that it's too hard to try it at home? Not at all. Over centuries, French home cooks have learned to develop a cuisine that is easy to prepare, great to share with your family, and not too expensive.

The French Pantry

Many things have changed since Julia Child returned from France and began cooking French food in the United States. The biggest and best change is that it is now easier to find ingredients that you need to cook classic French food.

French Staples

The following are some French staples that you should invest in before you begin cooking.

La Moutarde de Dijon

La moutarde de Dijon (Dijon mustard) can be found in every French refrigerator, just as ketchup is found in an American refrigerator. It might look like American mustard, but it is very different in taste: much spicier and less tart. The French cannot think of eating meat without a pot of Dijon mustard on the table. It's also a great ingredient to cook with, as you will see in this book, for pork or rabbit, for example.

Try to choose a real French brand, like Maille or Amora. Both brands are well distributed all over the United States now. Whole grain "ancient recipes" for Dijon mustard are also great for cooking a sauce or to serve with meats. You can get very elegant types of mustard, like the *moutarde d'Orléans*, or the violet mustard from Brive. (They should both be in your suitcase when you come back from traveling in France!)

Espelette Pepper

Le piment d'Espelette is a mild red chili pepper that is grown in the southwest of France, in the Basque country. It actually can only be produced in a very limited area of this region, and was first used only in Basque cuisine. But its discreet spiciness makes it a great ingredient in many French recipes, such as *Piperade* or *Pate de Campagne*. It's hard to find and quite expensive in the United States, but you can use paprika as a substitute.

Bouquet Garni

The "garnish bouquet" can be found in almost all recipes of savory slow-cooked dishes. It's a bundle of herbs, usually tied together with a string. There's no real list of ingredients that should be in it; it's mostly bay leaf, thyme, and parsley, but it can also contain rosemary, chervil, or tarragon. Some cooks put the herbs in a small sachet, like a tea bag, to be able to remove it afterwards. You can also just put the herbs in the pot and not worry about removing them; the flavor stays even longer. (Except, of course, for the bay leaf, which should be removed and never eaten.)

Onion and Clove

A great way to give flavor to savory dishes is often the onion and cloves. Peel the onion and insert four cloves in it, then add to the cooking broth for intense flavor that will wow all of your guests.

Stock

Chicken, beef, or vegetable stock is mandatory in a French cooking pantry. The French never use the liquid version, but always have a few boxes of bouillon cubes at home. It's a dehydrated version of the stock that is very convenient to use, almost as a regular spice. It is very useful for slow-cooking recipes and soups, and doesn't take much space in the pantry! The French also use it to give flavor to the water when cooking pasta or rice. Bouillon cubes are always salty, so try to add less or no salt when using one.

Cornichons

Forget about huge pickles: The French always think small! A bottle of *cornichons,* gherkins, is mandatory in every French refrigerator. These very small (around 1–2 inches) pickled cucumbers can now be found in American supermarkets pretty much everywhere you go. They are great to eat with *charcuterie* (meat products), *pot-au-feu* (beef stew), and are also great ingredients for some sauces.

Cooking Oil

Olive oil is used a lot in French cuisine, above all in *provençal* cuisine, but the French also believe that it's unhealthy to always use the same oil to cook. Sunflower oil (*huile de tournesol*) is used extensively for frying, walnut oil (*huile de noix*) is excellent in salads, and canola oil (*huile de colza*) is great used cold, in dressings, for example. Although canola oil has a bad reputation in the United States, it is seen as a great ally for good health in France, because of its high omega-3 content. Only use organic and/or extra-virgin canola oil.

Red Wine Vinegar

Vinegar is used daily in French cuisine. Red wine vinegar is the most commonly used (red wine was hard to preserve, and would turn easily into vinegar). Try to buy a bottle of good quality vinegar that isn't too sweet or too acidic. The *vinaigre à l'échalote*, red wine with shallots, is also great for *vinaigrette* and salads.

Duck Fat

Known as the butter from the southwest of France, duck fat gives incredible flavor to anything that cooks in it, and any inhabitant of southwest France will tell you that it's better for your health than other fats. (It's scientifically proven that they live longer and have less cardiac diseases than anywhere in France!) Beware, though: Fat is fat, and too much is never good!

Foie Gras

The liver of fattened duck or fattened goose is one of the tastiest traditions of French gastronomy. Canned *foie gras* is perfect for last minute fancy dinner, to be used on a *Tournedos Rossini*, or just as is, with sliced toasted bread and a good bottle of *Jurançon*, the sweet white wine that is produced in the Jurançon region southwest of France.

Crème Fraîche

French expats have the same first obsession when they come to the United States: finding a *crème fraîche*, or something that can be substituted for it without too much damage. The great thing is, some sorts of *crème fraîche* are now produced in the United States, and can be found in grocery stores like Trader Joe's, for example. For some recipes, Crema Mexicana is great to use, and easier to find on American shelves. Whipping cream can also be considered a substitute, for all recipes involving *crème fraîche liquide*, the liquid version of the crème.

Eau de Fleur d'Oranger

Orange blossom water is the secret of many pastries and desserts in France. It's a natural and simple way to perfume any dish with a sweet and soothing fragrance. Many French people who smell it will automatically talk about their mothers, and how great the kitchen smelled when she was preparing *crêpes* with just a tablespoon of *eau de fleur d'oranger*. A few drops of orange-blossom water in a bottle of water is also considered a great way to soothe a crying baby!

Crème de Marrons

This sweet chestnut spread is used a lot in easy recipes in France. It can be added to a bowl of yogurt or *fromage blanc*, or in a *crêpe*. It is hard to find in the United States, but it is relatively easy to make (see the recipe in this book!).

Wine

Always have a cheap bottle of red wine and white wine in your cupboard. Don't believe those who pretend that it's better to use an expensive wine like Chateau Latour to cook a *bourguignon*. They don't know very much about wine (Latour is a Bordeaux, and if you make a *bourguignon*, you'd better use Burgundy wine), and second, they don't respect good wine. A good wine must be sipped and shared, not cooked!

Cooking Equipment

There are many modern American kitchen gadgets that are very similar to the ones used in French kitchens. But some recipes call for a special instrument that may not be particularly common outside of France.

The Basics

French oven (Dutch oven): Call it Dutch if you want, but just buy one! A cast-iron pot was in every bride's trousseau when my mom got married, and she's still using her Le Creuset to this day. They are great to cook what French home cooks know how to do best: *mijoter,* slow cooking. Yes, they are expensive, but trust me, it's a great investment.

Ramekins are small ceramic bowls that can go in the oven. They are quite cheap, and can be used for very different recipes. You can put *pâté* or *rillettes* in them, and serve them directly to your guests. You can also cook *Œufs Cocottes* in them, serve sauces like *béarnaise* for *fondue bourguignonne*, and last but not least, they are very useful for making individual portions of mousse or *crème renversée*.

Useful, but Not Mandatory

Crêpe **pans** are incredibly helpful for new French cooks. Of course, you can try to make *crêpes* in a regular pan, but how can you play the flip-your-crêpe game with a heavy skillet? You can use a small, very light *crêpe* pan, and find it very useful for pancakes and crumpets, too.

A **fondue set** is more than just a creative gift bought for a friend's birthday that then stays in a box in their cupboard for years. A classic, simple ceramic set is not that expensive and can be used a lot! It's easy to plan a fondue night, and a great way to see friends and chat. This goes also for raclette sets.

The Typical French Meal

While modern life has taken its toll on some French traditions (yes, obesity is also increasing in France), there are still strong values in place that are essential to the French cuisine. When cooking your French meals, keep in mind that it's not all about the food. Sometimes, the people eating with you are just as important as how something tastes.

The Rules of French Dining

First, always eat together, and at the table. The elderly French would also add "and inside," because they considered having lunch in the garden to be vulgar. But apart from this tiny change (now French people love to eat *en terrasse*, on a café patio, for example, as soon as the sun allows it), most traditions have been kept throughout the years. Eating is the best moment of the day for everybody to relax together and share a nice moment of peace. And as the French popular saying goes: "It's something you have to do three times a day, every day of your life, so it better be great!"

Secondly, always eat at regular hours. People traditionally eat at very regular hours in France: noon for lunch, 7 P.M. for dinner in the countryside, 1 P.M. and 8 P.M. in big towns like Paris. Four o'clock in the afternoon is a time specifically loved by children. This is the hour of *goûter,* or snack. The hour is so strict that this afternoon snack is actually named after the time it's supposed to be taken: *quatre-heures,* or 4 P.M. French kids all know that there is no way they could snack before this wonderful time. And then suddenly, once it turns 4 P.M., chocolate and *Petits Pains au Lait* (Milk Buns recipe in Chapter 2) are at their reach! And they also know that they will not be able to eat anything again until dinnertime.

French adults have added another snacking time, right before dinner or lunch. It's called the *apéritif.* You have drinks (a beer, a glass of wine, a glass of Pastis) and savory things (peanuts, cold meats, cheese). It's a great way to have social time with friends, and a casual occasion. (You'd first invite new friends for *apéritif,* and then next time for dinner.)

Thirdly, you should always start with an *entrée*, an appetizer. (The French are always shocked at American menus calling a main dish the *entrée*! *Entrée* means "entering," it has to be at the beginning!) At lunch it's often *crudités*, or if it's a bigger occasion, *charcuterie*. At dinner, soups are appreciated, warm in winter and cold in summer.

You then have the *plat de resistance*, the main dish. Usually this dish is made up of meat or fish, with vegetables and whole grains. You should then follow with some cheese, of course. There are 30,000 types of *fromage* made in France! It usually comes with a green salad *en vinaigrette*.

Lastly, dessert. Of course, these rules all depend on what kind of occasions you're talking about. Dessert does not have to mean huge proportions. A dessert can be a fruit, cheese, or just a piece of camembert, and dinner could just be a great bowl of soup, a good piece of bread, and some applesauce. Just remember the two big rules of eating *à la française*: Take your time and enjoy it!

Basics of French Cooking

First things first: stop thinking that French food is fancy, and should therefore be hard to make. Of course, there are complicated dishes, but you don't need to be a four-star chef to cook French food on a daily basis!

The recipes in this book are not hard to follow, they just need three things:

- **Fresh ingredients.** Why try to cook strawberries in winter when pears and apples are at their best? Cooking food in season is healthier, more environment-friendly, and also means more flavor (don't get me started on these terrible winter tomatoes that never ever see true daylight and have no taste whatsoever). Of course, it reduces your options, but being limited has always been the best way to imagine new things! Try to go to the farmers' market, see what's in season this week, and cook with the best tools available: fresh and ripe vegetables!
- **Time.** Start thinking that time is on your side. Always take your time. Always simmer. Don't try to rush a *bourguignon*. Take 15 minutes a day ahead to prepare it, cover, and let it simmer gently for hours. *Mijoter*, that's the answer! Slow, slow cooking adds flavor naturally, and does the

job for you. And if you know there will be a time in the future when you'll be in a hurry, just cook twice as much as you need and freeze it!

- **Pleasure.** Try not to overdo it by preparing the most complicated appetizer, the most elaborate *plat de resistance,* and a crazy, difficult dessert. There is a chance you will slightly fail at one of the three (and you'll end up feeling terrible instead of enjoying your time with the people you wanted to see in the first place).

Try to focus on one dish, and go easy on the others. This is a great way not to overfeed your guests, and let them enjoy one little *chef d'œuvre.* They will always remember that time you did an amazing *cassoulet,* and also how relaxed and opened you were, sitting and chatting at the table with them.

CHAPTER 2

Petit Déjeuner (Breakfast)

Croissants

The iconic French breakfast pleasure! First thing on Sunday, Parisians line up at the boulangerie to buy croissants for the whole family, but the thing is, with a little time you can make them yourself!

INGREDIENTS | SERVES 6

⅓ cup whole milk

1 tablespoon baker's yeast

3 tablespoons sugar

2 teaspoons salt

7.5 ounces pastry flour

9 tablespoons butter, diced, at room temperature

2 egg yolks, beaten

Are Croissants French?

The first croissants were actually Austrian! There are many legends around its history, but the sure thing is that the recipe for the croissant we know today was developed in Paris. Croissants used to be more like a bun, and transitioned to the more familiar puff pastry dough in France.

1. Remove 2 tablespoons of milk from the ⅓ cup. In a small bowl, mix the 2 tablespoons of milk with the baker's yeast. Cover with a damp cloth and let it rest for 10 minutes.

2. In a large bowl, whisk the rest of the milk with the sugar and salt. Add the flour, then the baker's yeast mixture. Knead the dough, until combined. Cover with plastic wrap and leave the bowl in a warm room for 2 hours.

3. When it has doubled in size, knead the dough with your hands again; the dough should return to its previous size. Put it on a large parchment paper sheet. Shape it carefully into a ball. Using a knife, make a large cross incision about ⅛" deep on top of the ball. Using a rolling pin, roll it carefully until it's shaped like a star with 4 points, and about 1 inch high.

4. Put the butter in the middle. Fold the points of dough back toward the center over the butter, and flatten very gently, using a rolling pin. Roll until the dough is shaped in a rectangle, then fold it in three: Fold a first third over, then fold the two thirds over the third third. Roll it out again gently until you get a rectangle. Fold in three, wrap in plastic, and put in the refrigerator for one hour.

5. Repeat step 4 twice, and put back in the refrigerator for another hour.

6. Roll out the dough, until it's ⅛" thick. Using the tip of the knife, cut triangles of 5" and 6". Roll them up starting at the 5" base and put them on a baking sheet. Using a pastry brush, cover them with egg yolk. Keep at room temperature for one hour.

7. Preheat the oven to 350°F. Bake for 20 minutes.

8. Serve lukewarm or cold.

Pain au Chocolat (Chocolate Croissant)

French people love their pain au chocolat *so much that a popular singer even made a hit song about it! These are great for breakfast or for a goûter (snack).*

INGREDIENTS | SERVES 6

1 recipe Croissant dough (see recipe in this chapter)

24 squares of dark chocolate (Lindt 70%) or 1 cup chocolate chips

A Changing Name

Don't try to order a "chocolate croissant" next time you visit Paris. The name doesn't exist in France. *Croissant* stands for crescent moon, the shape of the pastry, and *pain au chocolat* is shaped like a rectangle. But depending on where you are in France, you'll order it differently: In the south, it's called a *chocolatine*.

1. Follow the croissant recipe up to the final time you remove it from the refrigerator. Roll out the dough and cut it into 5" × 13" wide rectangles.

2. Place 2 chocolate squares or 2 tablespoons chocolate chips at the center of a rectangle. Leave 1 inch of room at the bottom and the top of the rectangle. Fold the left third of the dough over the chocolate. Then add the same amount of chocolate on top of the folded part. Fold the right third of the dough over the chocolate.

3. Place a piece of baking parchment on a baking sheet. Put the *pains au chocolat* on the sheet. Using a pastry brush, spread the beaten egg yolks on the *pains au chocolat.* Leave at room temperature for 2 hours to rise.

4. Preheat the oven to 350°F. Brush egg yolk again on them again. Put in the oven and cook for 20 minutes.

5. Serve lukewarm or cold.

Pain Perdu (French Toast)

It always amazes French tourists visiting the United States to discover that their beloved pain perdu *is called French toast there. Back in France, it's mostly a leftover recipe, since most home cooks see it as a great way to use stale bread.*

INGREDIENTS | SERVES 4

4 large eggs

⅔ cup brown sugar, plus ⅓ cup to sprinkle after

1 teaspoon orange blossom water (if not, use vanilla extract)

1 cup whole milk

12 thick slices of whole-wheat bread, stale if possible

3 tablespoons butter

1. In a large bowl, whisk the eggs with the ⅔ cup of brown sugar and the orange blossom water. Whisk steadily until the mixture lightens in color, to a kind of white.

2. Pour the milk into another bowl. Dip each slice of bread first in the milk, then in the egg mixture. Lay them on a plate, and sprinkle all slices with the remaining brown sugar.

3. Heat a large nonstick skillet over medium-high heat. Melt the butter, making sure it doesn't brown. Fry the soaked bread in the pan, 2 minutes on each side. The slice should never stick to the pan, so don't hesitate to add butter. Serve immediately.

Pain Perdu Salé (Savory French Toast)

Because French toast doesn't have to be sweet, here is a savory recipe with dried porcini mushrooms.

INGREDIENTS | SERVES 4

3 tablespoons dried porcini mushrooms

4 large eggs

1 tablespoon Espelette pepper (or paprika)

1 cup whole milk

12 thick slices of stale bread

1 teaspoon salt

1 teaspoon ground black pepper

3 tablespoons butter

½ cup grated cheese

1. Put the dried mushrooms in a grinder or a blender and process for 30 seconds, until they become a powder. Break the eggs into a large bowl, and add the Espelette pepper or paprika. Add the dried mushroom powder, whisk well, and store in the refrigerator for a minimum of an hour.

2. Pour the milk into another bowl. Put each slice of bread first in the milk, then in the egg mix. Put all slices on a plate and sprinkle with salt and pepper.

3. Heat a large nonstick skillet over medium-high heat. Melt the butter, making sure it doesn't brown. Fry the slices in the pan, 2 minutes on each side. Don't hesitate to add butter. After flipping the slice, top with a tablespoon of grated cheese, and let the cheese melt. Serve immediately.

Chouquettes (Pastry Puffs)

In France, you would usually buy these funny round, sweet buns at the bakery to share at work in the morning with your colleagues.

INGREDIENTS | YIELDS AROUND 40 CHOUQUETTES

1 cup water
7 tablespoons butter, diced
¼ teaspoon salt
1 tablespoon sugar
1 cup flour
4 large eggs
1 cup pearl sugar

Temperature

As always when cooking pastry, it's easier to make this recipe with ingredients that are at room temperature. Try to take out the butter and the eggs an hour before, and keep them on the counter until you need to use them.

1. First, make the *pâte à choux*, a classic pastry dough. Pour the water into a medium saucepan, and bring to a boil over medium heat. Add the butter, the salt, and a tablespoon of sugar. As soon as it comes back to a boil, remove the pan from the heat.

2. Pour in the flour, and stir continuously with a wooden spoon. When the mixture is smooth, put the saucepan back on the stove over low heat, and stir until the dough no longer sticks to the spoon and the bottom of the saucepan.

3. Remove from the heat. Break the eggs in the saucepan, one by one, and stir well. The dough must be smooth, but not liquid.

4. Preheat the oven to 350°F.

5. Take 1 tablespoon of dough and make a small ball, then place it on a baking sheet lined with a sheet of parchment paper. Repeat. Make sure there's plenty of space between each ball, at least 1½" apart. Sprinkle 1 teaspoon of pearl sugar on each bun. Bake for 15 minutes.

6. Let cool before serving.

Baguette Viennoise au Chocolat (Chocolate Baguette)

This sweet baguette is sold either plain or with chocolate chips.

INGREDIENTS | YIELDS 3 BAGUETTES

⅔ cup whole milk (reserve 1 tablespoon)

1 packet (1½ tablespoons) of
  baker's yeast

4 cups flour

½ cup sugar

2 large eggs, beaten

¼ teaspoon salt

6 tablespoons butter, cut in small pieces,
  at room temperature

2 egg yolks, beaten

2 cups chocolate chips

The Austrian Influence

The French are always talking about *viennoiserie*, pastries from Vienna. There have been many morning pastries that have been inspired by eighteenth-century Austrian baked goods. Queen Marie Antoinette had an obsession for sweets: She was born an Austrian.

1. Take one tablespoon from the milk and put it in a small bowl with the baker's yeast. Combine well, then cover with a damp cloth. Keep in a warm room for 10 minutes.

2. In a large bowl, place the flour, the sugar, the remaining milk, the beaten eggs, and the salt. Add the baker's yeast mixture. First combine with a wooden spoon, then knead with your hands until the mixture is evenly textured.

3. Place the butter on the dough and knead again. Place the dough in the bowl of a stand mixer and knead for 10 minutes. Cover the bowl with a damp cloth, and leave at least one hour at room temperature, in a warm room.

4. When the dough has doubled in size, divide the dough in three. Flatten each piece, and roll it into a long *baguette*. With a pastry brush, spread the beaten egg yolks on the baguettes. Sprinkle each baguette with chocolate chips. Make sure there are chocolate chips on every side. Cover and leave for an hour in a warm room.

5. Preheat the oven to 350°F. Bake for 25 minutes.

6. Wait for the *viennoises* to cool, then enjoy them!

Petits Pains au Lait (Milk Buns)

These "little milk breads" are very simple and delicious. And quite healthy, too!

INGREDIENTS | YIELDS 6 *PETITS PAINS*

½ cup whole milk

1 packet (1½ tablespoons) of
  baker's yeast

2½ cups flour (divided)

2 tablespoons sugar

¼ teaspoon salt

6 tablespoons butter, cut in small pieces,
  at room temperature

¼ cup whipping cream

1 egg yolk, beaten

A Low-Cal Chocolate Croissant

Petits pains au lait are great with a good jam, or just plain at breakfast, but they are also "diet" *pain au chocolat*. It's common use in France to buy them at the *patisserie*, the pastry shop, with a bar of milk chocolate that you then stuff in the roll. Far less butter and fat than in the original version, and delicious too!

1. Pour the milk in a small saucepan, and place over low heat for a few minutes until it's lukewarm.

2. Pour the lukewarm milk into a large bowl and add the baker's yeast. Add 1 cup of flour, and stir well with a wooden spoon. Cover with a damp cloth, and leave in a warm room for half an hour.

3. Add the rest of the flour, the sugar, the salt, the butter, and the cream. Knead well with a stand mixer for 10 minutes. Cover with a damp cloth again and let rest in a warm room for 90 minutes.

4. Take some dough, the size of a small fist, and make small balls. With your fingers, roll each ball into a small baguette, the size of a hot-dog bun. Put them all on a parchment paper–lined baking sheet. Let rise for half an hour.

5. Preheat the oven to 350°F. Using a pastry brush, spread the beaten egg yolk on the buns. Bake for 20 minutes.

6. Wait for them to cool, and enjoy.

Brioche

It's not a bread, it's not a cake, it's something in between, and a delicious treat in the morning! Brioche is a classic petit déjeuner. You can slice it and spread jam on it, or just eat it plain.

INGREDIENTS | SERVES 4

2 cups flour

½ tablespoon salt

¼ cup sugar

1 tablespoon baker's yeast

4 large eggs at room temperature (divided)

9 tablespoons butter, at room temperature

⅓ cup sunflower oil

1 egg yolk

Let Them Eat *Brioche*!

Poor Queen Marie Antoinette went down in history as the first and only French queen to be guillotined, but also because of the famous quote she was supposed to have uttered when she was told Parisians were crowding the streets because they wanted bread. In fact, she never actually said, "Let them eat cake." She said "Let them eat *brioche*," which, as you'll see, is neither cake nor bread.

1. The day before making this treat, pour the flour, salt, sugar, baker's yeast, and two eggs into the bowl of a stand mixer. Use the knead utensil, and knead for 5 minutes.

2. Meanwhile, cut the butter in ½" cubes. Add half of the butter cubes to the stand mixer bowl, knead for 2 minutes, then add the other half and knead again for 2 minutes.

3. Wait for the dough to be smooth and even (it should not stick to the sides of the bowl anymore), and add the oil little by little. Don't stop the kneading. Add the other two eggs and knead again.

4. Let the *brioche* dough rest for 45 minutes at room temperature, covered by a damp cloth. Then knead it briefly again so that it returns to its previous size. Cover the bowl with plastic wrap and put in the refrigerator for 24 hours.

5. The next day, put the dough in a large meatloaf pan, or any regular rectangular pan. Beat the egg yolk in a small bowl, and spread it on the *brioche* with a pastry brush. Leave at room temperature for 2 hours. Preheat the oven to 300°F and bake for 30 minutes.

6. Unmold immediately and cut in ½" slices.

Gâche Vendéenne (Vendéenne Brioche)

This kind of smoother brioche is a tradition in Vendée, in the west of France, where it has been baked since the Middle Ages.

INGREDIENTS | SERVES 6

1 vanilla pod
½ cup whole milk
1 packet (1½ tablespoons) baker's yeast
2 eggs, beaten
3⅔ cups flour
1 teaspoon salt
½ cup sugar
½ cup butter, diced and at room temperature
2 tablespoons *crème fraîche* or whipping cream
1 tablespoon orange blossom water
1 egg yolk, beaten

Room Temperature

The secret of most baker's yeast–based recipes is being able to let the dough rise in a warm room. Professional bakers, who use their oven constantly, don't have this kind of problem, but if you have a harsh winter or your air conditioning is on, try to put the dough next to a heater, for example. Some people even put it under their duvet cover!

1. Slice outer layer of the vanilla pod in half lengthwise. In a small saucepan, add the milk and the sliced vanilla pod. Heat over medium heat and stop before it reaches the boiling point. Put aside.

2. Take 2 tablespoons of warm milk from the saucepan, and combine with the baker's yeast in a small bowl. Put a damp cloth on it and put in a warm room for 10 minutes.

3. Meanwhile, in a small bowl beat the 2 eggs with a fork. In the stand mixer bowl, pour the flour, the salt, sugar, the beaten eggs, and the butter, and knead for 10 minutes.

4. Take the vanilla pod out of the saucepan, put it on a flat surface, and scrape the inside of the pod with a paring knife. Add the vanilla milk to the stand mixer. Keep kneading and add the vanilla seeds, the cream, the yeast mixture, and the orange blossom water. Knead until the mixture is smooth.

5. Cover with a cloth and let it rise in a warm room for 6 hours. Then flatten the dough and put it in a large meatloaf pan, or shape it into a large roll that you lay on a parchment paper–lined baking sheet. Let it rise for another hour.

6. Preheat your oven to 350°F. Using a pastry brush, spread the beaten yolk on the surface of the dough. With a knife, cut a slit in the middle of the *gâche*. Bake for 30 minutes.

7. Serve with a nice jar of jam or hazelnut spread.

Fromage Blanc (Smooth Cottage Cheese)

The French not only love cheese, they love dairy products in general. At breakfast, women love their nice bowl of fromage blanc, with a few teaspoons of sugar, or honey, or jam, or Crème de Marrons (chestnut cream—see recipe in this chapter).

INGREDIENTS | SERVES 4

4 cups whole milk

4 drops of rennet (you can buy some easily online on cheesemaking websites)

Choose Your Milk

If you can, use raw milk straight from the farm. It is easier to have the milk curdle the way you want. Be sure to first bring the milk to a boil to kill all bacteria. Then leave it at room temperature, and use it when it has cooled down enough. You can also use 1% or 2% milk, but the resulting *fromage* is less smooth.

1. Pour the milk into a medium saucepan. Over medium-low heat, bring it slowly to a temperature of 95°F (measure with a thermometer).

2. Pour the milk into a large bowl, and add 4 drops of rennet. Cover the bowl with a cotton cloth and put in a room where the temperature is over 68°F for at least 12 hours.

3. After 12 hours, the milk should be curdled. Put a large strainer in a sink, cover it with a clean cotton cloth, and pour the curdled milk in the strainer.

4. Pour the strained solids slowly in a bowl, and put in the refrigerator. Serve in small bowls, with jam, honey, or *Crème de Marrons* (see recipe in this chapter). You can store it for 24 hours in the refrigerator.

Pâte à Tartiner aux Noisettes (Hazelnut Spread)

This chocolate and hazelnut spread is beloved by kids. It is perfect on a fresh baguette or with a sweet crêpe. And it is healthier than Nutella, which is full of palm oil.

INGREDIENTS | YIELDS 2 (12-OUNCE) JARS OF SPREAD

1 cup whipping cream

2 tablespoons sugar

1 cup dark chocolate chips

7 ounces hazelnut paste

1½ tablespoons sunflower oil

1. Pour the cream and the sugar into a medium saucepan. Bring to a boil over medium heat. Stir well as it's heating up.

2. In a large bowl, pour the chocolate chips and the hazelnut paste, and stir with a wooden spoon. Pour the boiling cream and sugar mixture on top. Stir well, then add the oil. Stir steadily until the mixture is smooth and combined. Pour into the jars, and let cool.

3. After 1 hour, store in the refrigerator. This spread should be taken out of the refrigerator and left to rest at room temperature for 30 minutes before using it.

Confiture de Fraises (Strawberry Jam)

Strawberry jam is on every French table at breakfast, for the most traditional national petit déjeuner: simple baguette with butter and jam.

INGREDIENTS | YIELDS 8 (12-OUNCE) JARS OF JAM

4 pounds strawberries, cut in half
4 cups white sugar
Juice of ½ lemon

Jam Paradise!

If you spoon out the small foam that can appear at the top of the saucepan, put it on a plate and let it cool. This sweet mousse is loved by kids. In France, this special treat is sometimes called *le paradis*, paradise.

1. In a large bowl, put the halved strawberries with the sugar and the juice of half the lemon. Stir to combine. Cover with plastic wrap and leave for at least 12 hours.

2. In a heavy-bottomed saucepan (in copper if possible, but you can use a French/Dutch oven, for example), pour the strawberries mixture and bring slowly to a boil over medium-low heat. Stir well with a wooden spatula.

3. When bubbles start appearing, take the strawberries out of the pot with a slotted spoon, and put them back in the large bowl.

4. When the sugar mixture reaches 220°F, or the "pearl moment" (a drop of the jam keeps its round shape on a cold plate), put the strawberries back in the saucepan. Stir well and cook for 15 minutes on very low heat. Then take the pot off the heat and pour the jam into jars, leaving ½" headspace on top before sealing.

5. Put the jars head down and let them cool for a few hours before storing or tasting the jam.

Chocolat Chaud (Hot Chocolate)

Hot chocolate is a traditional part of a kid's breakfast in France, but it has been "stolen" by adults who love to drink it to warm up winter mornings and rainy afternoons. Here is the most traditional version of the recipe. It's a bit bitter, but nonetheless delicious!

INGREDIENTS | SERVES 2

1½ cups water

1 pound dark (black) chocolate (such as Valrhona, Lindt) in chocolate bars, chopped

2 cups whole milk

A Queen's Delicacy

Hot cocoa was first served in France at the palace of Versailles, under the reign of Louis XIV. Queen Marie-Thérèse was very fond of it, and ordered all her maids to prepare some for her every day. You could only have it in Versailles, and if you were part of the court. At the time, some doctors said it could cure diseases, and that it was an aphrodisiac.

1. In a small saucepan, bring the water to a boil over high heat. Pour in the chocolate. Reduce the heat to its lowest setting and stir well, until the mixture is smooth.

2. Fill a larger saucepan about halfway with water. Bring to a boil over high heat, then reduce to low. Put the smaller chocolate saucepan in the water, so it stays at a good temperature.

3. Pour the milk in another saucepan. Place the pan over medium heat, and remove the pan just before the milk boils.

4. Pour the milk into a small serving pitcher.

5. Serve in cups. Fill a cup to the halfway point with the chocolate, and add hot milk from the jug, depending on how strong you like your hot chocolate.

Crème de Marrons (Chestnut Cream)

This chestnut spread is usually bought from the store, but if you have some time, you can make it at home. It's used in a lot of desserts, and is delicious at breakfast with fromage blanc, yogurt, or crêpes.

INGREDIENTS | YIELDS 2 (12-OUNCE) JARS

1 pound chestnuts, peeled (about 2 pounds unpeeled)
1 vanilla bean
½ pound sugar
2 cups water

A Nineteenth-Century Tradition

Crème de marrons was originally invented in 1885 by a manufacturer who was making *marrons glacés*, candied chestnuts, and wanted to use all the leftovers to make something else. The original recipe featured part chestnuts purée, part candied chestnuts.

1. Fill a large saucepan with water, bring to a boil, and put the chestnuts in it for 20 minutes. Drain them, then pour the chestnuts into a blender, and process until smooth.

2. Slice top outer layer of the vanilla pod in half lengthwise. Pour the sugar, the vanilla pod, and the 2 cups of water in another saucepan. Put over medium-low heat and simmer for 5 minutes, stirring often. Add the chestnuts to the saucepan; stir well, then reduce the heat to low and simmer for 20 minutes.

3. When the mixture sticks to your wooden spoon, remove from heat, and pour it in jars.

4. Seal the jars and put them upside down for a day if you want to store them (about 1 year). Put in the refrigerator and let it cool down at least 2 hours before using.

Œufs Mouillettes (Boiled Eggs)

The French are not very into eating eggs or savory things at breakfast. But there's one egg dish that they love to eat first thing in the morning: this œuf à la coque mouillettes.

INGREDIENTS | SERVES 4

4 slices of whole wheat bread

2 tablespoons butter

2 slices of prosciutto or *jambon blanc* (ham)

6 eggs

A Dip Breakfast Culture

The runny soft-boiled egg of *œufs à la coque* are a big symbol of how French love to dip bread in things in the morning. Most people love to dip their jam or butter bread *baguette* slices in their morning coffee or tea!

1. Toast the slices of bread, then spread butter on them. Cut them in long sticks about ½" wide. They are called *mouillettes*, because you are going to wet them (*mouiller*) by dipping them in the egg.

2. Cut the ham slices into ½" strips, and lay them on the sticks of buttered toast.

3. Fill a large saucepan with water and bring to a boil over high heat. With a tablespoon, plunge the eggs in the boiling water and leave them for 4 minutes.

4. Fill a large bowl with ice water. When the eggs are boiled, transfer with a slotted spoon to the ice water for 10 seconds.

5. Put an egg in an egg cup, and use a knife to cut off the top of the egg.

6. Serve the egg cups with the *mouillettes* to dip into the soft-boiled eggs.

CHAPTER 3

Entrées (Appetizers)

Escargots (Snails)

There's only one real thing to know about cooking escargot: The secret is in the butter.

INGREDIENTS | SERVES 4

½ pound butter

1 medium shallot, peeled and diced

2 garlic cloves, peeled and diced

3 tablespoons chopped parsley

1 teaspoon salt

1 teaspoon ground black pepper

24 snails (generally in cans of 12, so 2 cans)

24 snail shells

½ cup white wine

An *Entrée* is Not an *Entrée*!

A French tourist in the United States might be very confused while reading an American menu: *Entrées* are not main dishes in France, but starters.

1. Take the butter out of the refrigerator, cut it in small cubes, and keep at room temperature for at least 30 minutes.

2. Put shallot and the garlic cloves in a blender. Add the parsley, the salt and the pepper, and the butter. Process for 1 minute, until you get a smooth butter. Place in the refrigerator for 20 minutes.

3. Preheat the oven to 450°F.

4. Wash and dry the snails. Spoon out a full teaspoon (about the size of bean) of the flavored butter, and put it inside a snail shell. Put the snail in, then cover with another spoonful of flavored butter again: The shell must be totally full. Repeat for each snail shell.

5. Put the snail shells in a baking pan (or even better, in a special *escargot* pan if you own one!). Pour the white wine into the bottom of the pan, then put in the oven. Bake for 8 minutes.

6. Serve them immediately, in the pan, very hot, with bread to dip in the sauce.

Escargots aux Tomates Cerises (Snails with Cherry Tomatoes)

This version of snails with cherry tomatoes is more modern and a perfect start for summer dinner. It's also great for apéritif, or cocktail hour.

INGREDIENTS | SERVES 4

24 cherry tomatoes, halved

2 teaspoons salt, divided

1 medium shallot, peeled and diced

2 garlic cloves, peeled and diced

3 tablespoons chopped parsley

1 teaspoon ground black pepper

½ pound butter, diced, at room temperature

24 snails (generally in cans of 12, so 2 cans)

¼ cup breadcrumbs

1. Put the halved tomatoes on a plate, and sprinkle with one teaspoon of salt on the cut side. Turn the halves face down, so that the juices get out.

2. Preheat the oven to 350°F. Peel the shallot and the garlic cloves. Dice them and put them in a blender. Add the chopped parsley, 1 teaspoon salt, 1 teaspoon pepper, and the butter. Process for 1 minute until you get a smooth butter, then put in the refrigerator for 20 minutes.

3. Spoon out a teaspoon of the butter, and wrap it around the snail, making a ball. Put in a cherry tomato half. Repeat for 11 more cherry tomato halves.

4. Put the tomatoes in a baking pan. Sprinkle bread crumbs all over. Place the 12 remaining cherry tomato halves on each snail-filled tomato, like little hats. Bake for 15 minutes.

5. Serve them immediately, in the pan, very hot, with toothpicks to pick them up.

Harengs Pommes à l'Huile (Herring and Potato Salad)

You can find this marinated herring and potato salad on the menu of any good Parisian bistrot.

INGREDIENTS | SERVES 4

2 pounds small potatoes

2 teaspoons salt, divided

2 teaspoons ground black pepper, divided

4 tablespoons white wine vinegar (or cider vinegar)

6 tablespoons canola oil

2 tablespoons white wine

8 smoked herring fillets in oil, drained

1 big red onion, peeled and thinly sliced

1 tablespoon chopped chives

1. Fill a large saucepan with water. Add the unpeeled potatoes and bring to a boil over high heat. Boil for 20 minutes.

2. In a medium bowl, prepare a vinaigrette dressing by combining 1 teaspoon salt, 1 teaspoon pepper, and the vinegar. Stir well, then add the oil, tablespoon by tablespoon, stirring vigorously.

3. With a slotted spoon, take the potatoes out of the saucepan and peel them immediately. (Be careful! They will be very hot.) Put them in a large bowl. When they are all peeled, pour the white wine over them, and sprinkle 1 teaspoon of salt and 1 teaspoon of pepper. Toss well.

4. Add the onion slices to the potatoes, pour in the vinaigrette dressing, and toss well. Lay 2 herring fillets on each plate, and add a serving of potatoes and red onions. Sprinkle chives on the potatoes, and repeat for other plates.

5. Serve immediately, while the potatoes are still lukewarm.

Poireaux Vinaigrette (Leeks Vinaigrette)

Another bistrot classic, and a great way to cleanse your system (leeks have a very diuretic effect). The poached egg is a great protein option.

INGREDIENTS | SERVES 4

8 medium leeks
1 teaspoon salt
1 teaspoon ground black pepper
1 teaspoon Dijon mustard
4 tablespoons red wine vinegar
1 shallot, peeled and diced
6 tablespoons canola oil
2 tablespoons white vinegar
4 large eggs, very fresh

1. Soak the leeks in cold water, heads down, to take out all the sand. Then dry them and cut off the green parts. Fill a large saucepan with cold water, bring to a boil, then plunge the remaining white part of the leeks in boiling water. Reduce to a simmer and cook for 25 minutes.

2. In a medium bowl, combine the salt, the pepper, the Dijon mustard, and the vinegar.

3. Add the shallot to the boiling water. Stir well, then add the canola oil, tablespoon by tablespoon, stirring vigorously.

4. Fill another saucepan with water, add the white vinegar, and bring to a boil over very high heat. Break your eggs into the boiling water one by one, using a tablespoon to shape each into a ball. Cook for 3 minutes. Prepare a medium bowl of ice cubes. Using a slotted spoon, take the eggs out and lay them on the ice cubes.

5. When the leeks are cooked, drain them and slice them in half. Put 4 halves of lukewarm leeks on each plate. Sprinkle the Dijon and vinegar dressing on them. Then put an egg on top.

6. Serve immediately, and enjoy the "cracking" of the poached egg over the lukewarm leeks!

Pâté de Campagne (Country Pâté)

A good baguette and some great pâté can make an awesome lunch. But this popular charcuterie is mostly eaten as an appetizer.

INGREDIENTS | SERVES 8

½ pound pork belly

¼ pound beef or chicken liver

1 shallot, peeled and diced

1 tablespoon salt

1 tablespoon ground black pepper

1 tablespoon Espelette pepper (or paprika)

3 pounds sausage meat

1 tablespoon thyme plus 6 stalks of fresh thyme

1 tablespoon chopped parsley

3 fresh bay leaves

Charcuterie Etiquette

French *charcuterie* is usually served with a good baguette, a pot of *cornichons* pickles, and good butter. Some people like to spread butter on the bread, then spread pâté, and add *cornichons* on top, making a French sandwich.

1. Chop the pork belly and the liver in small pieces. Put them in a blender. Process for 1 minute. Add diced shallot to the blender. Add salt, pepper, and Espelette pepper. Process for another minute.

2. In a large bowl, combine the sausage meat with the pork belly and liver mixture. Add thyme and diced parsley. Mix everything with your hand.

3. Press the mixture into a meatloaf pan. Place bay leaves and fresh thyme stalks on the top of the meat. Cover with plastic wrap, and leave in the refrigerator for 24 hours at least.

4. The next day, preheat the oven to 360°F. Pour cold water in a very large baking pan (to a depth of about 1"). Remove the plastic wrap and place the meatloaf pan in this baking pan. Cook for 90 minutes.

5. Serve cold.

Rillettes de Porc (Pork Spread)

This dish may take seven hours of simmering, but this pork spread makes the best baguette sandwich ever, and a great appetizer as well.

INGREDIENTS | SERVES 10

4 pounds pork shoulder, rind cut off and reserved

3 pounds pork belly, rind cut off and reserved

4 tablespoons salt

2 tablespoons ground black pepper

3 bay leaves

2 tablespoons thyme

1. Chop the pork shoulders in big chunks. Cut the pork belly in ½"-wide strips.

2. Put a large French oven (or any cast-iron pot) over medium-high heat. Brown the pork belly in it for 2 minutes, then reduce the heat to medium-low and allow the meat to soften slowly. Add the chunks of pork shoulder and stir well. All sides should get slightly brown. Cook the meat for about 15 minutes.

3. Cover with cold water, put the lid back on the pot, and cook on medium heat for 1 hour, stirring often.

4. Add salt, pepper, bay leaves, thyme, and the pork belly rind. Reduce the heat to the lowest level, and simmer for 6 hours.

5. After the full 7 hours of cooking, remove and discard the rind and the bones. Turn off the heat and let the pot cool at room temperature. When the pot is cold enough, the fat should float over the meat. Using a spoon, skim the fat out and put it in a separate bowl. Then stir the meat with a wooden spatula. Pour the meat into ramekins. Cover them with plastic wrap and put in the refrigerator for 24 hours.

6. Serve cold, with *cornichons*, bread, and butter, or in a sandwich.

Rillettes de Lapin (Rabbit Spread)

Yes, it's a rabbit spread, which means it's low in calories and delicious!

INGREDIENTS | SERVES 6

1 (3-pound) rabbit
½ pound duck fat
1 large onion, peeled and thinly sliced
2 tablespoons thyme
1 bay leaf
1 tablespoon rosemary
2 cups white wine
1 tablespoon salt
1 tablespoon ground black pepper

1. Chop the rabbit in big chunks.

2. Put a large French oven (or any cast-iron pot) over medium-high heat, and melt the duck fat. Add the onion slices, stirring well in the fat (they must soften, but not get too brown, about 5 minutes). Add the rabbit parts, and brown them on each side. Add the thyme, the bay leaf, and rosemary, and stir well. Cook slowly for a total of 10 minutes.

3. Pour the white wine all over the meat and the onions. Bring to a boil over high heat. Add salt and pepper. When the wine boils, add enough water to cover the ingredients. Bring to a boil again. Then, at boiling point, reduce the heat to the lowest level. Cover the pot. Simmer for at least 4 hours.

4. With a fork, shred the meat in pieces and remove the bones from the flesh. The meat should shred very easily. Pour through a strainer if there still is liquid in the pot. Discard the liquid. Put the meat in a large bowl and stir it with a fork till the mixture is even and smooth.

5. Place the meat in a meatloaf pan or in small ramekins. Cover them in plastic wrap and put in the refrigerator for 24 hours.

6. Remove bay leaf and serve cold, with *cornichons*, bread, and butter.

Rillettes de Saumon (Salmon Spread)

*This recipe has been seen a lot in the last decades in France,
offered as a healthier alternative to pork rillettes!*

INGREDIENTS | SERVES 4

1½ pounds fresh salmon fillets, with no skin

2 large egg yolks

2 tablespoons olive oil

1¼ cups plain yogurt

Juice of ½ lemon

5 ounces smoked salmon, diced

6 tablespoons salted butter, diced, at room temperature

2 tablespoons chives, minced

1 teaspoon salt

2 teaspoons ground black pepper

1. Fill a large saucepan with water, bring to a boil over high heat, then poach the salmon fillets in the water for 8 minutes. Take them out with a slotted spoon and put them in the refrigerator for 15 minutes.

2. Dice the smoked salmon slices into pieces of about ½". In a medium bowl, whisk the egg yolks, the olive oil, yogurt, and the lemon juice.

3. In a large bowl, crumble the poached salmon with your fingers. Take the bones out.

4. Add the smoked salmon and use a fork to combine with the poached salmon. Add the butter, the minced chives, and salt and pepper, and combine well with the fork. Add the egg yolk and yogurt mixture. Stir well.

5. Pour into a meatloaf pan, or into small ramekins. Wrap in plastic wrap and put in the refrigerator for 12 hours.

6. Serve cold with toasted bread.

Gougères de Bourgogne (Cheese Puffs)

These delicious cheese puffs were created in Burgundy. They make a great hors d'oeuvre before serving Bœuf Bourguignon (see recipe in Chapter 10). They are also a treat at cocktail hour with a nice glass of Champagne!

INGREDIENTS | SERVES 8

1 cup water
½ teaspoon salt
4 tablespoons butter
1 cup flour
3 large eggs, beaten
2.5 ounces Gruyère cheese (or aged Cheddar), cut in ½" cubes

1. Preheat the oven to 400°F.

2. In a medium saucepan, place the water, salt, and the butter. Bring to a boil over high heat. Stir well. When water has reached the boiling point, pour in the flour immediately. Stir very steadily with a wooden spatula. Reduce the heat to medium-low. Stir again for about 2 minutes or until the mixture is smooth. The dough should dry slightly.

3. Take the saucepan off heat and let it cool a little, then pour the beaten eggs over the dough. Stir well, never stopping. Beat it vigorously until the mixture is really smooth, but not too thick.

4. Add the cheese cubes and beat well for 2 minutes at least, until the cheese melts in the dough.

5. Using a tablespoon, make small balls of dough and put them on a parchment paper–lined baking sheet. Bake for 25 minutes, or until the *gougères* are golden.

6. Serve lukewarm.

Gâteau de Foies de Volailles (Chicken Liver Cake)

This chicken liver cake is a great tradition in Lyon, and one of the reasons why the town is considered the French capital of gastronomy.

INGREDIENTS | SERVES 4

1 tablespoon olive oil

1 (28-ounce) can of diced tomatoes

1 bay leaf

1 tablespoon thyme

1 teaspoon salt

1 teaspoon ground black pepper

1 cup whole milk

2 slices of bread

1 medium onion, peeled and diced

1 garlic clove

2 tablespoons parsley

3 chicken livers

3 large eggs, white and yolks separated

1. In a medium saucepan, heat a tablespoon of olive oil over medium heat. Pour in the diced tomatoes and their juice, the bay leaf, the thyme, salt, and pepper. Stir with a wooden spatula, and cook slowly for about 10 minutes, stirring often. Remove bay leaf. Reduce the heat to low, cover, and simmer until serving.

2. In a small bowl, pour the milk; soak the bread in it. Then take out the bread and put it in the blender. Discard the milk. Add onion, garlic, and parsley to the blender. Process for 30 seconds. Add the chicken livers and process for 1 minute.

3. In a large bowl, pour the chicken liver mixture. Add 3 yolks, and stir again.

4. Preheat the oven to 350°F. Butter a large baking pan.

5. In a bowl, beat the egg whites until the whites hold firm peaks, and then add them to the mixture, stirring slowly.

6. Pour the mixture into the baking pan and bake for 50 minutes. Serve lukewarm, with the tomato sauce on the side in a gravy boat.

Asperges Blanches en Sauce Laurence (Asparagus in Light Sauce)

White asparagus are the symbol of spring at a French greengrocer. They are very low in calories and great in flavor. Enjoy them by dipping them in a vinaigrette dressing, or this very light sauce.

INGREDIENTS | SERVES 4

2 pound white asparagus, peeled, with bottoms trimmed

⅔ cup *crème fraîche* (or Greek yogurt, for a low-calorie recipe)

1 teaspoon salt

2 teaspoons ground black pepper

2 tablespoons chives, chopped

2 tablespoons red wine vinegar

1. Fill a very large saucepan with cold water. Bring to a boil over high heat. When the water boils, add the asparagus. Cook for 20 minutes.

2. Meanwhile, prepare the *sauce Laurence*. In a medium bowl, combine the *crème fraîche*, salt, pepper, and the chives, and stir well. Add the red wine vinegar and stir again, until the sauce gets evenly mixed. Pour in small individual bowls.

3. With a slotted spoon, remove asparagus from pan, dry them a little, and lay them all on a large rectangular plate.

4. Serve the asparagus lukewarm. You can either eat them with a fork and knife or savor them "family style," by grabbing the asparagus like a stick and dipping it in sauce.

Maquereaux au Vin Blanc (Mackerel in White Wine)

Mackerel marinated in white wine is a very popular appetizer. And very healthy!

INGREDIENTS | SERVES 4

1 bottle of white wine (Sauvignon blanc)

1 onion, medium, peeled and diced

2 carrots, peeled and thinly sliced

¾ cup cider vinegar or white wine vinegar

2 bay leaves

2 tablespoons thyme

3 cloves

1 teaspoon red chili peppers

1 teaspoon salt

2 teaspoons ground black pepper

1 lemon

2 mackerel fillets

1 pound small potatoes

1. In a medium saucepan, pour the white wine. Add the onion slices, the sliced carrots, vinegar, bay leaves, thyme, cloves, red chili peppers, and salt and pepper. Bring to a boil over high heat. Cover and reduce the heat to its lowest setting. Simmer for 20 minutes.

2. Preheat the oven to 350°F. Cut the lemon into thin slices and reserve. Take a baking dish, and lay the fillets in it. Cover them with the lemon slices. Pour the white wine reduction over them. Put in the oven and cook for 10 minutes. Remove from the oven, let it cool, then cover the pan in plastic wrap and put in the refrigerator for 12 hours.

3. The next day, fill a large saucepan with cold water, and plunge the small potatoes (unpeeled) in it. Bring to a boil and cook for 20 minutes. Serve the cold mackerel fillets with the boiled potatoes.

Soufflé au Fromage (Cheese Soufflé)

Cheese soufflé is a big symbol of French cuisine. It has also caused stress and anxiety for hundreds of French home cooks who have seen it "fall" before the guests arrive. Try to put it in the oven exactly 30 minutes before serving!

INGREDIENTS | SERVES 4

2 cups whole milk

8 tablespoons butter

4 ounces flour, plus 1 tablespoon for the dish

1 teaspoon ground nutmeg

1 teaspoon salt

1 teaspoon ground black pepper

6 large eggs, whites and yolks separated

5.5 ounces cheese (Gruyère, Cheddar, Comté), diced

Soufflé Secrets!

Make sure that your egg whites are firm enough by putting a teaspoon in them. When you do this, a spoonful of the beaten egg whites should keep their shape when scooped up. After buttering the dish, pour a tablespoon of flour in it, shaking the dish to make sure the flour spreads everywhere inside. Do not touch the inside of the dish after that. And most importantly, *never* open the oven while it's baking.

1. In a medium saucepan, bring the milk to a boil over medium heat.

2. Melt the butter in a large saucepan over medium-low heat. Pour in the flour and stir immediately, until it combines with the butter in a thick mixture. Season with the nutmeg, salt, and pepper. Slowly pour in the boiled milk, stirring constantly until the sauce is smooth and thick.

3. Remove from heat and let the sauce cool down. Then add two egg yolks and stir well. Add the cheese cubes and stir again. Add two more egg yolks and stir until smooth, then add the last two egg yolks, still stirring.

4. Preheat the oven to 375°F.

5. Using a handheld electric or stand mixer, beat the egg whites until they are very firm. Add them slowly to the egg and cheese mixture: First pour in a third, stir carefully, then add another third, and the last one, always very slowly.

6. Butter and flour a round 8" and 3" deep dish (preferably ceramic). Pour in the mixture and bake for 30 minutes, or until the top browns slightly.

7. Serve immediately.

CHAPTER 4

Œufs (Egg Dishes)

Œufs Mimosa (Deviled Eggs)

You may say deviled eggs, but the French say œufs mimosa. Named after the yellow flowers, these simple eggs are perfect to start a lunch or on a buffet table.

INGREDIENTS | SERVES 6

8 large eggs
½ cup mayonnaise
4 tablespoons diced chives
1 teaspoon salt
1 teaspoon ground black pepper

1. Fill a large saucepan with water, bring to a boil over high heat, and add the eggs. Prepare a bowl of ice water. Boil the eggs for 10 minutes, then remove the eggs to the ice water bath.

2. Peel the eggs and cut them in half lengthwise. Spoon out the egg yolks into a small bowl and mash them with a fork. Mix ⅔ of the mashed egg yolks with the mayonnaise, half the chives, salt, and pepper. With a teaspoon, fill each boiled egg half with the mayonnaise-yolk mixture.

3. Sprinkle the last third of the mashed egg yolks and the chives on the eggs. Serve cold.

Œufs Mayo

A regular dish in old-fashioned bistrots, these are a symbol of a typical Parisian lunch. All restaurants fight to be on the Top Ten List of the best Œufs Mayo in Paris!

INGREDIENTS | SERVES 6

2 egg yolks
1 teaspoon salt
1 teaspoon ground black pepper
1 tablespoon Dijon mustard
1 tablespoon red wine vinegar
1 cup oil (such as olive, canola, or sunflower)
1 tablespoon boiling water
8 eggs

1. In a small bowl, whisk the egg yolks with the salt, pepper, Dijon mustard, and the vinegar. Add 2 tablespoons oil drop by drop while continuing to whisk. Then pour in the rest of the oil slowly, still whisking until the mustard mayonnaise is thick.

2. Fill a large saucepan with water and bring to a boil over high heat. Boil the eggs for 10 minutes. Prepare a bowl of ice water and place the eggs in it after they are cooked. Peel them and cut them in half.

3. Lay them on a serving plate, add a teaspoon of the mustard mayo to each half, and serve cold.

Œufs Meurette (Poached Eggs in Red Wine Reduction)

Another great tradition from Burgundy. And remember, there's no alcohol left in a wine reduction, so have more than one!

INGREDIENTS | SERVES 4

2 tablespoons butter, divided

½ pound bacon sliced in *lardons* (small strips)

1 large onion, peeled and minced

1 carrot, peeled and thinly sliced

1 cup minced mushrooms

2 cups red wine

⅔ cup beef stock

2 bay leaves

1 tablespoon thyme

1 teaspoon salt

1 teaspoon ground black pepper

3 tablespoons white vinegar

8 eggs

1. Put a medium saucepan over medium-high heat. Melt 1 tablespoon butter slowly with half of the bacon, for 3 minutes. Add the diced onion and cook for 5 minutes. Make sure the *lardons* and the onions brown slowly together. Add the carrot and the mushrooms and stir well. Cook for 5 minutes, then pour in the red wine and bring to a boil over high heat. When the liquid has reduced to a third of its original amount, pour in the stock. Add the bay leaves, thyme, salt, and pepper. Reduce the heat to low and simmer until the sauce has reduced to a third of its original amount.

2. Fill another medium saucepan with water and the vinegar, and bring to a boil over high heat. Crack the eggs into the water one by one, and nudge each into a round shape with a tablespoon. Reduce the heat to low and poach the eggs for 3 minutes.

3. In a nonstick skillet, melt 1 tablespoon of butter with the other half of the diced bacon, and fry over high heat.

4. Serve in small bowls, first pouring in the wine sauce, then placing two poached eggs in the sauce, then sprinkling on the fried diced bacon.

Œufs Cocotte (Eggs in Ramekins)

A typical family dish, Œufs Cocotte can be served as an appetizer or an entrée.
Try to use the freshest eggs you can for an even better taste.

INGREDIENTS | MAKES 4 RAMEKINS

1 tablespoon butter

1 teaspoon salt

1 teaspoon ground black pepper

1 tablespoon spices of your choice
(ground nutmeg, cumin, paprika, etc.)

⅔ cup *crème fraîche* or crema Mexicana

4 large eggs

3 tablespoons fresh chives, minced

Added Pleasures

This is a basic recipe, but the idea of *Œufs Cocottes* is to try to cook it with different flavors inside the cream. You can also add fried bacon at the bottom of the ramekin, mushrooms, smoked salmon, or heads of green asparagus. Some cooks even put ½ a teaspoon of caviar in it.

1. Preheat the oven to 350°F.

2. Butter four ramekins. Sprinkle salt and pepper in the bottom of each one. You can also sprinkle various spices, like ground nutmeg, or cumin, paprika, etc.

3. In a small saucepan, heat the *crème fraîche* or crema Mexicana over medium-high heat, and stir continuously. Remove from heat right before it begins to boil. Pour 2 tablespoons of warm cream in each ramekin, and break an egg on the top of each one. Be careful not to break the egg yolk.

4. Cook in a *bain-marie*: Pour water to a depth of 1" in a larger dish, then put the smaller ramekins in it. Put in the oven and bake for about 6 minutes. Watch closely; the egg whites should not be transparent anymore, but the egg yolk should still be runny.

5. Sprinkle about 1 tablespoon minced chives over each pot. Serve the *Œufs Cocottes* directly in their ceramic ramekins, with toasted bread on the side.

Œufs Cocotte Sauce Aurore
(Eggs in Ramekins with Aurore Sauce)

This version of the Œufs Cocotte has tomatoes, and is served with another traditional French sauce called Aurore, which means dawn.

INGREDIENTS | MAKES 6 RAMEKINS

6 large eggs

2 cups tomato sauce

¾ cup *crème fraîche* or crema Mexicana

1 teaspoon salt

1 teaspoon ground black pepper

Sauce Aurore

Sauce Aurore is one of the most classic sauces in the French cuisine. The traditional sauce is actually made with a roux, to which you add tomato sauce and butter. But the name is now used for any kind of sauce that has tomato sauce in it.

1. Preheat the oven to 350°F.

2. Separate the egg yolks from the whites. Reserve the egg yolks. In a medium bowl, whisk the egg whites quickly with a fork.

3. In another bowl, combine the tomato sauce and the cream, then add the egg whites and stir well. Divide the sauce among 6 ramekins, and cook in a *bain-marie*: Pour water in a larger dish (at least 1" high), then put the smaller ceramic dishes in it. Put in the oven and bake for 5 minutes.

4. Spoon an egg yolk into each ramekin, on top of the tomato sauce, and cook for another 5 minutes. Watch carefully; the white should cook, but the yolk should still look runny.

5. Sprinkle salt and pepper on each ramekin, and serve with toasted bread to dip in.

Œufs Brouillés à la Truffe
(Scrambled Eggs with Black Truffles)

A classy version of scrambled eggs, with the wonderfully tasty black truffle. Simple and chic, it's a perfect breakfast or brunch after a Christmas dinner!

INGREDIENTS | SERVES 6

1 fresh truffle (about 1.5 ounces)
10 eggs
1 teaspoon salt
1 teaspoon ground black pepper
2 tablespoons butter

The Legendary *Truffe Noire*

You should always buy fresh truffles when in season. Yes, it's expensive, but its crazy flavor is worth it. Store it in your refrigerator in an airtight container with your eggs: after one day, the eggs will be perfumed as well!

1. The day before, put the truffle and the eggs in the same airtight container, and keep in the refrigerator.

2. Brush the black truffle (never wash it with water, as it would take the flavor out). Peel the truffle carefully: pull apart the skin peels, and then dice the main piece into small sticks. Reserve.

3. In a large bowl, beat the eggs firmly with salt and pepper.

4. Heat a nonstick skillet over very low heat, and melt the butter. Pour the beaten eggs and immediately whisk them, never stopping, as the eggs slowly start to cook. Stop after around 3 minutes (they should be kept creamy).

5. Take the skillet off of the heat, add the black truffle skins, and stir well.

6. Serve immediately, sprinkling the black truffle sticks on top.

Œufs Pochés Sauce Mornay (Poached Eggs in Mornay Sauce)

Perfect for brunch or breakfast, these poached eggs are served in a traditional French sauce. Sauce Mornay was invented in the nineteenth century in Le Grand Véfour, a renowned Parisian restaurant that is in the Palais Royal gardens.

INGREDIENTS | SERVES 6

4 tablespoons unsalted butter, divided

⅓ cup flour

2 cups whole milk

2 egg yolks

3 tablespoons grated cheese

2 tablespoons white vinegar

6 eggs

1. First, prepare the Mornay sauce: Heat a medium saucepan over medium-high heat. Melt 3 tablespoons of butter, add the flour, and stir well. Let it brown a little, until you obtain a roux (3–5 minutes). Remove saucepan from the heat.

2. Pour in all the milk and whisk well. Put back on low heat. Whisk well, and don't stop stirring until it's very thick. Remove from heat and allow to cool to lukewarm.

3. Add the egg yolks and stir well. Add the grated cheese and stir again.

4. Preheat the oven to 450°F.

5. Fill a medium saucepan with water and the white vinegar, and bring to a boil over high heat. One by one, break the eggs into the water, nudging each of them into a nice round shape with a tablespoon. Reduce the heat to low and poach for 3 minutes. Prepare a bowl of ice water. When the eggs are done poaching, lift them out with a slotted spoon and transfer them to the ice water bath.

6. Butter a large baking dish and pour half of the sauce in it. Place the poached eggs in the dish, and pour the rest of the sauce over them.

7. Bake for 10 minutes, and serve immediately with grilled toast.

Omelette au Jambon Fromage (Ham and Cheese Omelet)

*What is more French than a good, simple omelet? Most French
like their omelets simple with just cheese and ham.*

INGREDIENTS | SERVES 4

8 eggs
1 teaspoon salt
1 teaspoon ground black pepper
⅓ cup grated cheese
2 slices of thinly chopped cooked ham
2 tablespoons butter
2 tablespoons chopped chives
1 tablespoon chopped fresh parsley

The Best Omelet in the World?

The most famous omelet in France was invented by *la mère Poulard*, an old French woman who lived in Normandy, on the island of Mont Saint-Michel. She created it to feed the tourists and the pilgrims who came to visit this beautiful historical place, and made a fortune doing so. Decades after her death, the fluffiness and smoothness of her omelet is still legendary: In Mont Saint-Michel, the restaurant she owned still serves it. But the original recipe is still a well-kept secret.

1. Break the eggs in a large bowl, add the salt and pepper, and beat the eggs firmly. Add the cheese and the ham, and beat again until the mixture is smooth and even.

2. Heat a nonstick frying pan over medium heat. Melt the butter, making sure that the butter spreads evenly in the pan, and pour the egg mixture. With a wooden spatula, stir the eggs immediately on the surface for a few seconds, especially around the edges of the pan, while quickly rotating the pan over the fire. Then let it cook.

3. When the bottom of the omelet is golden, and the top is still a little bit runny, use the wooden spatula to fold one third of it toward the center.

4. Grip the handle of the pan, tilt the pan down, and let the omelet fall to the edge. Flip the remaining edge over as the omelet leaves the pan.

5. Garnish with chives and parsley, and serve immediately.

Omelette aux Escargots (Snail Omelet)

*There are as many French omelette recipes as there are ingredients in
your cupboard! This one is a great way to rediscover snails.*

INGREDIENTS | SERVES 4

24 snails (2 cans of 12 precooked
  escargots)
6 eggs
1 teaspoon salt
1 teaspoon ground black pepper
2 tablespoons butter
2 shallots, peeled and diced
2 spring onions, diced
2 anchovy filets, drained
1 tablespoon fresh parsley, chopped

Do You Like Your *Omelette* Dribbling?

Most French cooks would tell you that they
like their *omelette* to dribble, *baver*. This
means to still be runny.

1. Wash and rinse the snails. Dry them and reserve.

2. In a large bowl, beat the eggs firmly, with salt
   and pepper.

3. Warm a nonstick frying pan over medium heat. Melt
   the butter. Make sure that the butter spreads evenly in
   the pan. Sauté the shallots and spring onions in the
   pan for 5 minutes, then add the anchovy fillets and the
   parsley. Stir, and add the snails.

4. Pour the egg mixture into the pan. With a wooden
   spatula, stir the eggs immediately on the surface for a
   few seconds, especially around the edges of the pan,
   while quickly rotating the pan over the flame. Then let
   it cook, while continuously rotating the pan. When the
   bottom of the omelet is golden, and the top is still a
   little bit runny, fold one third of it with a wooden
   spatula. Grip the pan's handle, tilt the pan down, and
   let the omelet fall to the edge. Flip the remaining edge
   over as the omelet leaves the pan.

5. Serve with an arugula salad.

Omelette aux Cèpes (Mushroom Omelet)

Fall in France is always a great season for fun. It means spending your Sunday trying to find mushrooms in the woods, and then cooking them in a delicious omelette. Finding cèpes (from the Boletus genre of mushroom) is like winning the lottery!

INGREDIENTS | SERVES 4

8 eggs

1 teaspoon salt

1 teaspoon ground black pepper

4 tablespoons butter, divided

1 cup wild mushrooms (preferably Boletus), diced

1 garlic clove, peeled and sliced

2 tablespoons fresh parsley, chopped, and a sprig of parsley

Be Careful

If you have a *cèpe*, brush it gently, dusting the dirt off. Never wash it, or it will lose its flavor!

1. Break the eggs in a large bowl and beat them with salt and pepper.

2. In a medium saucepan, melt 2 tablespoons of butter on medium heat. Add the mushrooms and stir well, then add the garlic. Cook on medium-low heat for 5 minutes, till the water of the mushrooms releases. Take the garlic slices out of the pan, then add the chopped parsley to the mushrooms. Remove the pan from the heat.

3. Warm a nonstick frying pan over medium heat. Melt 2 tablespoons butter in it. Make sure that the butter spreads evenly in the pan. Pour the egg mixture into the pan, and immediately start to stir on the surface for a few seconds, especially around the edges of the pan, while quickly rotating the pan over the flame. Then let it cook, while continuously rotating the pan.

4. When the omelet is half cooked, pour in the mushrooms. When the bottom is golden, grip the pan's handle, tilt the pan down, and let the omelet fall to the edge. Fold the side nearest to you to the center by a third, and then flip the remaining edge over as the omelet leaves the pan.

5. Top with the sprig of parsley and serve.

Œufs en Gelée (Jellied Eggs)

This is a traditional entrée or appetizer that is always very dramatic, so serve it at your next dinner party.

INGREDIENTS | SERVES 4

¼ ounce of gelatin

2 cups chicken stock

2 tablespoons port wine

1 tablespoon chopped parsley

1 tablespoon chopped cilantro

4 teaspoons diced tomatoes

2 tablespoons white vinegar

1 slice cooked ham

4 eggs

1. Soften the leaves of gelatin by putting them under cold water. In a medium saucepan, warm the chicken stock over medium heat, then add the gelatin leaves and the port, and stir well.

2. Pour ½" of the gelatin mixture into 4 small ceramic or glass bowls, dividing it evenly among the bowls. Add 1 teaspoon diced parsley and 1 teaspoon chopped cilantro to each bowl. Add 1 teaspoon diced tomatoes in each bowl too.

3. Fill a large saucepan with water, add the white vinegar, and bring to a boil over high heat. Break one egg after each other into the boiling water, shaping each into a ball using a spoon. Reduce the heat to low and cook for 3 minutes. Prepare a medium bowl of ice cubes. Using a slotted spoon, take the eggs out and put them on ice immediately.

4. When the gelatin is firmer, add one poached egg to each bowl. Cut the ham in ½" slices and place some in each bowl. Then cover with the rest of the gelatin. Make sure the gelatin is still lukewarm. Let the jellied eggs cool and put in the refrigerator.

5. To unmold, put 1" warm tap water in a large dish, and place the bowls in it. Run a sharp knife around border and unmold the jellied eggs on a plate.

CHAPTER 5

Crudités (Raw Salads)

Carottes Râpées (Grated Carrots)

One of the most common appetizers at lunch, a side of grated carrots often appears as one of the famous French crudités. Always on the school or cafeteria menu!

INGREDIENTS | SERVES 4

8 carrots, peeled
Juice of 1 lemon
1 teaspoon salt
1 teaspoon ground black pepper
2 tablespoons olive oil
2 tablespoons fresh cilantro or parsley

Follow the Carrot!

The French have tons of expressions about carrots, but their favorite must be *les carottes sont cuites*, which means that the carrots are cooked. This strange saying was used during WWII by the British Broadcasting Corporation anchors as code to talk to the French Resistance. Folk beliefs say that carrots are supposed to make you a nice and polite person, and help babies have a pink bottom!

1. Grate the carrots with a box grater (using the largest holes) or a mandoline slicer. It should make flecks of carrots about 2" long. Place the grated carrots in a large salad bowl.

2. Sprinkle the freshly squeezed lemon juice on the grated carrots. Toss well.

3. Add a teaspoon of salt and a teaspoon of pepper. Toss well, cover with plastic wrap, and leave in the refrigerator for at least 3 hours. You can eat the salad right away, adding the oil and tossing, but it is tastier when you let the carrots marinate in the lemon.

4. Five minutes before serving, add the 2 tablespoons of olive oil and toss well. Add the parsley or cilantro, and toss again.

5. Serve as a raw appetizer, or add a poached egg and make it a light lunch.

Champignons à la Grecque (Greek Mushrooms)

This mushroom salad is supposed to be Greek, but you can only find this recipe in France, where you will see this mushroom salad in every charcutier traiteur, the traditional pork and catering shop found in every small town.

INGREDIENTS | SERVES 4

½ cup water

1 cup white wine

3 tablespoons tomato paste

1 cup button mushrooms, washed and trimmed

1 fennel, cut in ½" cubes

1 onion, peeled and diced (or 3 spring onions)

15 coriander seeds

1 tablespoon sugar

1 tablespoon thyme

Juice of 1 lemon

2 bay leaves

2 tablespoons olive oil

¼ teaspoon salt

¼ teaspoon ground black pepper

1. In a medium saucepan, pour the water and the white wine. Add the tomato paste and stir well. The paste should completely dissolve in the liquid. Add the mushrooms, the fennel, and the onions. Stir well and reduce the heat to low.

2. Add the coriander seeds, sugar, thyme, lemon juice, the bay leaves, and olive oil. Stir again. Cover and simmer for at least 1 hour. Remove from heat, stir well, then add salt and pepper. Leave in the refrigerator for at least half a day.

3. Serve very cold, as an appetizer.

Fenouil Confit (Fennel Salad)

This simple fennel salad is great in the summer and very low in calories. It was inspired by Lebanese cuisine, which is dear to the hearts of French people.

INGREDIENTS | SERVES 4

1 teaspoon salt

1 teaspoon ground black pepper

Juice of 1 lemon

2 tablespoons olive oil

1 tablespoon ground cumin

2 fennel bulbs, thinly sliced

1. In a large salad bowl, combine the salt and the pepper with the juice of the lemon. Stir well, then add the olive oil slowly, whisking energetically for the sauce to blend well.

2. Add the ground cumin and stir, then add the fennel slices and toss until all the fennel slices are damp with sauce. Cover the bowl with plastic wrap, and put in the refrigerator for 2–3 hours minimum (the lemon will "cook" the fennel).

3. Serve cold. You can also do the same recipe with diced cabbage, and make a French-Lebanese coleslaw!

Salade de Tomates et de Fromage de Chèvre
(Tomato and Goat Cheese Salad)

This is the French version of the Caprese salad. Mozzarella usually isn't used in French cuisine, but a fresh goat cheese is perfect!

INGREDIENTS | SERVES 4

6 organic tomatoes
1 tablespoon kosher salt
2 tablespoons fresh parsley
8 fresh basil leaves
2 tablespoons olive oil
1 tablespoon cider vinegar
1 teaspoon ground black pepper
½ pound fresh goat cheese, cut in slices

1. At least one hour before serving time, wash the tomatoes, cut them into thin slices, and put them in a large bowl. Sprinkle them with kosher salt and stir well. Cover with plastic wrap and put in the refrigerator for a minimum of 1 hour. This way the juice of the tomatoes is released, and will mix with the oil to make a great dressing.

2. Five minutes before serving, wash the parsley and the basil leaves, and chop them in small slices. Add to the tomatoes and toss well. Add olive oil, cider vinegar, and the pepper. Toss again.

3. Cut the fresh goat cheese in thin slices (the same thickness as the tomatoes) and add them to the serving bowl at the last minute (fresh goat cheese tends to melt in the sauce). Toss right before serving.

Salade de Pissenlit (Dandelion Salad)

*Young dandelion leaves are very healthy, and have a great peppery
flavor that marries well with bacon and eggs.*

INGREDIENTS | SERVES 4

½ pound dandelion leaves

2 tablespoons white vinegar

4 eggs

4 ounces bacon, cut in ½"-wide slices

2 slices of bread (slightly stale is best),
  cut in ½" cubes

¼ teaspoon salt

¼ teaspoon ground black pepper

A Detox Herb

Dandelion leaves have been used in French
cuisine and in the French pharmacy for a
long time. Their diuretic properties, when
cooked, are well known. In the Middle
Ages, people used to make an elixir out of
them and drink some every day for one
month during spring.

1. Make sure the dandelion leaves are very young. When
   harvested later, they are still totally edible, but their
   flavor is bitter. Wash and dry them.

2. Fill a medium saucepan with water, add the 2
   tablespoons of white vinegar, and bring to a boil over
   high heat. When the water boils, poach the eggs in it,
   using a tablespoon to shape each into a ball. Reduce
   the heat to low and cook them for 3 minutes. Prepare a
   bowl of ice cubes. After 3 minutes, remove the eggs
   with a slotted spoon and put them on ice.

3. Preheat a nonstick skillet over medium-high heat for 1
   minute. Put the bacon slices in it. If the bacon is fatty
   enough, you don't need to add fat for frying. If not, you
   can add one tablespoon butter. Add the bread cubes
   and fry them in the bacon fat, stirring (they must
   brown on each side).

4. Place the dandelion leaves in a large bowl, and then
   add the bacon strips and croutons, and pour all the fat
   that is still in the skillet over it all. Sprinkle with salt
   and pepper, and toss well.

5. Add the poached eggs on the salad at the last minute,
   and serve immediately.

Salade de Betteraves et de Mâche (Beets and Greens Salad)

Cooked beet salad is very popular in France. Add a mâche salad (greens) and walnuts, and you have a great healthy appetizer, full of antioxidants, iron, and omega-3 fatty acids.

INGREDIENTS | SERVES 4

2 tablespoons white vinegar

3 or 4 beets (around 1 pound), washed and trimmed

1 tablespoon cider vinegar

¼ teaspoon salt

¼ teaspoon ground black pepper

2 tablespoons organic canola oil, divided

½ pound *mâche* salad

½ cup whole walnut halves

1. Fill a medium saucepan with water, add the 2 tablespoons of vinegar, and bring to a boil. When the water boils, put the beets in it, and set the heat to low. Cover and leave for 1 hour. The water is going to turn pink, but it's normal!

2. In a large bowl, combine the cider vinegar with salt and pepper, add one tablespoon of canola oil, stir well, then add the other tablespoon of canola oil, whisking until the mixture is smooth.

3. Take the beets out of the pink water (you can also keep them in the water for 4 to 5 days in the refrigerator; the vinegar helps keep them fresh and tasty). Peel the beets, and cut them into ½" cubes. Be careful to do this in the sink and with an apron on: The pink will stain your clothes, your kitchen, and your hands badly! But it goes away easily with water and soap.) Put the *mâche* salad in the bowl, and then add the walnuts.

4. Add the beets to the salad and toss well. Serve as an appetizer.

Concombre en Sauce Blanche (Cucumber in White Sauce)

*A very refreshing appetizer, and very low in calories, too! The authentic version
is made with crème fraîche, but this one is better for your waistline.*

INGREDIENTS | SERVES 4

1 cucumber, peeled and thinly sliced
1 tablespoon kosher salt
2 tablespoons chives, chopped
½ cup Greek yogurt or plain yogurt
1 teaspoon red wine vinegar
1 teaspoon ground black pepper

1. Put the cucumber slices in a large bowl and sprinkle them with kosher salt. Cover in plastic wrap and leave for at least 1 hour in the refrigerator, so that the cucumber can release its juices.

2. Take the bowl out of the refrigerator and add the chives and the yogurt. Toss well. Add the teaspoon of red wine vinegar, toss again, and add pepper.

3. Leave in the refrigerator until served. The salad should be eaten very cold.

Chou Rouge en Salade (Red Cabbage Salad)

*This is the easiest crudités recipe you can find. A French version of
coleslaw, but much wiser in terms of calorie count!*

INGREDIENTS | SERVES 4

1 teaspoon salt
1 teaspoon ground black pepper
1 tablespoon red wine vinegar
4 tablespoons olive oil
1 tablespoon green anise seeds
½ medium red cabbage, minced

1. In a large bowl, whisk salt and pepper with the red wine vinegar, then add the olive oil slowly while whisking continuously. Add the green anise seeds to the dressing. Put the minced red cabbage in the dressing and toss well. Cover with plastic wrap.

2. Leave in the refrigerator for 3 hours before serving.

Haricots Verts en Salade (French Beans Salad)

The best way to enjoy fresh French beans in the summer!

INGREDIENTS | SERVES 4

2 teaspoons salt, divided, plus more to taste

2 pounds French beans, washed and trimmed

1 teaspoon ground black pepper (plus more to taste)

1 tablespoon red wine vinegar

1 medium shallot, peeled and diced

3 tablespoons olive oil

2 tablespoons fresh parsley, chopped

1. Fill a large saucepan with water, add a teaspoon of salt, and then bring to a boil. Add the French beans to the boiling water, and leave for 10 minutes without covering the saucepan. Prepare a large bowl full of ice. Using a slotted spoon, take the French beans out of the saucepan and immediately put them on ice.

2. In a large salad bowl, combine the salt and the pepper with the red wine vinegar. Add the diced shallot and stir well, then slowly add the tablespoons of olive oil, one after the other, stirring continuously, until it is smooth.

3. Mix the chopped parsley with the French beans, sprinkle on more salt and pepper, toss well, and serve.

Courgettes en Salade (Zucchini Salad)

To enjoy this salad more, it's better to use organic zucchini. This way you don't have to peel the skin, which will add flavor to the dish.

INGREDIENTS | SERVES 4

4 organic zucchini

1 teaspoon salt

1 teaspoon ground black pepper

Juice of 1 lemon

4 tablespoons olive oil

2 tablespoons fresh cilantro, minced

2 tablespoons fresh mint, minced

1. Don't peel the zucchini. Wash them carefully and dry them. Cut them in half, and take the seeds out.

2. Using a vegetable peeler, make long zucchini strips, as long as the vegetable if possible, like spaghetti.

3. In a large bowl, whisk salt and pepper with the lemon juice, then add the olive oil slowly. Add the cilantro and the mint to the dressing.

4. Add the zucchini strips, toss well, cover, and leave in the refrigerator for an hour before serving.

Céleri Rémoulade (Celery Rémoulade)

Along with Carottes Râpées, this raw vegetable appetizer is one of the most common at lunch.

INGREDIENTS | SERVES 4

2 pounds celery, peeled

1 lemon, halved

1 tablespoon plus 1 teaspoon salt, divided

1 cup French Mayonnaise (see recipe in Chapter 22)

3 tablespoons fresh parsley or tarragon, minced

1 tablespoon drained capers

3 *cornichons* (gherkins)

1 teaspoon ground black pepper

Not As Spicy As the American Version

Rémoulade sauce is one of the first things taught at a French classic culinary school. But it's very different from the Louisiana version, which is almost always red and very spicy, a great American derivative of the classic sauce that was brought to the United States by the first French settlers.

1. Rub the peeled celery with one half of the lemon so that it doesn't turn brown. Julienne the celery stalks: Use your best knife to cut it into long, thin strips, similar to matchsticks.

2. Fill a large bowl with ice water. Fill a medium saucepan with water, add 1 tablespoon of salt, and bring to a boil over high heat. Blanch the celery slices by adding to boiling water for 2 minutes, then removing them and plunging them in ice water.

3. Put the blanched celery slices in a large salad bowl, and season with the juice of the other half of the lemon.

4. In a separate bowl, make your mayonnaise. Mince the herbs, and add them to the mayonnaise with the capers. Cut the *cornichons* in very thin slices, and add them as well.

5. Add the mayonnaise sauce to the celery slowly, mixing well. Season with remaining salt and pepper. Leave in the refrigerator for at least 1 hour before serving.

Salade Piémontaise (Potato Salad)

Another hors d'oeuvre that bears the name of a foreign region
(Piedmont is in Italy), but is typically French.

INGREDIENTS | SERVES 4

8 potatoes

1 shallot, peeled and minced

6 *cornichons* (gherkins), thinly sliced

2 slices of ham (or pork roast), cut in
½" squares

4 tomatoes

4 eggs

1 egg yolk

1 tablespoon Dijon mustard

⅔ cup olive oil

2 tablespoons *crème fraîche* or
crema Mexicana

1 teaspoon red wine vinegar

1 teaspoon salt

1 teaspoon ground black pepper

1. Fill a large saucepan with cold water, add the potatoes, and bring to a boil over high heat. Boil the potatoes for 20 minutes. Prepare a large bowl of ice water. With a slotted spoon, take the potatoes out, and put them in the ice water. When cool, dry them and peel them.

2. Put the shallot, *cornichons*, ham, tomatoes, and potatoes in a large salad bowl.

3. Fill a medium saucepan with water, and bring to a boil over high heat. Prepare a bowl of ice cubes. Boil 4 eggs for 10 minutes, then remove them with a slotted spoon and put them on the ice. When cool, peel the eggs and slice them in half.

4. In a separate bowl, prepare the sauce: Make a quick mayonnaise, whisking an egg yolk with one tablespoon of Dijon mustard, adding the olive oil slowly. When the sauce is thick, add the *crème fraîche*, whisk well, then add the red wine vinegar to the sauce and stir again. Add salt and pepper, stir well, and pour over the potatoes and tomatoes. Toss well and add the hardboiled eggs.

5. Cover and keep in the refrigerator for an hour before serving.

Salade de Lentilles Vertes du Puy (Green Lentil Salad)

*Full of antioxidants, this lentil salad is perfect in winter, and a
must for pregnant women: It's full of folic acid!*

INGREDIENTS | SERVES 4

½ cup bacon, cut in ½"-wide strips

2 shallots, peeled and minced

1 carrot, peeled and thinly sliced

1 cup dried French green lentils

½ cup white wine

1 bay leaf

1 tablespoon thyme

1¼ teaspoons salt, divided

1¼ teaspoons ground black
  pepper, divided

1 teaspoon Dijon mustard

1 tablespoon red wine vinegar

4 tablespoons olive oil

Lentilles du Puy: A Gem from the Center of France

French green lentils are special, and mostly come from a little town in the center of France called *Le Puy*. They are so good that their nickname is *"vegetal caviar"*!

1. Put a large saucepan over medium-high heat. Put the bacon in it, let it "sweat" some of its fat, then add the diced shallots and stir well. Reduce heat to medium. Add the carrots, making sure they brown slightly on each side (about 1 minute), and then add the lentils.

2. Pour in the white wine, stir well, and then bring to a boil over high heat. Add the bay leaf and the thyme. Cover with cold water, bring to a boil once more, and then sprinkle with ¼ teaspoon salt and ¼ teaspoon pepper. Reduce to low heat and simmer for at least 20 minutes. The water should totally evaporate. Remove from the heat, and let cool. Remove bay leaf.

3. Meanwhile, prepare the dressing: In a salad bowl, stir the mustard with the red wine vinegar, salt, and pepper. Add olive oil slowly and stir well. Pour the lentils in the salad bowl, stir well, then cover and leave in the refrigerator until served. Serve cold.

Salade de Haricots Blancs (White Bean Salad)

Haricots blancs *are a frequently used legume in French cuisine. The best for this recipe are Haricots tarbais, but they are hard to find in the United States, so you can use fresh navy beans here.*

INGREDIENTS | SERVES 6

6 tablespoons olive oil, divided

2 medium carrots, peeled and minced

4 spring onions, peeled and minced

2 garlic cloves, peeled and crushed

1 bay leaf

1 tablespoon thyme

1 pound fresh navy beans or 2 cups dried

1 tablespoon kosher salt

2 tablespoons cider vinegar

1 teaspoon salt

1 teaspoon ground black pepper

2 tablespoons minced parsley

1. In a large saucepan, heat 1 tablespoon of olive oil over medium-high heat. Add carrots, onions, crushed garlic cloves, bay leaf, and thyme. Stir well and cook for 5 minutes.

2. Add the navy beans, pour in 4 cups of water, stir well, and then cover and reduce the heat to low. Simmer for 30 minutes. Add kosher salt 5 minutes before turning off the heat. Remove bay leaf.

3. In a large bowl, combine cider vinegar with salt and pepper. Add 5 tablespoons of olive oil, one at a time, whisking well.

4. Drain the navy beans, dry them, and pour them in the large bowl. Mince the parsley, add it to the navy beans, and toss well. Serve lukewarm.

Salade de Pastèque et Feta (Feta and Watermelon Salad)

Yes, feta cheese is Greek, but France is the second biggest consumer (and producer!) of this great goat cheese. And in summer, it's very refreshing in this watermelon and arugula salad.

INGREDIENTS | SERVES 4

¾ cup fresh feta cheese, cut in ½" cubes

1 pound watermelon, cut in ½" cubes

2 cups arugula

1 teaspoon fresh mint, finely chopped, plus 6 mint leaves for garnish

¼ teaspoon salt

¼ teaspoon ground black pepper

1 tablespoon balsamic vinegar

4 tablespoons olive oil

1. In a large salad bowl, combine the feta, watermelon, arugula, and mint. Sprinkle with salt and pepper, toss well, then cover in plastic wrap and put in the refrigerator.

2. In a small bowl, combine balsamic vinegar and olive oil, whisking well until it is homogeneous. Five minutes before serving, pour the balsamic vinegar and olive oil dressing on the salad. Toss well. Add the mint leaves on top for decoration (and taste!).

3. Serve as fresh as you can, as an appetizer or a side dish (with grilled chicken, for example).

CHAPTER 6

Soups

Potage Bonne Femme (Leek, Potato, and Carrot Soup)

This recipe literally means "good woman soup." It's one of the easiest, most popular family soups in France, especially in the winter season.

INGREDIENTS | SERVES 4

6 tablespoons butter

½ pound carrots, thinly sliced

½ pound leeks, thinly sliced

1 pound potatoes, peeled and thinly sliced

6 cups water

1 bay leaf

1 tablespoon thyme

1 teaspoon salt

1 teaspoon ground black pepper

1. Put a large saucepan over medium-high heat. Melt the butter in the saucepan. Add the vegetables, stir well so they can all caramelize slightly in the butter. Cook for 8–12 minutes.

2. Pour the water on the vegetables, add the bay leaf and the thyme, sprinkle with salt and pepper, and bring to a boil. Reduce to a low heat, and simmer for 45 minutes. Take the bay leaf out.

3. Serve the soup as is, with the diced vegetables floating. You can add a tablespoon of *crème fraîche* just before serving.

Soupe au Lard et au Chou (Soup with Bacon and Cabbage)

This cabbage soup is typical of the kind you would have eaten on a French farm years ago. It is very comforting in the winter season.

INGREDIENTS | SERVES 4

1 pound unsliced bacon, or pork belly, cut in ½"-wide slices

½ pound ham, cut in ½"-wide slices

1 medium cabbage, shredded

3 medium carrots, peeled and thinly sliced

4 medium potatoes, peeled and thinly sliced

1 turnip, peeled and thinly sliced

2 medium leeks, thinly sliced

1 large onion, peeled and minced

1 bay leaf

1 teaspoon ground black pepper

1. Fill a large saucepan with cold water. Add the pork and the ham. Bring to a boil over high heat. After 10 minutes, use a wooden spoon to skim the foam out.

2. Add all the vegetables to the saucepan. Add a bay leaf, bring to a boil over high heat, and then reduce to a low heat. The soup should simmer for at least 2 hours. Add a teaspoon of pepper at the end, and take out the bay leaf.

3. Serve the soup very hot.

Potage Julienne (Julienne Soup)

This soup is the best way to learn a basic technique of French cuisine: the julienne, which means cutting the vegetables in long thin strips.

INGREDIENTS | SERVES 4

1 tablespoon butter

1 tablespoon ground nutmeg

4 medium potatoes, peeled and julienned

3 medium carrots, peeled and julienned

1 turnip, peeled and julienned

1 large onion, peeled and julienned

4 stalks of celery, julienned

8 cups water

1 bay leaf

1 tablespoon thyme

1 teaspoon ground black pepper

1 teaspoon salt

4 ounces French peas

1. Put a large saucepan over medium-high heat. Melt the butter in the saucepan. Then add the ground nutmeg and stir. Add all the vegetables one by one (except the French peas), stir well, and make sure they get slightly brown in the butter (about 8–12 minutes). Cover with water, add the bay leaf and the thyme, reduce the heat to its lowest, and simmer gently for two hours.

2. Half an hour before serving, add salt and pepper, and French peas. Remove bay leaf.

3. Serve the soup as is. You can add a tablespoon of butter and ½ cup of croutons just before serving.

Add Lettuce!

You can also add fresh lettuce at the end of this recipe. Just wash it and shred it into thin strips, and add it to the pan a half hour before serving. Sorrel and cabbage can also be added.

Soupe de Cresson (Watercress Soup)

Watercress soup is very healthy. Watercress is full of antioxidants, and can also improve your vision and cure eye problems. This is a low-calorie version of the recipe and a great detox soup.

INGREDIENTS | SERVES 4

2 cups chicken stock

6 cups water

2 bunches of upland watercress, about ½ pound

1 teaspoon salt

1 teaspoon ground black pepper

½ cup *crème fraîche* or crema Mexicana

1. Bring the chicken stock and the water to a boil over high heat, in a large saucepan.

2. Wash the watercress, take the roots off, chop the bunches in half, and add to the boiling chicken stock. Add salt and pepper, then reduce the heat and simmer for 20 minutes.

3. With a slotted spoon, take out the watercress leaves, put them in a blender with 1 cup of the stock, and process well. Put back in the saucepan with the stock, stir well, and simmer for another 5 minutes.

4. Serve as is, and add a tablespoon of *crème fraîche* in each bowl.

Soupe Poireau Pommes de Terre (Potato Leek Soup)

Leeks and potato soup is the most basic, and maybe the most popular, soup in France.

INGREDIENTS | SERVES 4

3 medium leeks

1 tablespoon butter

1 pound medium potatoes, peeled and diced

1 teaspoon salt

1 teaspoon ground black pepper

1 cup chicken stock

3 cups water

1. Wash the leeks in cold water, dry them, and remove and discard the green parts. Cut them in thin slices.

2. Place a large saucepan over medium-high heat and melt the butter slightly. Add leeks and cook for 2 minutes. Add the potatoes and stir well with a wooden spatula. Add salt, pepper, stock, and water.

3. Bring to a boil over high heat, and then reduce to low and simmer for 20 minutes. Put all ingredients in a blender, and process for 2 minutes.

4. Serve warm.

Soupe de Fanes de Radis ou de Carottes
(Radish and Carrot Leaves Soup)

Part of the art of the good French home cook is to be able to use all the leftovers, and never waste anything. This soup of radish or carrot leaves is a good example.

INGREDIENTS | SERVES 4

2 tablespoons butter

1 medium onion, peeled and sliced

2 bunches of radish or carrot leaves, chopped

3 medium potatoes, peeled and sliced

1 cup chicken stock

3 cups water

1 teaspoon salt

1 teaspoon ground black pepper

4 tablespoons *crème fraîche* or crema Mexicana

1. In a large saucepan, melt the butter over medium-high heat. Add the onion and cook for 5 minutes, stirring regularly. Add the leaves, stir well, reduce the heat, and cook for 5 minutes, stirring regularly. Add the potatoes, cook for another 5 minutes, and then pour in the chicken stock and the water.

2. Bring to a boil over high heat, add salt and pepper, then reduce the heat to low, and simmer for 20 minutes.

3. Using a slotted spoon, take out the leaves, onions, and potatoes, and put them in a blender with 1 cup of stock. Process well until smooth.

4. Put the purée back in the saucepan with the stock, stir well, and simmer for another 5 minutes.

5. Serve as is, and add a tablespoon of cream to each bowl.

Soupe aux Orties (Nettle Soup)

Nettle soup is a culinary mystery. How can such a stingy plant be so sweet when eaten? One thing is for sure: It is also very good for the health of your kidneys, or to prevent bloated feet.

INGREDIENTS | SERVES 4

1 pound fresh stinging nettles
4 tablespoons butter
1 medium onion, peeled and thinly sliced
4 cups water
1 pound potatoes, peeled and diced
1 teaspoon salt
1 teaspoon ground black pepper
½ cup *crème fraîche* or crema Mexicana

How to Pick Stinging Nettles

Springtime and the beginning of summer are the best seasons to pick stinging nettles; later in the year, the plant is too tough. Go for the upper leaves, and try to pick them on a dry day, since the leaves will be easier to store.

1. With gloves on, choose the leaves that are on top of the nettle stalks. Wash them thoroughly and let them dry.

2. In a large saucepan, melt 2 tablespoons butter over medium heat, then add the stinging nettle leaves and the onion slices. Cook for 5 minutes, stirring constantly.

3. When the color of the leaves has whitened slightly, pour in the water and add the potatoes. Cook for 30 minutes over medium heat.

4. Take out one cup of the cooking liquid, pour it in a bowl, and reserve. Pour the rest of the soup in a blender. Process well for 2 minutes. Then pour into a large serving bowl. Use the cup of leftover cooking liquid to add as much as you need to get the thickness of soup that you want. Add salt and pepper at the last minute. Leave on low heat until the moment you serve.

5. Serve in individual bowls, and add a tablespoon of *crème fraîche* to each serving.

Velouté à la du Barry (Cauliflower Cream Soup)

Invented in the eighteenth century for Jeanne du Barry, King Louis XV of France's last maîtresse en titre (his official mistress), this cauliflower cream soup is now a French classic.

INGREDIENTS | SERVES 4

1 tablespoon kosher salt

1 medium cauliflower, cut into chunks

1 medium onion, peeled and diced

1 tablespoon olive oil

2 small potatoes, peeled and diced

1 cup chicken stock

1 cup whole milk

1 cup whipping cream

1 teaspoon salt

1 teaspoon ground black pepper

8 fresh cilantro leaves

Velouté: A Different Kind of Soup

French traditional soups are divided into various types: *Soupe* is usually home cooked; *potage* is a more delicate, refined soup. *Velouté* is a creamier version of *potage*.

1. Fill a large saucepan with cold water, add a tablespoon of kosher salt, and bring it to a boil over high heat.

2. Add cauliflower to the boiling water and cook for 5 minutes. The cauliflower chunks should be soft after this process. Dry them well.

3. In another large saucepan, cook the onion with the olive oil over medium-low heat for 3–5 minutes. Then add the diced potatoes, stir well, and cook for 5 minutes. Add the cooked cauliflower and pour in the chicken stock. Add the milk and the cream, stir well, season with salt and pepper, and simmer for 20 minutes. The vegetables must be very tender.

4. Transfer to a food processor or a blender, and process for at least 5 minutes. The *velouté* must be extremely smooth. Put back in the saucepan, and simmer very slowly until serving.

5. Add 2 cilantro leaves to each bowl of soup before serving.

Crème de Châtaignes (Cream of Chestnut Soup)

*Chestnuts are definitely a symbol of the winter season, and they
are delicious in this comforting and creamy soup.*

INGREDIENTS | SERVES 4

8 cups water

1 leek, cut in small slices, green part discarded

1 onion, peeled and minced

1 carrot, peeled and cut in small slices

1 celery stalk, cut in small slices

1 bay leaf

1 clove

1 tablespoon thyme

1 teaspoon salt

1 teaspoon ground black pepper

1 shallot, peeled and minced

2 tablespoons salted butter

1 pound peeled and cooked chestnuts

2 cups *crème fraîche* or crema Mexicana

1. In a large saucepan, combine the water, vegetables, bay leaf, clove, thyme, salt, and pepper. Bring to a boil and then reduce the heat and simmer for 1 hour.

2. In another large saucepan over medium heat, cook the shallot in the salted butter until soft, about 3–5 minutes. Add the chestnuts, stir well, and let it cook for around 5 minutes.

3. Pour the vegetable stock over the chestnuts and bring to a boil over high heat. Take the bay leaf and the clove out, then reduce the heat to its lowest, cover, and simmer for 45 minutes.

4. Transfer to a food processor or a blender, and process for at least 5 minutes: The *velouté* must be extremely smooth. Pour back in the saucepan. Add the cream, stir well, bring to a boil over high heat, and cook for 5 minutes.

5. Serve the *crème* as soon as you can.

Soupe à l'Oignon Gratinée (Onion Soup au Gratin)

One of the most famous soups in French cuisine, this grated cheese and onion soup is supposed to be a great way to fight a bad hangover!

INGREDIENTS | SERVES 4

2 medium onions, peeled and very thinly sliced

4 tablespoons butter, divided

1 tablespoon flour

1 cup white wine

5 cups beef stock

1 teaspoon salt

1 teaspoon ground black pepper

4 large slices of whole-grain bread

½ cup grated *Gruyère* or *Comté* cheese

A Royal Tradition

Legend has it that onion soup was actually invented by French king Louis XV in the eighteenth century. One night he was hungry and couldn't find anything at his hunting lodge except onions and bread.

1. Preheat the oven to 450°F.

2. Heat a large saucepan over medium-high heat, and cook the onions with 3 tablespoons butter. Stir constantly with a wooden spatula for about 5 minutes. When the onions are golden, sprinkle the flour in and let the onions brown slightly. Pour the white wine over the onions, bring to a boil over high heat, and then pour in the beef stock. Add salt and pepper, cover, reduce to medium-high heat, and cook for 10 minutes.

3. Spread the rest of the butter on the slices of bread, and toast them in the hot oven, flipping them to make sure each side gets slightly browned.

4. Pour the soup into 4 ovenproof soup bowls or a large casserole dish. Cover with the grilled toast, and sprinkle generously with grated cheese. Leave in the oven for 10 minutes. Don't allow the grated cheese to get too brown.

5. Serve very hot.

Soupe à la Tomate (Tomato Soup)

A very simple tomato soup, with rice to thicken it.

INGREDIENTS | SERVES 4

1 medium onion, peeled and diced
1 carrot, peeled and diced
2 tablespoons olive oil
1 tablespoon flour
1 (28-ounce) can diced tomatoes
3 cups water
1 teaspoon salt
1 teaspoon ground black pepper
1 tablespoon white sugar
2 tablespoons chopped parsley
1 cup chicken stock
3 tablespoons rice

1. In a large saucepan, cook the diced onion and the diced carrots in olive oil over medium-low heat, stirring well for about 5 minutes. Add the tablespoon of flour and stir again with a wooden spatula. Pour in the diced tomatoes (with the juice from the can), and stir again.

2. Add the water, sprinkle with salt and pepper, then add the sugar and parsley. Bring to a boil, then lower the heat and simmer for 45 minutes.

3. Meanwhile, in a smaller pan, bring the chicken stock to a boil, add the rice, and cook for 20 minutes.

4. When the tomatoes are cooked, put them in a blender, process well, then put back in the saucepan. Add the chicken stock and the rice to the larger saucepan, bring to a boil, then reduce to medium heat for 10 minutes. Stir well.

5. Serve immediately.

Soupe Courgettes et Boursin

A low-calorie and easy soup, with a French cheese that can be found easily in the United States: garlic and fine herbs Boursin cheese.

INGREDIENTS | SERVES 4

1 onion, peeled diced

4 tablespoons olive oil, divided

6 organic zucchini (4 minced, and 2 cut in thin slices)

5 cups chicken stock

1 (5.2-ounce) package garlic and fine herbs Boursin cheese

½ cup sliced almonds

1. In a large saucepan, cook the diced onion with 1 tablespoon olive oil over medium-high heat for 5 minutes. When it is golden, add the zucchini. Make sure they brown slightly on each side. Pour in the chicken stock and bring to a boil, and then reduce heat to low and simmer for 20 minutes.

2. Add half of the Boursin cheese to the saucepan, stir well, and simmer for another 5–10 minutes.

3. Meanwhile, heat 2 tablespoons of olive oil in a nonstick skillet over medium heat and cook the sliced almonds, stirring them frequently with a wooded spatula. The slices should toast slightly on each side. After 2 minutes, remove them from the heat and put them in a small bowl.

4. Over medium-high heat, pour another tablespoon of olive oil in the skillet. When it is hot, add the sliced zucchini. Stir them, using a wooden spoon. Once they are slightly golden brown, remove from the heat.

5. Put the cooked diced zucchini and stock in a blender and process until smooth. Put back in the large saucepan or in a large serving bowl. Crumble the other half of the Boursin cheese, and add it to top of the soup. Then add the thin slices of fried zucchini.

6. Sprinkle the sliced almonds on top of everything and serve.

Garbure (French Ham and Vegetable Stew)

This soup is very traditional in the southwest of France. Delicious, comforting, but high in calories.

INGREDIENTS | SERVES 6

6 duck legs preserved in fat (*confit*)

3 leeks, cut in 1" slices

1 large onion, peeled and diced

12 cups water

1 cabbage, cut in big chunks

1 turnip, peeled and cut in slices

3 medium carrots, peeled and cut in slices

2 celery stalks, cut in slices

6 medium potatoes, peeled and cut in slices

½ pound of Bayonne ham or smoked ham hock

1 tablespoon Espelette pepper (or paprika)

3 garlic cloves, peeled and diced

½ teaspoon salt

2 (29-ounce) cans of cannellini beans

1. Cook the duck legs in a very large French oven or a very large pot until all the fat is rendered for about 15 minutes, over low heat. When all the fat is rendered, take the legs out and put on a plate, and pour the rendered fat in a bowl. Reserve.

2. Put the pot (or French oven) over low heat and melt 4 tablespoons of the reserved duck fat. Add the sliced leeks and the onion. Stir very often for about 10 minutes, making sure the leeks don't turn brown. Then fill the pot with water and bring to a boil over high heat.

3. Add the vegetables (cabbage, turnip, carrots, celery, potatoes) and the ham. Add the tablespoon of Espelette pepper or paprika, the garlic, and the salt. Cover, reduce the heat to low, and simmer for at least 2 hours, stirring from time to time and spooning the foam and the fat out. The longer you can leave the pot on very low heat, the better the *Garbure* will be.

4. About 20 minutes before serving, add the cannellini beans and the *confit* duck legs, and put on medium heat.

5. On each plate, serve first the vegetables, then a piece of ham, then a piece of duck leg, and pour broth over it all.

Soupe de Potiron au Cumin (Pumpkin Soup with Cumin)

Halloween is not a traditional holiday in France, but the French sure do know their pumpkins all right! This savory pumpkin soup with a cumin twist is a good example.

INGREDIENTS | SERVES 4

1 large onion, peeled and diced

1 tablespoon olive oil

2 pounds pumpkin, peeled and cut in chunks

1 teaspoon salt

1 teaspoon ground black pepper

1 tablespoon ground cumin

4 cups water

1 cup chicken stock

4 fresh cilantro leaves

1. In a large saucepan, cook the diced onion in olive oil over medium-high heat. Stir with a spoon until the onion is translucent, about 3–5 minutes. Add the pumpkin, stir well, then add salt, pepper, and cumin. Pour in the water and the chicken stock, and bring to a boil over high heat. When reaching the boiling point, reduce the heat to low, cover, and simmer for 20 minutes.

2. With a slotted spoon, take the vegetables out and put them in a blender. Add one cup of the cooking liquid to the blender, process until smooth, and pour back in the saucepan.

3. Stir well, simmer for another 10 minutes, and serve with cilantro leaves in each plate. You can also sprinkle cumin seeds on top of the bowls if you have some.

Soupe de Potiron au Lait (Pumpkin Milk Soup)

Although sweet, this pumpkin in milk soup is served as an appetizer or even a main dish at dinner, mostly in the countryside. You can serve it with small cubes of stale baguette that you dip in the soup, or plain. It's also so sweet that it can make a nice warm dessert.

INGREDIENTS | SERVES 4

4 cups water

2 pounds pumpkin, peeled and cut in chunks

3 cups whole milk, divided

1 teaspoon cinnamon

For a Peachy Complexion

Pumpkins are rich in beta-carotene, which is great for your complexion. It is high in important antioxidants and low in calories. And it is rich in flavor!

1. In a large saucepan, bring the water to a boil over high heat. Add the pumpkin, reduce to medium heat, and cook for 20 minutes. When the pumpkin is soft, take it out of the water with a slotted spoon and put it on a plate and reserve.

2. Empty the saucepan, then fill it with 2½ cups milk, and heat it again on medium-low heat. Meanwhile, put the pumpkin in a blender with the remaining ½ cup milk. Process until smooth, and pour the pumpkin back in the saucepan with the warm milk. Stir well and simmer for 10 minutes.

3. Add the cinnamon at the last minute, stir well, and serve immediately.

Soupe à l'Oseille (Sorrel Soup)

Sorrel has long been a favorite among French chefs, and sorrel soup is the best way to discover its amazing flavor.

INGREDIENTS | SERVES 4

3 tablespoons butter
1 shallot, peeled and minced
1 garlic clove, diced
1 pound sorrel, chopped
3 potatoes, peeled and diced
1 teaspoon ground black pepper
1 teaspoon salt
1 cup chicken stock
4 cups water
1 cup whipping cream
4 tablespoons *crème fraîche*

Watch Your Sorrel!

The French love sorrel so much that they use it to talk about money. For instance, the French version of "take the money and run" is *Prends l'oseille et tire toi*—take the sorrel and run.

1. In a large saucepan, melt the butter over medium heat. Add the minced shallot, stir well, turn the heat to medium-low, cover, and cook gently for 5 minutes, stirring from time to time.

2. Add garlic to the saucepan. Stir well and add the chopped sorrel. Reduce the heat to the lowest level. Cook and stir well for around 5 minutes.

3. Add potatoes to the pot with the salt and pepper. Stir well, then immediately pour in the chicken stock and water. Bring to a boil over high heat, then reduce the heat to medium and cook for 15 minutes.

4. Put everything in a blender, process until very smooth, then put back in the saucepan. Add the whipping cream, stir well, and then put back on very low heat for 5 minutes.

5. Serve hot, and add a tablespoon of *crème fraîche* to each bowl to add smoothness.

Soupe à l'Oseille Légère (Light Sorrel Soup)

This is a low-calorie version of the classic sorrel soup, but nonetheless delicious! You can also make it with spinach, or with a combination of half spinach and half sorrel.

INGREDIENTS | SERVES 4

2 tablespoons olive oil
1 shallot, peeled and minced
1 garlic clove, diced
1 pound sorrel, chopped
1 cup chicken stock
4 cups water
2 eggs

1. Heat the olive oil in a large saucepan over medium-high heat.

2. Put the shallot in the saucepan and cook with olive oil. Stir well for 5 minutes over medium-low heat. Add garlic and sorrel to the pot. Stir well and cook for 3 minutes.

3. Cover with chicken stock and water. Bring to a boil over high heat, then reduce the heat to medium, cover, and cook for 15 minutes.

4. Pour in a blender, process until very smooth, then put back in the saucepan. Turn the heat to medium-high and cook for at least 5 minutes. Reduce the heat to low and simmer until serving time.

5. About 5 minutes before serving, whisk the two eggs together in a separate bowl. Make sure the soup is hot (but not boiling). Whisk it, pour in the eggs, and immediately go back to whisking very firmly. This will add smoothness and volume to the soup without adding the same amount of calories that cream does!

6. Serve immediately.

Velouté de Champignons (Cream of Mushroom Soup)

Cream of mushroom soup is a very common and popular winter soup.

INGREDIENTS | SERVES 4

2 tablespoons butter

1 medium shallot, peeled and diced

1 pound mushrooms (half diced, half undiced)

Juice of ½ lemon

1 garlic clove, peeled and diced

2 tablespoons fresh parsley, minced, and 4 parsley sprigs

½ cup white wine

1 cup chicken stock

1 cup water

½ cup *crème fraîche* or crema Mexicana

1 teaspoon salt

1 teaspoon ground black pepper

1 teaspoon Espelette pepper or paprika (optional)

1. In a large saucepan, melt the butter over medium-low heat. Add the diced shallot, stir well, and cook for around 5 minutes. Add diced mushrooms to the shallots. Stir well. Meanwhile, put the other half of the mushrooms (undiced) in a bowl, and sprinkle lemon juice on them so that they won't get brown.

2. Add garlic and parsley to the pan of mushrooms. Reduce the heat to low and cook for around 5 minutes, until the mushrooms get really soft.

3. Pour in the white wine and bring to a boil over medium-high heat. Let the wine reduce to about half, then add the chicken stock and the water and bring back to a boil over high heat. Add the rest of the mushrooms, stir well, and reduce heat to low. Let simmer for 15 minutes.

4. Pour everything into a blender and process until smooth, around 2 minutes. Pour back in the saucepan, add the cream, whisk well, and add salt and pepper. If you use the optional Espelette pepper, add it now. Simmer on very low heat until dinnertime.

5. Serve with a sprig of parsley in each bowl.

Velouté d'Asperges (Cream of Asparagus Soup)

This soup can be made with either green or white asparagus. If you use the white ones, make sure you peel them well.

INGREDIENTS | SERVES 4

2 pounds asparagus

6 cups water

1 cup chicken stock

2 cups crema Mexicana or sour cream

1 teaspoon salt

1 teaspoon ground black pepper

1 tablespoon ground nutmeg

1 tablespoon butter

8 leaves of fresh chervil (you can use parsley)

A Dieter's Dream

Both green and white asparagus are perfect for a foodie who would like to watch his or her figure while enjoying good food. It's very low in calories, and a great way to cleanse the system. It is also a great vegetable for pregnant and nursing women, because it's rich in B_9 vitamins.

1. Peel the asparagus (only slightly if you're using green asparagus), cut off about 2 inches of the tips, put them in a bowl, and reserve. Cut off the bottom of each asparagus (about 1") and discard. Then dice the rest of the asparagus spears.

2. Fill a large saucepan with water and chicken stock, bring to a boil over high heat, and add the diced asparagus and the asparagus tips. Boil for 5 minutes. With a slotted spoon, take the diced asparagus and the tips out. Reserve in two different bowls. Remove saucepan with the remaining broth from heat.

3. Fill another saucepan with the cream, and add salt, pepper, and nutmeg. Bring to a boil over medium-high heat and stir well. The cream should reduce to about a third.

4. Pour the diced asparagus in a blender. Add one cup of the broth from the saucepan, and process until very smooth. Add the purée to the cream, whisk well, then simmer on low heat for 5 minutes, stirring from time to time and making sure it never boils. Just before serving, warm the asparagus tips by stirring them in melted butter in a saucepan over low heat.

5. Serve in individual bowls, adding two chervil leaves and some asparagus tips on top of each bowl.

CHAPTER 7

Cold Soups

Soupe Froide de Courgettes au Fromage de Chèvre (Cold Zucchini Soup with Goat Cheese)

Goat cheese, zucchini, and mint are a great refreshing combination in this chilled green soup.

INGREDIENTS | SERVES 4

4 small organic zucchini, diced
2 tablespoons olive oil, divided
1 onion, peeled and diced
1 garlic clove, diced
1 cup chicken stock
3 cups water
1 teaspoon salt
1 teaspoon ground black pepper
2 tablespoons fresh mint, minced, and 8 mint leaves
5 ounces goat cheese

A New French Tradition

Cold or chilled soups have appeared in France only in the last fifty years, after the refrigerator became a common household appliance. But they have settled onto the typical summer menu quite nicely.

1. Reserve half of the diced zucchini in a bowl.

2. In a large saucepan, heat 1 tablespoon olive oil on medium-high heat, and add the diced onion. Stir well for about 3 minutes, until they become transparent. Then add the diced garlic (green part discarded), and half of the diced zucchini. Stir well and brown slightly for 2 minutes.

3. Cover with chicken stock and water, add salt and pepper, stir well and cook for 20 minutes on low heat. Pour into a blender. Add the minced mint. Process well for about 4 minutes. Pour the puréed soup in a serving bowl.

4. Heat a nonstick skillet over medium-high heat, add 1 tablespoon of olive oil, and the other half of the diced zucchini. Cook them slowly for 5 minutes, stirring and reducing the heat if necessary. Then pour in the bowl, cover with plastic wrap, and put in the refrigerator for at least 2 hours.

5. Five minutes before serving, crumble the goat cheese over the soup and stir. Decorate with mint leaves on the top.

Soupe Glacée à l'Avocat (Chilled Avocado Soup)

To really enjoy this chilled avocado soup, you have to make it one day ahead.

INGREDIENTS | SERVES 4

1 cup chicken stock

2 cups water

1 cup arugula

Juice of 1 lemon

3 avocados

1 teaspoon salt

1 teaspoon ground black pepper

1 teaspoon Espelette pepper
(or paprika)

4 bacon slices

2 tablespoons olive oil

Omega-3 Delight

Avocado is one of these super foods that you love to love. It's packed with omega-3 fatty acids and fiber, and has great benefits for the health of your heart and your skin.

1. Fill a medium saucepan with the chicken stock and the water, and bring to a boil over medium-high heat. Add the arugula, and boil for 5 minutes. Using a slotted spoon, take the leaves out, put them in a blender, add a cup of the stock, and process until smooth. Pour the blended arugula leaves back in the saucepan, bring back to a boil, and keep on medium-high heat for 5 minutes after the boiling point.

2. In a large serving bowl, spoon out the avocado flesh and mash with a fork, stirring the lemon juice in. Add salt, pepper, and Espelette pepper, then mash again until the avocados are really smooth.

3. Slowly pour the boiling stock onto the avocados, stirring well, adding more liquid only when the mixture is smooth. At the end, the mixture must be even and somewhat thick. Cover and put in the fridge for 12 hours at least.

4. The next day, dice the bacon slices and fry them in the olive oil. Dry them with a paper cloth, put in a bowl, and reserve.

5. Serve the soup as is, adding the bacon pieces on top of each bowl.

Soupe de Melon au Champagne
(Chilled Melon and Champagne Soup)

What's more elegant than starting a dinner with a chilled Champagne soup? This cold soup is a perfect summer appetizer.

INGREDIENTS | SERVES 4

2 *charentais* melons (or 1 American cantaloupe), about 2 pounds

2 cloves

2 tablespoons fresh mint, minced, and 8 mint leaves

½ cup Champagne or sparkling wine

4 thin slices of Serrano ham, cut in ½"-wide strips

How to Choose a Melon

Charentais melons are one of the finest fruits of a French summer, and there's a whole art to choosing them. You should weigh them with your hand (the heavier, the tastier), then take a look at the stalk. If it's already detaching itself, that means it's ripe enough.

1. Cut the melon in two, take out the seeds, and spoon out the flesh. Make a dozen melon bowls by using a teaspoon: They should look like ice cream balls, but smaller. Reserve the melon balls, and put in the refrigerator. Spoon out the rest of the flesh into a large bowl.

2. In a blender, pour the melon flesh, the cloves, the minced mint, and the Champagne, and process until very smooth. Place immediately in the refrigerator. If you want to serve the soup in a couple of hours, pour it in a container and leave in the freezer for an hour, then move it to the refrigerator for the last hour.

3. Serve the soup in individual bowls. First ladle in the soup, then the melon balls, then the ham. Add mint leaves to the top.

Soupe de Pastèque Froide (Cold Watermelon Soup)

This soup is a savory way to rediscover watermelon.

INGREDIENTS | SERVES 4

3 pounds watermelon

1 cucumber, peeled and diced into
 ½" cubes

1 red bell pepper, seeded and diced

1 onion, peeled and diced

2 garlic cloves, peeled and diced

1 cup orange juice

3 tablespoons balsamic vinegar

1 teaspoon salt

1 teaspoon ground black pepper

1. Cut the watermelon in big chunks and take the seeds out. Take about a half cup of the watermelon, and cut it in small ½" cubes. Reserve and store in the refrigerator.

2. Put ⅓ of the cucumber cubes in a bowl, and store in the refrigerator.

3. Pour the remaining cucumber, red pepper, watermelon chunks, onion, garlic, orange juice, and vinegar into a blender and process well, for about 5 minutes.

4. Pour the puréed soup in a serving bowl, add salt and ground pepper, then add the reserved cubes of watermelon and cucumber. Cover and put in the refrigerator for at least 2 hours

5. Serve with a bottle of hot sauce on the table.

Soupe Froide à la Betterave (Chilled Beet Soup with Feta)

The color of this soup is a thrill in itself! Beets with feta is both sweet and so refreshing.

INGREDIENTS | SERVES 4

4 beets (1 pound)

3 tablespoons white vinegar

1 cup chicken stock

2 cups water

1–2 tablespoons rice vinegar or
 cider vinegar

1 teaspoon salt

1 teaspoon ground black pepper

5 ounces feta cheese in bulk, cut in
 ½" cubes

How to Cook Beets the French Way

The most traditional way to cook beets in France is to roast them slowly in a 300°F oven. Just put them in a dish (after cutting the leaves off) and let them roast for at least 2 hours. Then peel them once they are cool.

1. If you don't have time to roast the beets, you can boil them. Wash them, take off the leaves, and trim them at each end. Fill a large saucepan with water, add the white vinegar, and bring to a boil over high heat. Put the beets in the boiling water, then reduce the heat to low and simmer for 30 minutes.

2. Peel the beets (careful of staining your hands! You can wear plastic gloves to keep this from happening) and cut them in small cubes. Fill a medium saucepan with the chicken stock and water, and bring to a boil over high heat. Add the beets and reduce the heat to low, simmering for 5 minutes.

3. Pour into a blender and process well, for about 4 minutes, then pour into a serving bowl. Add the rice vinegar or the cider vinegar, stir well, and add salt and pepper. Cover and put in the refrigerator for at least 2 hours.

4. About 5 minutes before serving, mix the feta into the soup.

Soupe Glacée de Tomates au Basilic
(Chilled Tomato Soup with Basil)

The French Provençal *version of gazpacho, this chilled tomato soup is much less garlicky and full of basil flavor.*

INGREDIENTS | SERVES 4

2 tablespoons olive oil, divided

1 medium onion, peeled and diced

1 medium carrot, peeled and diced

1 garlic clove, peeled and diced

1 celery stalk, diced

1 bay leaf

1 tablespoon thyme

1 (28-ounce) can of diced tomatoes

1 tablespoon tomato paste

2 cups chicken stock

3 cups water

1 teaspoon salt

1 teaspoon ground black pepper

3 tablespoons fresh basil leaves

1. In a large saucepan, heat 1 tablespoon of olive oil, and cook the diced onion over medium heat, stirring well, for about 5 minutes. Add the carrot, garlic, and celery, and cook for another 5 minutes, stirring very often.

2. Add the bay leaf and the thyme; stir well for around 1 minute.

3. Pour the diced tomatoes in the saucepan, with the juice, and add the tomato paste. Stir well, then add the chicken stock and the water. Bring to a boil, add salt and pepper, then reduce the heat to medium and cook for 20 minutes.

4. Take the bay leaf out, and pour everything in a blender. Process well for 4 minutes, then pour in a large bowl. Cover the bowl and put it in the refrigerator for 2 hours.

5. Five minutes before serving, process the basil leaves (except 4 that you will use for decoration) and 1 tablespoon of olive oil in the blender for about 1 minute, until it makes a paste.

6. Serve in individual bowls, adding a basil leaf and a tablespoon of basil paste at the center of each bowl.

Soupe Glacée de Petits Pois à la Coriandre
(Chilled Pea Soup with Cilantro)

This ice-cold soup is perfect for hot summer days spent lounging in the garden.

INGREDIENTS | SERVES 4

1 pound peas (preferably fresh, but frozen is all right)

3 tablespoons olive oil

1 dozen spring onions, diced

1 head romaine lettuce, shredded

1 tablespoon fresh cilantro, minced, and 4 cilantro leaves

1 cup chicken stock

1 cup water

1 teaspoon salt

1 teaspoon ground black pepper

1 teaspoon curry powder

1. Put 4 tablespoons of fresh peas in a bowl and reserve. If you're using frozen peas, place them with 4 tablespoons in a bowl of warm water to thaw slowly.

2. In a large saucepan, heat the olive oil and cook the onions over medium heat, stirring well for about 5 minutes. Add the peas, stir well, and then add the shredded lettuce. Let everything cook and reduce for another 5 minutes.

3. Put the minced cilantro in a medium saucepan with the chicken stock and the water. Add salt and pepper. Stir well, and bring to a boil over high heat. When it begins to boil, reduce to a low heat, cover, and simmer for 20 minutes.

4. Meanwhile, fill a medium saucepan with water, and bring to a boil over high heat. Prepare a medium bowl of ice cubes. Pour the fresh peas you reserved earlier into the boiling water and cook for 5 minutes. The peas should stay crunchy and *al dente*. Remove them and put them on the bed of ice.

5. Pour the onion mixture and peas in a blender, and process well for around 5 minutes. Pour the mixture in a serving bowl, add the *al dente* peas, and put in the refrigerator for 2 hours.

6. Serve in individual bowls, adding a cilantro leaf and a pinch of curry powder to the center of each bowl.

Soupe Froide de Concombre (Cold Cucumber Soup)

The hydrating powers of the cucumber makes it a great vegetable for summer, iced soup included!

INGREDIENTS | SERVES 4

2 medium cucumbers, peeled, seeded, and diced

1 teaspoon kosher salt

1 garlic clove, peeled and diced

1 cup chicken stock

1 (7-ounce) container of Greek yogurt

Juice of 1 lemon

1 teaspoon salt

2 teaspoons ground black pepper

8 mint leaves

1. Reserve 4 tablespoons of diced cucumber and put them in a bowl. Put 1 teaspoon kosher salt on them, stir well, cover in plastic wrap, and reserve in the refrigerator.

2. Pour the unreserved cucumbers, garlic, chicken stock, and Greek yogurt in the blender. Process until very smooth.

3. Pour into a serving bowl, add lemon juice, salt, and pepper, and stir well. Cover and put in the refrigerator for 1 hour.

4. Before serving, pour the reserved diced cucumber into the soup. Decorate with mint leaves. Serve very cold.

Soupe de Pois Chiches Glacée (Cold Chickpea Soup)

This iced cold soup with garbanzo beans is inspired by North African cuisine, which is a big influence on today's French home cooking.

INGREDIENTS | SERVES 4

2 (7-ounce) containers Greek yogurt

1 (15-ounce) can garbanzo beans, drained

1 teaspoon cumin

1 teaspoon ground ginger

1 teaspoon Espelette pepper (or paprika)

1 tablespoon plus one teaspoon olive oil, divided

1 teaspoon salt

1 teaspoon ground black pepper

4 cilantro leaves

1. Put 1 Greek yogurt and half of the second one in the blender. Reserve the leftover yogurt.

2. Add the garbanzo beans to the blender with the cumin, ginger, Espelette pepper, and olive oil. Process until smooth. Pour back in a serving bowl, sprinkle with salt and pepper, and put in the refrigerator for about 1 hour.

3. Serve in individual bowls, adding a drop of olive oil, a cilantro leaf, and a teaspoon of Greek yogurt to the center of each bowl.

Soupe d'Asperges Vertes Glacée (Cold Asparagus Soup)

This delicious cold soup has smoked salmon for the omega-3 benefit!

INGREDIENTS | SERVES 4

14 ounces green asparagus, peeled

1 tablespoon butter

1 teaspoon salt

1 teaspoon ground black pepper

2 cups chicken stock

1 cup whipping cream

1 tablespoon diced chives

4 ounces smoked salmon, cut in ½" squares

1. Cut off the asparagus heads. Fill a saucepan with water, bring to a boil over high heat, and poach the heads for 2 minutes. Take them out with a slotted spoon and reserve.

2. In a medium saucepan, melt the butter over medium heat. Cook the rest of the asparagus in it for 2–3 minutes, adding salt, pepper, and the stock, and simmer for 15 minutes.

3. Put in the blender, add the cream, and process until smooth. Pour in a large bowl, and put in the refrigerator for 2 hours.

4. Serve in individual bowls, sprinkling diced chives and smoked salmon in each.

Soupe de Radis Glacée (Cold Radish Soup)

Radishes and cucumber come together perfectly in this refreshing appetizer.

INGREDIENTS | SERVES 4

2 bunches of radishes
2 teaspoons plus one pinch salt, divided
2 teaspoons ground black pepper
1 medium organic cucumber, shredded
2 garlic cloves
4 coriander seeds
Juice of 1 lemon
2 cups regular plain yogurt
8 mint leaves

About Radishes

French radishes are actually a little different from American ones. They are longer, thinner, and less peppery. In any case, always make sure you have some in your pantry: In France, *n'avoir plus un radis*, to be without radishes, means being completely out of money.

1. Reserve half the radishes. Cut the first bunch of the radishes in very thin slices, almost transparent, then sprinkle 1 teaspoon salt and pepper on them and put in the refrigerator. Sprinkle the shredded cucumber with 1 teaspoon salt and put in the refrigerator as well.

2. Pour the rest of the radishes in a blender, with the rest of the cucumber, garlic cloves, coriander seeds, and lemon juice. Process well for 2 minutes, then add the yogurt. Process again for 2 minutes. Pour in a serving bowl, cover it with plastic wrap, and put in the refrigerator for 1 hour.

3. After an hour minimum, take the cucumber slices out of the refrigerator, pick them up and squeeze them over the sink. Add the cucumber slices to the serving bowl, stir well, then add half of the radish slices and stir again. Sprinkle 1 teaspoon of ground pepper, and a pinch of salt. Dice 4 mint leaves.

4. Serve in individual bowls, adding the rest of the radish slices and sprinkling diced mint on top of each. Add one mint leaf to each bowl.

Soupe Vichyssoise

The mother of all cold soups à la française, *it's a simple cold version of* Potage Bonne Femme *with milk.*

INGREDIENTS | SERVES 4

2 tablespoons butter

1 onion, peeled and diced

3 leeks, thinly sliced (discard the green part)

2 potatoes, peeled and diced

1 teaspoon salt

1 teaspoon ground black pepper

½ cup chicken stock

1 cup whole milk

⅓ cup *crème fraîche*

8 parsley sprigs

A Very American French Soup

Vichyssoise is nowhere to be found in old French cookbooks. It was invented in New York by a French chef, Louis Diat, at the beginning of the twentieth century. Diat was born near the town of Vichy; hence the name. One century later, the recipe has crossed the Atlantic and is popular in France!

1. In a large saucepan, melt the butter on low heat. Add the diced onion and cook slowly, stirring often, for 5 minutes. Then add the leeks (only the white parts, cut in very thin slices), and cook slowly for another 5 minutes. Add the potatoes, salt, and pepper, and stir well. Add the chicken stock, bring to a boil over high heat, then reduce to a simmer. Add the milk, stir well, and simmer for 30 minutes over very low heat.

2. Pour into a blender and process until very smooth. Pour the mixture into a serving bowl, and let it cool at room temperature for about 30 minutes. You can then add the cream. Stir well, and put in the refrigerator for 1 hour.

3. Decorate with parsley sprigs, and serve very cold.

CHAPTER 8

Salades Composées (Salads)

Salade Landaise (Landes Salad)

This salad is as generous as the region it is named after. Les Landes, in the southwest of France, is famous for inhabitants who love to party and eat well. You can also add foie gras on top of it.

INGREDIENTS | SERVES 4

1 tablespoon plus 1 teaspoon salt, divided
1 pound French beans, trimmed
1 medium shallot, diced
1 tablespoon red wine vinegar
1 teaspoon ground black pepper
2 tablespoons olive oil
10 cherry tomatoes, halved
4 duck gizzards, trimmed and chopped
4 cups curly endive lettuce (frisée)
12 slices smoked duck bacon
2 ounces pine nuts

1. Fill a medium saucepan with water, add a tablespoon of salt, and bring to a boil over high heat. Fill a medium bowl with ice water and set aside.

2. Add French beans to the boiling water and boil for 7 minutes. With a slotted spoon, remove beans from the saucepan and immediately plunge them into the ice water. Reserve.

3. Put the shallot in a large salad bowl. Add vinegar, 1 teaspoon salt, and pepper, stir well, then add the olive oil and stir to combine. Stir in the tomatoes.

4. Heat a large nonstick skillet over high heat. Add gizzards to the skillet and let them cook in their fat, sautéing for 3–5 minutes, until they lose their blue color and turn slightly red. Remove from skillet and keep warm.

5. Add the lettuce and the French beans to the salad bowl and toss with the cherry tomatoes and shallot dressing.

6. Divide the lettuce mixture among 4 salad plates. Top with the smoked duck bacon and gizzards.

7. Sprinkle pine nuts over the salads and serve immediately.

Salade Niçoise

This is the most famous French salad, and it's definitely the healthiest. This salad was invented in Nice, along the Mediterranean coast. It's a perfect example of the celebrated Mediterranean diet.

INGREDIENTS | SERVES 4

3 large eggs
1 garlic clove, peeled
1 tablespoon red wine vinegar
1 teaspoon salt
1 teaspoon ground black pepper
3 tablespoons olive oil
4 cups mixed salad greens
3 medium tomatoes, thinly sliced
4 green onions, thinly sliced
8 anchovy fillets in olive oil, drained
1 (5-ounce) can tuna in olive oil
6 large basil leaves, shredded
½ cup small black olives

The Real Recipe!

Niçoise salad is so loved in France that it has been adapted in a thousand ways: some add potatoes, French beans, etc. It infuriates the inhabitants of Nice, who fight for their original recipe. In fact, an organization to save the "real Niçoise salad" gives a prize each year to the chef who is the most faithful to the recipe.

1. Fill a medium bowl with ice water and set aside. Place eggs in a small saucepan and cover with water. Bring to a boil over high heat. Boil eggs for 10 minutes. Remove eggs from water with a slotted spoon, then plunge them into ice water. Reserve.

2. Rub the garlic clove on the inside of a large salad bowl, crushing the clove as you do so.

3. Add vinegar, salt, and pepper to the bowl and stir well. Whisk in olive oil.

4. Add the salad greens and toss to coat. Add tomatoes and green onion and toss again.

5. Add anchovies and tuna and stir again. Remove eggs from water and peel and quarter them. Add to the salad.

6. Add basil leaves and the olives just before serving.

Salade Lyonnaise

This salad comes from Lyon, also known as the capital of French gastronomy, because so many great chefs started there. But there's nothing to be scared of with this recipe. It's really easy, and relies on the first commandment of French cuisine: great fresh produce.

INGREDIENTS | SERVES 4

½ pound of bacon, cut in ½"-wide slices

1 medium shallot, peeled and diced

2 tablespoons white vinegar

4 eggs

1 curly endive lettuce (*frisée*), at least 4 cups

1 teaspoon salt

1 teaspoon ground black pepper

Two Dressings

You can either serve this salad with a very simple dressing made with only the bacon fat and the caramelized shallots, or make another dressing with 1 teaspoon Dijon mustard, 1 tablespoon red wine vinegar, and 2 tablespoons vegetable oil, whisked firmly.

1. Heat a nonstick skillet over medium heat. Add the *lardons* (sticks of bacon) and the diced shallot. Stir them well and cook slowly for around 7 minutes.

2. Fill a medium saucepan with water, add the white vinegar, and bring to a boil over high heat. Poach your eggs in the boiling water: Break them one by one into the water and nudge each immediately in a round shape with a tablespoon. Reduce the heat to low and cook for 3 minutes.

3. In a large salad bowl, put the curly lettuce, then the bacon and the caramelized shallot, along with the warm bacon fat that is still in the skillet. Toss the salad, add salt and pepper, and toss again.

4. Top the salad with the poached eggs and serve.

Salade Auvergnate

The volcanic mountains of Auvergne in the center of France are the source of some of the best cheeses and charcuterie in the country. It's also a region of harsh weather, which explains why the recipe is comforting and perfect in winter!

INGREDIENTS | SERVES 4

6 medium potatoes, in their skin

1 tablespoon kosher salt

1 tablespoon cider vinegar

1 teaspoon salt

1 teaspoon ground black pepper

1 teaspoon Dijon mustard

3 tablespoons walnut oil (or vegetable oil)

4 cups mixed greens salad

2 slices of cured ham, cut in ½"-wide sticks

1 pound young Cantal cheese (a strongly flavored young cow cheese), cut in ½"-wide sticks

1 shallot, peeled and diced

1 tablespoon diced chives

1. Fill a large saucepan with water. Add the potatoes and a tablespoon of kosher salt.

2. Bring to a boil over high heat, then cook for 20 minutes. Dry them, peel them, and cut them in thin slices.

3. In a large salad bowl, combine the cider vinegar, salt, and pepper, and stir well. Add the mustard and stir well, then add the oil little by little, whisking until the dressing is totally smooth and uniform.

4. Add the salad, toss well for about 3 minutes, then add the potatoes, ham, and cheese. Add the diced shallot and the chives, and toss again.

5. Serve as a main dish.

Salade du Nord

The endives, blue cheese, apples, and walnuts in this salad pay homage to the cuisine of northern France.

INGREDIENTS | SERVES 4

Juice of 1 lemon
6 endives, thinly sliced
2 apples, peeled
1 tablespoon red wine vinegar
1 teaspoon Dijon mustard
1 teaspoon salt
1 teaspoon ground black pepper
3 tablespoons canola oil
½ pound blue cheese, cut in ½" cubes
½ cup walnuts halves

The Vampire Salad

Northern France is not particularly blessed with sunny weather, but when it comes to growing endives, the climate is perfect. This very strange salad never sees the sun before it comes to the grocery store. It grows mostly in total darkness.

1. In a bowl, pour half the lemon juice on the endives. Reserve.

2. In another bowl, sprinkle the other half of the lemon juice on the apples, and reserve.

3. In a large bowl, stir the red wine vinegar with the Dijon mustard, salt, and pepper. Then add the canola oil little by little, whisking constantly, until the dressing is thick and smooth.

4. Add the endives, stir well, then add the apples and stir again. The endives and the apples must really soak up the dressing. Then add the cheese and the walnuts, and stir again.

5. Keep at room temperature until serving.

Salade Camarguaise

There are no salad leaves in this salad, because it's based on the main crop in the region it's named after. Camargue in the South of France is the only area in the country where wild rice is grown.

INGREDIENTS | SERVES 4

1 tablespoon kosher salt

1 cup rice

Juice of 1 lemon

1 teaspoon salt

1 teaspoon ground black pepper

3 tablespoons olive oil

1 medium red bell pepper, seeded and chopped in ½" squares

2 medium tomatoes, thinly sliced

12 anchovies fillets in olive oil, drained

1 (5-ounce) can tuna in water, drained

¼ cup black olives, pitted

1. Fill a large saucepan with water, and bring to a boil over high heat. Add a tablespoon of kosher salt and the rice. Cook for 18 minutes. Drain the rice and reserve.

2. Put the lemon juice in a large salad bowl. Sprinkle with teaspoon of salt and a teaspoon of pepper and stir. Add the olive oil slowly and whisk well, until the dressing is even and thick.

3. Add the rice, the bell pepper, the slices of tomatoes, the drained anchovy fillets, tuna, and black olives. Toss well. Cover with plastic wrap and put in the refrigerator for one hour.

4. Serve cold.

Salade Marocaine

There are large North African communities in France, and they have had a great influence on French cuisine. It's unclear if this Moroccan salad recipe is actually made in Morocco, but it's always a big hit in France! It's also a perfect vegan meal, with vegetables and legumes.

INGREDIENTS | SERVES 4

Juice of 1 lemon

1 teaspoon salt

1 teaspoon ground black pepper

3 tablespoons olive oil

6 carrots, peeled and grated

1 (15-ounce) can garbanzo beans, drained

2 oranges, peeled and sectioned

1 tablespoon ground cumin

2 tablespoons fresh cilantro, minced, plus 8 cilantro leaves

1. In a large salad bowl, pour the lemon juice, salt, and pepper, and stir well. Slowly add the olive oil, whisking constantly and firmly, until the dressing is smooth and thick.

2. Place grated carrots in the salad bowl and toss well. Add garbanzo beans and toss again.

3. Add oranges to bowl. Toss well, then add the ground cumin and stir again. Minced the cilantro thinly, reserving 8 leaves for decoration.

4. Put in the refrigerator for an hour, to make sure the lemon and the cumin have time to really settle in the ingredients. Add the 8 cilantro leaves on top before serving.

Salade Parisienne

This is the mother of all salades completes: literally a full salad, as in full of the ingredients you need to eat at lunch in order to go on with your day in a crazy, busy city like Paris. It's the kind of salad the real parisienne would have on a daily basis at the bistrot around the corner!

INGREDIENTS | SERVES 4

½ cup fresh button mushrooms, thinly sliced

Juice of ½ lemon

4 eggs, boiled, peeled and halved

1 teaspoon Dijon mustard

1 teaspoon salt

1 teaspoon ground black pepper

1 tablespoon red wine vinegar

3 tablespoons olive or canola oil

4 cups romaine lettuce, leaves shredded

½ pound Gruyère cheese, cut in ½" cubes

1 ham steak, cut in ½" squares

½ cup fresh parsley, chopped

1. Sprinkle mushrooms with lemon juice so that they don't turn brown.

2. Fill a medium saucepan with water, bring to a boil over high heat, and cook the eggs for 10 minutes. Prepare a bowl of ice water. Put the boiled eggs in the ice water, and peel them when cool. Cut them in half.

3. In a large salad bowl, stir the mustard with the salt and pepper, then add the vinegar and stir well. Add the olive oil little by little, whisking well, until you get a smooth and thick dressing. Add the shredded romaine leaves, stir well, then add the mushrooms, the Gruyère cheese, and the ham. Add the chopped parsley.

4. Put the hard-boiled eggs on top of the salad before serving.

Salade de Chèvre Chaud (Hot Goat Cheese Salad)

Another Parisian bistrot classic. This salad is perfect in winter to help you warm up, but it's not too heavy a meal.

INGREDIENTS | SERVES 4

2 garlic cloves, peeled

4 slices of bread

1 pound goat cheese, cut in ½" slices (or 4 *crottins* of goat cheese)

1 teaspoon ground black pepper

2 tablespoons chives, chopped

½ pound bacon slices, cut in ½" sticks

1 tablespoon red wine vinegar

1 teaspoon Dijon mustard

1 teaspoon salt

1 teaspoon ground black pepper

3 tablespoons canola oil

6 cups mixed greens salad

12 cherry tomatoes, halved

Crottin

Crottin is a typical round goat cheese from the Loire Valley. The most famous is called *Crottin de Chavignol*. It is made in the very small village of Chavignol, not far from another great culinary village, Sancerre. A glass of white Sancerre is actually the best wine to drink with this recipe.

1. Preheat your broiler. Rub garlic on the slices of bread. Cut the slices of bread in two halves. Put a disk or slice of goat cheese on top of each piece of bread, sprinkle pepper and chopped chives on them, then put them on a parchment paper–lined baking sheet. Put in the oven for 10 minutes, or as long as it takes the cheese to melt and slightly brown.

2. Heat a nonstick skillet over medium-high heat, and cook the bacon for 5 minutes. Remove bacon, pouring the bacon fat into a salad bowl.

3. Combine vinegar, Dijon mustard, salt, and pepper in the same bowl. Add the oil little by little, and whisk steadily. Add the mixed greens, toss well, then add the bacon and the cherry tomatoes, and top with the goat cheese toast.

4. Serve immediately.

Salade Alsacienne (Alsatian Salad)

Alsace is the land of great sausages and charcuterie, partly because of its proximity to Germany. That's why frankfurter sausage is used in this American adaptation of the Alsatian salad.

INGREDIENTS | SERVES 4

4 large eggs, boiled and peeled, halved
6 medium potatoes
4 frankfurter sausages
1 medium shallot, peeled and diced
1 tablespoon chives, diced
1 teaspoon Dijon mustard
1 tablespoon red wine vinegar
1 teaspoon salt
1 teaspoon ground black pepper
3 tablespoons canola oil
4 cups romaine lettuce
2 tomatoes, thinly sliced
1 ham steak, cut in ½" squares
½ pound Cheddar, cut in ½" cubes

1. Fill a large saucepan with water and bring to a boil over high heat. Add the eggs and cook for 10 minutes. Prepare bowl of ice water, and transfer the eggs to the ice water as soon as they are boiled. Peel them when cool, and cut them in half.

2. Put the potatoes in a medium saucepan, fill it with water, bring to a boil, and cook for 20 minutes.

3. Meanwhile, warm the frankfurter sausages in a smaller saucepan, over medium-low heat.

4. Peel the potatoes and cut them in thin slices. Then cut the warm sausages in ½" slices.

5. In a salad bowl, combine the diced shallot, chives, and mustard. Add the vinegar, salt, and pepper. Stir well, then add the oil little by little, whisking firmly. Add the romaine leaves and the tomatoes, toss well, then add the potatoes, the ham, the cheese, and the sausage slices.

6. Serve immediately.

Salade de Foies de Volaille (Salad with Chicken Livers)

Chicken liver is full of iron, and is a great inexpensive ingredient! This salad is a favorite among students: You can look like a great chef without spending too much.

INGREDIENTS | SERVES 4

2 thick slices of bread (stale is better), cut ½" cubes
1 garlic clove, peeled
1 tablespoon butter
2 tablespoons olive oil, divided
12 chicken livers (approximately 1 pound)
1 teaspoon Dijon mustard
1 teaspoon salt
1 teaspoon ground black pepper
2 tablespoons red wine vinegar
3 tablespoons canola oil
4 cups arugula
2 tomatoes, sliced

Butter? Oil? Or Both?

It is usually said that France is divided in two parts: North of the Loire Valley, people cook only with butter, while in the south of France, they cook with oil. It is sometimes easiest to just use both! Combining oil and butter allows you to cook more easily and with more flavor.

1. Rub the bread slices with garlic. Heat a nonstick skillet over medium-high heat, melt the butter in it, then add 1 tablespoon olive oil. Swirl to combine, then add the bread cubes, stir them well in the butter and oil, and let them get slightly brown on each side, about 3–5 minutes.

2. Pour the croutons in a bowl, put the skillet back on the heat, and add remaining tablespoon of olive oil over medium-high heat. Add the chicken livers and cook them for 10 minutes, stirring often, until their color changes on each side.

3. Meanwhile, combine the Dijon mustard, salt, and pepper in a large bowl.

4. Remove the chicken livers from the skillet, and put aside. Pour the red wine vinegar in the skillet. Deglaze, then pour the vinegar and the fat of the chicken liver into the large bowl. Stir well. Add the canola oil slowly. Whisk well.

5. Add the arugula, toss well, then add the sliced tomatoes. Add the bread croutons, toss again, then add the livers on top at the end.

6. Serve immediately.

Taboulé (Tabbouleh)

This couscous salad is very popular in the summer. It's inspired by the Lebanese original tabbouleh, but is much more filling, and is therefore often served as a main dish at picnics, for example.

INGREDIENTS | SERVES 4

1 pound couscous
Juice of 2 lemons
¾ cup olive oil
6 medium tomatoes, peeled and diced
3 small spring onions, peeled and diced
1 medium cucumber, diced
4 tablespoons fresh mint, minced
4 tablespoons fresh cilantro, minced
1 teaspoon salt
1 teaspoon ground black pepper

1. In a large salad bowl, combine the couscous with the lemon juice and the olive oil. Stir well.

2. Prepare a large bowl of ice water. Fill a medium saucepan with water, bring to a boil over high heat, then turn off the heat and add the tomatoes. Leave them in the water for 1 minute, then take them out and plunge them in the ice water.

3. Add the tomatoes, onion, and cucumber to the couscous, and stir well.

4. Add the mint, cilantro, salt, and pepper, and stir again. Use a fork to prevent the couscous from getting sticky. Cover. Put in the refrigerator for at least one night.

5. Serve very cold.

Salade de Truite au Pamplemousse (Smoked Trout and Grapefruit Salad)

This smoked trout and grapefruit recipe is great to bring a splash of summer to your winter! It's also very good for your health: Trout and avocado are full of omega-3 fatty acids.

INGREDIENTS | SERVES 4

Juice of 1 lemon
1 teaspoon salt
1 teaspoon ground black pepper
2 tablespoons canola oil or olive oil
4 cups romaine lettuce, shredded in two
1 tablespoon dill, minced
2 smoked trout fillets, cut in 2" slices
1 grapefruit, peeled and cut in slices
1 avocado, peeled and cut in 1" cubes

1. In a large salad bowl, stir the lemon juice with the salt and pepper, then add the oil little by little, whisking well until you get a smooth and thick dressing.

2. Add the romaine leaves, and toss well. Then add the dill, trout, grapefruit, and avocado. Toss well; "tire" your salad!

3. Serve cold.

CHAPTER 9

Quiches and Savory Pies

Quiche Lorraine

The first and most famous French savory pie: Quiche Lorraine!

INGREDIENTS | SERVES 4

3 large eggs

½ cup *crème fraîche* or crema Mexicana

½ cup whole milk

½ teaspoon salt

1 teaspoon ground black pepper

1 teaspoon ground nutmeg

1 *Pâte Brisée* dough (see recipe in Chapter 22)

4 ounces cooked ham steak or bacon, cut in ½" sticks

3 ounces cheese (Comté is the best, but Gruyère or Cheddar will do), roughly grated

A Tradition in the East of France

Quiche is a symbol of Lorraine, a region in the east of France that is dear to the French, because of its history (it was invaded by the Germans in the nineteenth century and wasn't returned to France until WWI), but also because of its food. Quiche is the best example. In Lorraine, people will always welcome you with a *quiche de bienvenue*, a welcome pie.

1. Preheat the oven to 350°F.

2. In a bowl, whisk the eggs well, then add the cream and whisk until very smooth. Add the milk slowly and whisk well again. Add the salt, pepper, and nutmeg, then stir again.

3. Roll out the dough to a 13" diameter circle on a parchment paper sheet. Take a 12" tart pan, and place the dough and the parchment sheet in it. Fold the overhanging dough under and crimp the edges. Cut away the excess parchment paper that extends past the rim. Then, with a fork, make small holes all over the dough.

4. Spread the ham slices or the bacon all over the dough. Pour the egg and cream mixture on it. Spread the grated cheese all over the quiche. Bake on the top rack of your oven for 20 minutes, then move the quiche to the lower rack for another 20 minutes. Then turn off the oven and leave the quiche inside while it cools, with the door slightly open.

5. Serve lukewarm with a salad, or cold the next morning, at brunch or for a picnic.

Quiche Lorraine sans Pâte (Crustless Quiche Lorraine)

A low-calorie version of the traditional quiche, this crustless and cream-free quiche is a great light dish.

INGREDIENTS | SERVES 4

¾ cup flour

4 large eggs

1½ cups whole milk

1 teaspoon salt

1 teaspoon ground black pepper

1 teaspoon ground nutmeg

4 ounces ham steak, cut in 1" long and ½" wide sticks

4 ounces grated cheese (Comté or Gruyère)

1. Preheat the oven to 350°F.

2. In a stand mixer, or in a large bowl, mix the flour and the eggs. Add the milk slowly, then season with salt, pepper, and nutmeg.

3. Butter the inside of a 10" round baking dish. Lay the ham and the grated cheese all over the bottom of the dish. Pour the egg and milk mixture in the dish. Bake on the top rack of your oven for 30 minutes.

4. Serve lukewarm with a salad, or cold the next morning, at brunch or for a picnic.

Quiche au Thon (Tuna Quiche)

Tuna and tomato quiche is an easy last-minute recipe with ingredients you always have in your pantry.

INGREDIENTS | SERVES 4

1 medium onion, peeled and diced

1 tablespoon olive oil

1 (5-ounce) can tuna

1 small (14.5-ounce) can tomato sauce

1 tablespoon thyme

4 large eggs

2 tablespoons *crème fraîche*

1 teaspoon salt

1 teaspoon ground black pepper

1 *Pâte Brisée* dough (recipe in Chapter 22)

4 ounces grated cheese (Emmental or Comté)

1. Preheat the oven to 350°F.

2. In a nonstick skillet, cook the diced onion in the olive oil over medium-high heat for 3–5 minutes. Then add the tuna and reduce heat to low. Add the tomato sauce and the thyme. Stir, and simmer for 10 minutes.

3. Beat the eggs and the cream together in a medium bowl, add salt and pepper, and stir.

4. Butter a 12" tart pan, put the dough in it, and fold under the overhanging dough. Pour in the tuna and tomato mixture, then sprinkle the grated cheese. Add the eggs and the cream mixture. Bake 35 minutes.

5. Serve warm with a salad.

Quiche Courgettes et Menthe (Zucchini Quiche with Mint)

This zucchini mint quiche is inspired by Corsican cuisine, where mint and goat cheese are often paired. A must-have in the summer!

INGREDIENTS | SERVES 4

4 eggs
½ cup *crème fraîche* or crema Mexicana
½ cup whole milk
12 mint leaves, minced
¾ teaspoon salt
1 teaspoon ground black pepper
1 teaspoon nutmeg
1 tablespoon olive oil
2 large zucchini, grated (leave the skin if they are organic, otherwise peel them)
1 *Pâte Brisée* dough (see recipe in Chapter 22)
3.5 ounces goat cheese, cut in ½" cubes
1 garlic clove, diced

1. Preheat the oven to 350°F. Position a rack on the higher level, and another one at the bottom.

2. In a bowl, whisk the eggs well, then add the cream and whisk until very smooth. Add the milk slowly and whisk well again. Add the minced mint leaves, salt, pepper, and nutmeg, and stir again.

3. Put a nonstick skillet over medium-high heat, pour in the oil, then add the grated zucchini. Cook for around 5 minutes, stirring regularly. They should shrink and be a little bit brown. Remove from heat and reserve.

4. Roll out the dough to a 13" round piece on a sheet of parchment paper. Take a 12" tart pan and lay the dough with the parchment paper in it. Fold the overhanging dough under, and crimp the edges of the crust. Cut away the parchment paper that extends past the rim. Then, with a fork, make small holes all over the pie dough.

5. Pour the zucchini into the dish. Add the cubes of goat cheese. Make sure the ingredients are evenly spread. Sprinkle with the diced garlic. Pour the egg and cream mixture over it. Bake on the top rack of your oven for 20 minutes, then put the quiche on the lower rack for another 20 minutes. Then turn off the oven and leave the quiche inside, with the door slightly open.

6. Serve lukewarm with a salad, or cold the next morning, at brunch or for a picnic.

Quiche au Poulet et aux Champignons (Quiche with Chicken and Mushrooms)

This chicken and mushroom quiche is a great way to use the leftovers of a grilled chicken. Perfect for a winter Sunday evening!

INGREDIENTS | SERVES 4

1 *Pâte Brisée* dough (see recipe in Chapter 22)

2 tablespoons butter

2 cups uncooked macaroni

½ cup mushrooms, thinly sliced

1 cup of *Béchamel* sauce (see recipe in Chapter 22)

½ cup grated cheese

1 tablespoon curry powder

½ cup *crème fraîche* or crema Mexicana

¾ teaspoon salt

1 teaspoon ground black pepper

2 cups grilled chicken meat, shredded

1. Preheat the oven to 350°F. Roll out the dough to a 13" circle.

2. Spread butter on a 12" tart pan, or roll out your dough on a parchment paper sheet and lift it into the pie plate. Fold the overhanging dough under, and crimp the edge of the crust. Trim excess parchment from the edge. With a fork, make small holes all over the pie dough.

3. Pour the uncooked macaroni over the dough, making sure they cover it completely. The weight will prevent the dough from distorting too much. Put the unfilled pie shell in the oven on the lower rack, and cook for 20 minutes.

4. Meanwhile, in a bowl, combine mushrooms with *Béchamel* sauce, grated cheese, curry powder, and cream. Add salt and pepper, and stir again.

5. Take the baked crust out of the oven. Take out the pasta and discard. Spread the chicken meat in the crust, then pour the mushroom mixture over it. Put the pie back in the oven, and cook for 20 minutes on the top rack of the oven.

6. Serve lukewarm, with a green salad.

Quiche au Saumon et aux Poireaux
(Salmon and Leeks Quiche)

This salmon and leeks quiche is very healthy: it's full of omega-3 fatty acids from the fish, antioxidants from the leeks, and good proteins from the eggs! You can also use tuna in place of salmon.

INGREDIENTS | SERVES 4

1 tablespoon thyme

1 bay leaf

1 pound fresh salmon fillets

1 tablespoon butter

4 medium leeks, trimmed, green parts discarded, and chopped

1 *Pâte Brisée* dough (see recipe in Chapter 22)

1 tablespoon Dijon mustard

3 large eggs, beaten

½ cup *crème fraîche* or crema Mexicana

¾ teaspoon salt

1 teaspoon ground black pepper

Parlez-Vous Quiche?

Quiche is actually derived from the Alsatian word *Küchen* or *Kuche*, which means cake. When in France, be careful when using the *quiche* word; it can also mean being a little dumb!

1. Preheat the oven to 350°F. Fill a medium saucepan with water, add the thyme and the bay leaf, and bring to a boil over high heat. Poach the salmon in the boiling water for 5 minutes. Then take it out with a slotted spoon and put on a plate. Reserve.

2. In a nonstick skillet, melt the butter over medium-low heat, then add the chopped leeks. Brown them slowly on each side for two minutes, then add ½" of water to the pan. Stir well, and simmer for 15 minutes.

3. On a parchment paper sheet, roll out the dough into a 13" circle. Lay in a 12" tart pan. Fold the overhanging under, crimp the edge of the crust, and trim the excess parchment paper. Then, with a fork, make small holes all over the pie dough. Spread the mustard on the dough. Shred the salmon into the pie shell, then add the leeks, making sure they are evenly spread.

4. In a bowl, beat the eggs firmly, then add the cream. Add the salt and the pepper, and whisk well. Pour over the salmon and the leeks. Put the pie on the top rack in the oven, and cook for 35 minutes.

5. Serve lukewarm with a salad, or eat cold the next day.

Quiche aux Asperges (Asparagus Quiche)

This green asparagus quiche is perfect for early spring picnics!

INGREDIENTS | SERVES 4

7 ounces green asparagus, trimmed at the base

3 large eggs, beaten

½ cup *crème fraîche* or crema Mexicana

½ cup whole milk

¾ teaspoon salt

1 teaspoon ground black pepper

1 *Pâte Brisée* dough (see recipe in Chapter 22)

Green or White?

You can also make this quiche with white asparagus. In that case, peel them very carefully (if not, there will be lot of threads in the asparagus and they will be difficult to cut), and cook them for 10 minutes in the boiling water.

1. Preheat the oven to 350°F.

2. Fill a large saucepan with water and bring to a boil over high heat. Fill a medium bowl with ice water and set aside. When the water boils, add the asparagus and boil for 3 minutes. Then drain them and put them immediately in the ice water bowl.

3. In a bowl, beat the eggs firmly, then whisk in the cream. Then add the milk little by little, whisking continuously. Add the salt and the pepper, and whisk again.

4. On a parchment paper sheet, roll the dough into a 13" circle. Lay it, with the parchment paper, on a 12" tart pan. Fold overhang under, and crimp the edge of the dough. With a fork, make small holes all over the pie dough. Lay the asparagus in a flower shape on the dough. Pour the beaten eggs and the cream over the asparagus. Put the quiche on the top rack of the oven, and cook for 35 minutes.

5. Serve lukewarm with a salad, or cold.

Quiche Roquefort et Brocolis
(Roquefort Quiche with Broccoli)

This broccoli and Roquefort cheese can be made with another blue cheese, like Fourme d'Ambert, for example.

INGREDIENTS | SERVES 4

1 pound broccoli florets (with 1" of stem attached)

3 large eggs, beaten

½ cup *crème fraîche* or crema Mexicana

½ cup whole milk

¾ teaspoon salt

1 teaspoon ground black pepper

1 *Pâte Brisée* dough (see recipe in Chapter 22)

7 ounces Roquefort cheese, cut in ½" squares

A Very Protected Cheese

Roquefort is the first French cheese that got a label of quality. It can only be made in the Roquefort area, with the milk of local sheep of selected breeds. This blue cheese has been a symbol of French gastronomy for years. The blue parts have also been used as medicine, for their antibacterial properties.

1. Preheat the oven to 375°F.

2. Fill a large saucepan with water and bring to a boil over high heat. When the water boils, add the broccoli florets and boil them for 7 minutes. Drain them and reserve.

3. In a bowl, beat the eggs firmly, then whisk in the cream. Add the milk little by little, whisking continuously. Add the salt and the pepper, and whisk again.

4. On a parchment paper sheet, roll the dough into a 13" circle. Lay it in a 12" tart pan, transferring the parchment paper too. Fold overhanging dough under, and crimp the edge of the crust. With a fork, make small holes all over the pie dough.

5. Lay the broccoli florets on the dough. Add the cheese. Pour the beaten eggs and the cream over them. Put the quiche in the oven, and cook for 30 minutes.

6. Serve lukewarm or cold.

Quiche Forestière (Forest Quiche)

This is a great fall recipe for quiche with mushrooms. Try using wild mushrooms; if not, regular button mushrooms are also very good.

INGREDIENTS | SERVES 4

½ pound mushrooms (diced)

1 tablespoon butter

2 tablespoons parsley, finely chopped

1 garlic clove, peeled and minced

1 teaspoon salt

1 teaspoon ground black pepper

1 *Pâte Brisée* dough (see recipe in Chapter 22)

4 large eggs, beaten

1 cup *crème fraîche* or crema Mexicana

1. Preheat the oven to 350°F. If you're using button mushrooms, wash and slice them thinly. If you have small wild mushrooms, brush them and cut them in two. If we're talking porcini-size mushrooms, then cut them in 1" cubes.

2. Put a nonstick skillet over medium heat, and melt the tablespoon butter in it. Add the mushrooms and stir well, using a wooden spatula. Add the parsley, stir again, then add the garlic, salt, and pepper, and stir well again. Reduce the heat to low and cook for 5 minutes, until the mushrooms release their liquid.

3. On a parchment paper sheet, roll the dough into a 13" circle. Transfer the dough and the parchment paper into a 12" tart pan. Fold overhanging dough under, and crimp the edge of the crust. Then, with a fork, make small holes all over the dough. Place in the refrigerator.

4. In a large bowl, beat the eggs firmly, then add the cream and whisk well. Add the mushrooms, stir well. Remove the pie crust from the refrigerator, and pour the mushroom and egg mixture in the pan. Put in the oven and cook for 30 minutes.

5. Serve lukewarm with a salad, or cold.

Pissaladière

The French provençal version of pizza! Pissaladière is a specialty of Nice, which is on the Mediterranean coast.

INGREDIENTS | SERVES 4

1 ready-made (13.8-ounce) pizza crust
4 pounds onion, peeled and thinly sliced
⅓ cup olive oil
1 garlic clove, unpeeled
1 bay leaf
1 tablespoon thyme
1 tablespoon rosemary
¼ teaspoon salt
1 tablespoon ground black pepper, plus extra for sprinkling
18 anchovy fillets, drained
36 black olives, unpitted

1. Roll out your dough on a parchment paper sheet, and stretch it to a 10" × 15" rectangle. Then put a damp cloth on it and let it rise till it doubles in height.

2. Peel the onions and cut them in very thin slices. Put a large nonstick skillet on medium-high heat. Add the olive oil and onion. Cook for 1 minute. Add the unpeeled garlic clove, the bay leaf, thyme, rosemary, salt, and pepper, stirring continuously. Reduce the heat to very low. Cover and simmer for around 45 minutes. From time to time, check the onions, stir them, and let the steam escape before putting the cover back on. They should slowly shrink and caramelize.

3. If there's still water at the end, bring the heat to high for 5 minutes, cover off. Remove garlic and the bay leaf.

4. Preheat your oven at 500°F. Uncover the pizza dough and re-roll until it's ⅛" thick. The *pissaladière* is always a rectangle, and it should be about the size of your baking rack or pizza stone. Spread the onions evenly on the dough. Then arrange the anchovy fillets on it in small rectangle shapes. Put an olive at the center of each rectangle. Put in the hot oven for 20 minutes. Just as you take it out of the oven, sprinkle with pepper.

5. Serve immediately.

Flammekueche

A tradition in Alsace, this bacon and cream pie was originally baked by farmers once or twice a month, after making their bread in a wood-fired oven.

INGREDIENTS | SERVES 4

2 cups flour

¼ cup plus 1 tablespoon canola oil

1 tablespoon plus ¼ teaspoon salt

⅓ cup water

⅔ cup *crème fraîche* or sour cream

⅓ cup cottage cheese or ricotta, drained

1 teaspoon ground black pepper

1 teaspoon ground nutmeg

3 medium onions, very thinly sliced

3 ounces bacon, cut into matchsticks

A Friendly Pie!

According to the Alsatian tradition, *Flammekueche* should be shared and eaten with the hands, and new pies should be made again and again until everybody is satisfied! A bottle of Gewürztraminer or schnapps should also pass among the guests.

1. In a large bowl, pour the flour. Make a hole in the center and pour in the ¼ cup oil, then add 1 tablespoon salt and the water. Knead well until you have a dough that you can roll out easily. You can also make it in a stand mixer, using the dough hook. Cover with a damp cloth and let it rest.

2. In a bowl, combine the cream and the cheese, the pepper, ¼ teaspoon of salt, and the ground nutmeg. Stir well, then add the tablespoon of canola oil.

3. Preheat the oven to 500°F. Roll the dough on parchment paper until it is very thin. The *Flammekueche* can be either round or square, but always thin crusted.

4. Spread the cream and cheese on the dough with a spatula, making sure there's about ½" of dough still bare on the edges. Sprinkle the onions all over the pie, then add the bacon pieces. They should be spread evenly. Put the pie and the parchment paper on a pizza stone or use a baking rack that you will place in the oven, then put in the oven for 8–10 minutes. The pie should be out of the oven when it starts to get brown.

5. Serve very hot.

Tarte à la Moutarde et à la Tomate (Mustard and Tomato Tart)

Dijon mustard adds spice and flavor to this very simple and gourmet savory pie. A must-cook in the summer!

1 tablespoon salt

5 medium tomatoes, sliced

1 pate *Pâte Brisée* dough (see recipe in Chapter 22)

3 tablespoons Dijon mustard

6 basil leaves, chopped

1 teaspoon ground black pepper

1 tablespoon thyme or rosemary

The Bacon Solution

Meat and bacon lovers can also layer 1 sliced medium onion on the mustard, then the tomato slices, and finally add ½ pound of bacon sliced in very thin matchsticks to the top. Add the same spices.

1. Preheat the oven to 400°F. In a bowl, sprinkle salt on the sliced tomatoes and reserve.

2. On a parchment paper sheet, roll the dough into a 13" circle. Lay the dough with the parchment paper on it in a 12" tart pan. Fold the overhanging dough under, and crimp the edges of the crust. Cut away the parchment paper that extends past the rim. Then, with a fork, make small holes all over the pie dough.

3. Spread the Dijon mustard evenly on the pie dough. Lay the tomato slices one by one on the mustard, starting at the edge of the dish first. Once you've finished the first circle, go on layering tomato slices in a spiral until you reach the middle. Sprinkle the chopped basil on the tomatoes, then sprinkle the pepper and thyme or rosemary. Put in the oven on the top rack for 15 minutes, then on the lower rack for another 15 minutes.

4. Serve very hot.

Tarte à la Tomate et au Fromage de Chèvre
(Tomato and Goat Cheese Salad)

Goat cheese and tomatoes make a very nice combination for this very simple tart.

INGREDIENTS | SERVES 4

1 teaspoon salt

5 medium tomatoes, thinly sliced

1 *Pâte Feuilletée* dough (see recipe in Chapter 22)

4 ounces fresh, soft goat cheese

1 teaspoon ground black pepper

1 tablespoon thyme

1 tablespoon rosemary

Land of the Goat Cheeses

France is the number-one producer of goat milk and goat cheeses in the world. There are lots of different types of shape, aging, and preserving techniques. In total, there are more than 1,001 registered goat cheeses in France!

1. Preheat the oven to 400°F.

2. Sprinkle salt on the tomato slices and reserve.

3. On a parchment paper sheet, roll your dough into a 13" circle. Lay the parchment paper and the dough in a 12" tart pan. Fold overhanging dough under, and crimp the edge of the crust. Trim the excess. Then, with a fork, make small holes all over the pie dough.

4. Spread goat cheese evenly on the pie dough. Sprinkle pepper on it. Lay the tomato slices one by one on the goat cheese, starting by following the edge of the dish first and spiraling into the middle. Sprinkle thyme and rosemary on the goat cheese. Put in the oven on the top rack for 15 minutes, then on the lower rack for another 15 minutes.

5. Serve very hot.

Tarte au Potiron

A pumpkin pie in France is not dessert, it's a savory dish. Discover this new way of enjoying fall's most generous vegetable!

INGREDIENTS | SERVES 4

1 *Pâte Brisée* dough (see recipe in Chapter 22)
1 tablespoon butter
2 medium onions, diced
⅓ pound bacon, cut into ½"-wide slices
1 pound pumpkin, peeled and cut in chunks
1 cup chicken stock
½ tablespoon salt
½ teaspoon pepper
1 tablespoon ground nutmeg
1 egg, beaten

1. Preheat the oven to 350°F and set a rack in the middle. On a parchment sheet, roll dough into a 13" circle. Lay the parchment paper and the dough in a 12" tart pan. Fold the overhanging dough under, and crimp the edges of the crust. Cut away the parchment paper that extends past the rim. Then, with a fork, make small holes all over the pie dough. Cover and put in the refrigerator.

2. Heat a medium nonstick skillet over medium heat. Melt the butter, then add the onion slices, stirring well so that they all touch the butter. Then add the bacon, stir well, and cook for 5 minutes.

3. Add the pumpkin chunks to the skillet, brown on each side, then pour in the chicken stock. Bring to a boil over high heat, add the salt, pepper, and nutmeg. Once the stock is boiling, reduce to a low heat and simmer for 30 minutes. Stir often. The stock should disappear, and the pumpkin turn into a marmalade. Take off the heat and let cool.

4. In a large bowl, beat the egg firmly, then add the pumpkin marmalade little by little. Take the crust out of the refrigerator and pour the pumpkin marmalade in it. Put in the oven for 40 minutes, on a rack set in the middle of the oven.

5. Serve hot, with a salad.

Tarte aux Oignons (Onion Tart)

You can either bake this onion tart with only onions, or add sliced bacon to it.

INGREDIENTS | SERVES 4

1 *Pâte Brisée* dough (see recipe in Chapter 22)

1 tablespoon butter

2 tablespoons vegetable oil

6 medium onions, thinly sliced

1 tablespoon flour

3 eggs

½ cup *crème fraîche* or crema Mexicana

½ cup whole milk

1 tablespoon Espelette pepper (or paprika)

½ tablespoon salt

½ teaspoon ground black pepper

1. Preheat the oven to 350°F and set a rack in the middle. On a parchment sheet, roll dough into a 13" circle. Lay the parchment sheet and the dough in a 12" tart pan. Fold overhanging dough under, crimp the edge of the crust and trim it. Then, with a fork, make small holes all over the pie dough. Cover and put in the refrigerator.

2. Heat the butter in a nonstick skillet over medium heat. Add the oil, then cook the slices of onions in it. They should get translucent, but not brown. Add the flour, stir well, and cook slowly for 3 minutes. Take off of the heat and let them cool.

3. In a large bowl, beat the eggs, then add the cream and whisk well. Slowly pour in the milk, again whisking firmly. Add the Espelette pepper, salt, and pepper, and stir well. Take the crust out of the refrigerator, and pour the onion mixture into it. Bake in the oven for 40 minutes.

4. Serve immediately.

CHAPTER 10

Plats Mijotés
(Slow-Cooked Main Dishes)

Bœuf Bourguignon

*What's more French than this slow-cooked beef in red wine? It's
also one of the easiest French traditional recipes.*

INGREDIENTS | SERVES 4

1 tablespoon butter

4 ounces bacon

1 large onion, peeled and thinly sliced

1 pound cubed beef roast or beef
cheeks (or ½ pound of both)

½ pound oxtail

1 bay leaf

1 tablespoon thyme

1 (25.3-ounce) bottle of red wine

1 cup chicken stock

1 teaspoon salt

1 teaspoon ground black pepper

4 medium carrots, peeled and diced

2 medium turnips (or 4 small), washed
thoroughly and trimmed

2 parsnips, peeled and cut in two

Wine and Time

Some people can argue for hours about
what kind of wine should be used in this
recipe: a Burgundy at all cost? The best
wine in your cellar? Any cheap cabernet
sauvignon does the trick. The real important ingredient here, as in all recipes of this
chapter, is time. Slow, slow cooking, and
low, low simmering.

1. Cut the bacon in ½"-wide sticks.

2. Put a large French oven over medium heat. You can
   also use a very large pot with a thick bottom. Melt the
   butter, and add the bacon. (If your pot is nonstick, you
   can skip the butter: The bacon fat is fat enough!) Stir
   for 1 minute, then add the sliced onion. Stir well and
   cook together for 3 minutes.

3. Add the beef to the onion and bacon. Make sure it gets
   browned on each side. Same for the oxtail; stir well.
   This should all take around 5 minutes. Add the bay leaf
   and the thyme, then pour in the red wine and the
   chicken stock.

4. Bring to a boil over high heat, then add the salt and
   the pepper. If the liquid doesn't cover all the
   ingredients, add water till they are all covered. Add
   carrots, turnips, and parsnips to the pot. When it
   comes to a boil, immediately cover and reduce the
   heat to low. Simmer for 3 hours, more if you can. It's
   even better on the next day.

5. Remove bay leaf. Serve dish with boiled potatoes or
   fresh pasta.

Pot-au-Feu (Pot Roast)

French pot roast is one of the pillars of French gastronomy. Alexandre Dumas, the famous French novelist who wrote The Three Musketeers, *famously said it had to be cooked more than 7 hours. And he was right!*

INGREDIENTS | SERVES 6

1 pound beef shank, in 2" chunks

1 pound beef roast, in 2" chunks

1 pound oxtail

4 cloves

1 large onion, peeled

1 bay leaf

1 tablespoon thyme

1 tablespoon parsley, chopped

1 teaspoon salt

1 teaspoon ground black pepper

4 medium carrots, peeled

4 leeks, green parts cut off

2 medium turnips, trimmed

1 pound bone marrows (ask your butcher to cut them every 2")

6 medium potatoes

One Day Early

The best thing to do is to cook the *Pot-au-Feu* the day before. Put it in the refrigerator overnight and in the morning, all the fat in the stock will have solidified. You can remove it to make an even leaner dish.

1. Fill a very large French oven, or cooking pot, with cold water. Add the beef shanks, the beef roast, and the oxtail. Bring to a boil over medium heat. Spoon out the foam that appears on the surface. When the water boils, cover and reduce the heat to its lowest. Simmer for 1 hour.

2. After an hour, nail the cloves in the peeled onion, and add it to the water. Add the bay leaf, thyme, parsley, salt, and pepper. Bring to a boil, and spoon out the foam again. When it has boiled again, cover and reduce the heat to low. Simmer.

3. After 2 hours, add the carrots and leeks to the stock. Let it simmer for as long as you can (1 hour minimum). Add the bone marrow and the potatoes 1 hour before serving. Before serving, spoon out the broth and put it into a large soup bowl. Remove bay leaf. Serve as an appetizer, with grilled slices of bread.

4. Take out the vegetables and the meat with a slotted spoon and layer them in separate dishes. Serve with a pot of *cornichons* and a jar of Dijon mustard on the table.

Carbonnade

Northern France is big on beer, so of course when they stew beef, they choose beer, not red wine!

INGREDIENTS | SERVES 4

1 tablespoon butter
1 tablespoon sunflower oil
2 medium onions, peeled and diced
½ pound bacon, cut in ½" slices
2 pounds beef shanks, cut in 1" cubes
1 bay leaf
1 tablespoon thyme
2 tablespoons raw sugar
1 teaspoon salt
1 teaspoon ground black pepper
4 cups stout beer

1. Take a medium French oven (or any cast-iron pot), and place over medium-high heat. Melt the butter, add the oil, combine well, and add the slices of onion. Stir well, then add the bacon slices. Cook for 3 minutes, stirring often, then add the beef cubes. Make sure they get browned on each side, about 5 minutes. Add the bay leaf and the thyme, stir well, then add the raw sugar, salt, and pepper, and pour in the beer.

2. Bring to a boil over high heat, then reduce to low, put the cover on, and simmer for 3 hours.

3. Serve warm, with boiled potatoes or French fries, and a nice glass of beer! Remove bay leaf before serving.

Bœuf Carottes (Beef and Carrot Stew)

This simple slow-cooked beef and carrot stew is always a success.

INGREDIENTS | SERVES 4

1 tablespoon butter
1 tablespoon sunflower oil
2 medium onions, peeled and sliced
2 pounds beef shanks, cut in 1½" cubes
12 medium carrots, peeled and
 thinly sliced
2 (12-ounce) bottles of ginger beer
1 bay leaf
1 tablespoon thyme
4 black peppercorns
1 teaspoon salt
1 teaspoon ground black pepper

1. Heat a medium French oven (or pot) over medium-high heat. Melt the butter and add the oil. Add the diced onions and cook for 3 minutes; they should start to look translucent. Brown the cubes of beef shanks on each side, for 3 minutes.

2. Add the carrots to the pot, stir well, and cook for 3 minutes.

3. Pour the ginger beer on the meat and the carrots. Stir again. Add the bay leaf and the thyme, then the peppercorns, the salt, and the pepper. Stir well and bring to a boil over high heat. Once it has reached the boiling point, reduce to the lowest heat, put the cover on, and simmer for 2 hours.

4. Remove bay leaf. Serve with a bowl of white rice.

Daube Provençale

*A tradition in Provence, daube is the beef bourguignon of the south of France,
full of Mediterranean flavors, but with the same main ingredient: time!*

INGREDIENTS | SERVES 4

1 tablespoon butter

1 tablespoon olive oil

2 medium onions, peeled and sliced

3 pounds beef shanks, cut in 2" cubes

2 carrots, peeled and thinly sliced

2 garlic cloves, peeled and diced

1 (25.3-ounce) bottle of red wine

3 tablespoons tomato paste

1 orange peel

1 bay leaf

1 tablespoon thyme

1 teaspoon salt

1 teaspoon ground black pepper

10 ounces pitted black olives

Doubtful *Daube* . . .

The name of the dish comes from the Provençal language, apparently from *adobar*, which means preparing something. In modern slang, *daube* means a very bad movie.

1. In a large French oven (or pot) melt the butter over medium-high heat. Add the oil, combine them well, and add the onions. Stir and cook slowly for 3 minutes, then add the beef shanks, browning them on each side, for 5 minutes.

2. Add carrots to the pot, stir well. Then add the garlic.

3. Pour in the red wine, and bring to a boil over high heat. Add the tomato paste, stir well, then add an orange peel, the bay leaf, thyme, salt, and pepper. Cover and reduce the heat to its lowest. Simmer for 3 hours. About 30 minutes before serving, add the black olives, cover again, and simmer for another 30 minutes.

4. Remove bay leaf before serving. Serve warm, with fresh pasta or polenta.

Blanquette de Veau (Veal Stew in White Sauce)

This veal stew in white sauce is a symbol of French cuisine bourgeoise, which was developed in France in the nineteenth century. It's a typical winter dish, the kind you like to prepare for the whole family on Sunday.

INGREDIENTS | SERVES 4

4 cups beef stock

3 pounds veal shoulder, cut in 2" cubes

1 medium onion, peeled

4 cloves

1 bay leaf

1 tablespoon thyme

1 teaspoon salt

1 teaspoon ground black pepper

3 medium carrots, peeled and thinly sliced

1 celery stalk, minced

2 leeks, green part cut out, sliced in two

2 tablespoons butter

1 pound whole mushrooms

4 egg yolks

Juice of 1 lemon

¾ cup *crème fraîche* or crema Mexicana

1. In a large cooking pot (preferably a French oven), pour the stock. Add the veal, the onion, cloves, bay leaf, thyme, salt, and pepper. If the stock doesn't cover the meat, add some water. Bring the pot slowly to a boil over medium heat. Cover the pot, reduce the heat to low, and simmer for 90 minutes.

2. Add the carrots, celery, and leeks; cover again and simmer for another 30 minutes. Remove bay leaf.

3. In a small saucepan, melt the butter over medium heat. Add the mushrooms and cook for 5 minutes. Add to the pot and simmer for another 30 minutes.

4. About 10 minutes before serving, use a slotted spoon to take the meat and vegetables out of the pot. Put in a serving dish and cover. Bring the liquid left in the pot to a boil over high heat. Wait until it has reduced by a third, then decrease the heat to low.

5. Beat the egg yolks in a bowl, add the lemon juice, the cream, and one ladleful of broth from the pot, and whisk continuously. When the broth is just simmering, pour the egg mixture in it, whisking constantly for 5 minutes, until the sauce thickens. Pour it on the vegetables and the meat.

6. Serve with white rice.

Baeckeoffe (Meat in White Wine)

A tradition in Alsace, this slow-cooked dish combines three sorts of meat: beef, pork, and lamb, marinated in white wine!

INGREDIENTS | SERVES 6

1 (25-ounce) bottle of white wine (Riesling or Sauvignon blanc)

3 medium onions

4 cloves

2 garlic cloves, peeled and diced

1 tablespoon parsley, chopped

3 leeks, greens cut out

1 bay leaf

1 tablespoon thyme

1 pound beef shank, cut in 2" cubes

1 pound lamb shoulder, cut in 2" cubes

1 pound pork shoulder, cut in 2" cubes

2 teaspoons salt, divided

2 teaspoons ground black pepper, divided

3 pounds potatoes, peeled and sliced

1 tablespoon duck fat

Two Stories, One *Baeckeoffe*

Some say that this recipe was invented by Lutheran Alsatian women, who left their pot to cook slowly at the baker's while they were attending the very long Sunday services. Other stories say it was invented by women for laundry day, the day in the week where they didn't have time to prepare a meal.

1. A day earlier, pour the white wine in a very large bowl.

2. Peel and mince 1 onion. Peel another one and insert the cloves into it. Add them to the wine. Add the garlic, parsley, leeks, bay leaf, and the thyme. Add the meat. Add 1 teaspoon salt and 1 teaspoon pepper, cover, and put in the refrigerator for one night.

3. The next day, peel the potatoes and two onions, and cut them in thin slices. Preheat the oven to 400°F. Take a very large French oven, or a very large dish (preferably ceramic) that has a cover. Spread the duck fat inside the pot. Put a layer of potatoes at the bottom, then put a layer of meat, then a layer of onions, then start over: a layer of potatoes, a layer of meat, a layer of onions, etc. Stop with a last layer of potatoes.

4. Pour the white wine marinade in the pot through a strainer. Remove bay leaf. Sprinkle a teaspoon of salt and pepper, then put the cover on. Put in the oven for 1 hour, then reduce the heat to 350°F and cook for 2 more hours.

5. Serve with a green salad.

Potée Auvergnate (Pork and Cabbage Stew)

A pork and cabbage stew invented in the mountains of Auvergne, where the harsh climate in winter makes it necessary to find strength and comfort over a good meal!

INGREDIENTS | SERVES 6

1 pound pork belly, cut in 3" chunks

3 pounds pork shoulder

1 bay leaf

1 tablespoon thyme

1 tablespoon parsley, chopped

1 teaspoon salt

1 teaspoon ground black pepper

1 onion

4 cloves

1 cabbage

1 tablespoon baking soda

4 medium carrots, peeled and cut in 3 chunks each

10 medium potatoes, washed and unpeeled

1. Fill a very large French oven or cooking pot with cold water.

2. Add the pork belly and the pork shoulder to the cold water. Bring to a boil over medium heat. Add the bay leaf, thyme, parsley, salt, and pepper. Peel the onion and nail the cloves in it. Add it to the water. When the water starts boiling, reduce to a low heat. Spoon the foam out. Cover and simmer for 2 hours.

3. Meanwhile, fill a large saucepan with water and bring to a boil over high heat. Wash the cabbage, take off the outer leaves, and cut it in 6 chunks. When the water boils, add the tablespoon of baking soda, then add the cabbage. Cook for 5 minutes and drain. The baking soda should help you digest the cabbage more easily.

4. After 2 hours of simmering the pork, spoon out the leftover foam, and add the cabbage and the carrots. Cover again, and simmer for another 30 minutes (or more!).

5. About 30 minutes before serving, add the potatoes (with their skin) to the pot. After 30 minutes, take out the potatoes and the vegetables with a slotted spoon and put them in a large presenting dish. Remove bay leaf. Take out the meat and put it on top. Each guest should help himself or herself to the vegetables and meat.

6. Serve with a jar of Dijon mustard.

Rôti de Porc à l'Orange (Orange Pork Roast)

Sweet and sour is not very common in French traditional cuisine, but it's often used to cook pork, as for this orange pork roast.

INGREDIENTS | SERVES 4

2 tablespoons butter

4 small shallots, minced

2 pounds pork roast

½ cup brandy (Cognac, if you can)

2 organic oranges

1 cup white wine

1 tablespoon thyme

1 tablespoon parsley, chopped

1 bay leaf

1 teaspoon salt

1 teaspoon ground black pepper

1. Heat a medium French oven (or pot) over medium heat.

2. Add the butter, and cook the shallots in it, stirring for about 3 minutes. Add the pork roast, and brown it on each side for 5 minutes. Then pour in the brandy (be careful of the possibility of flames!). Squeeze the juice from one orange and pour half of it over the pork roast; reserve the other half. Add the white wine, the thyme, the parsley, the bay leaf, salt, and pepper, and cover. Reduce the heat to low, and simmer for 1 hour.

3. Meanwhile, peel the other orange. Cut the orange peels in very thin slices. Fill a small saucepan with water, and bring it to a boil over high heat. Add the orange peels. Leave them for 1 minute, then take them out with a slotted spoon. Reserve. Cut the peeled orange in very thin slices.

4. About 5 minutes before serving, take the pork roast out of the pot and put it in a serving dish. Add the slices of orange to the pot, with the leftover juice. Remove bay leaf. Stir well and let the orange cook slightly for 2 minutes. Take out the orange slices with a slotted spoon, and layer them all around the pork roast in the serving dish. Lay the orange peels on top of the roast, to decorate. Pour the orange sauce in a gravy boat.

5. Serve immediately with white rice.

Petit Salé aux Lentilles (Pork with Lentils)

A pork classic for wintertime, which has to be cooked with the world-famous French lentils known as lentilles du Puy. It is traditionally cooked with petit salé pork, a pork that has been brined in salt for two days to preserve it longer. This recipe is adapted to traditional American pork.

INGREDIENTS | SERVES 4

1 tablespoon butter
8 ounces bacon, cut in ½"-wide slices
2 onions (1 peeled, 1 peeled and sliced)
2 pounds pork shoulder
2 carrots, peeled and thinly sliced
4 cups water
4 cloves
1 bay leaf
1 tablespoon thyme
1 teaspoon salt
1 teaspoon ground black pepper
1 cup *lentilles du Puy*

Add Sausages

Petit Salé is also often cooked with *saucisse de Morteau*. You can sometimes find this traditional smoked sausage in the United States. If not, you can also try a regular American smoked sausage. Make sure you prick small holes in it with a fork to prevent it from exploding. Add it to the pot just after the pork shoulder.

1. Put a large French oven or stove pot over medium heat. Melt the butter, then raise the heat to medium-high and add the bacon slices. Cook for 2–3 minutes, until the fat releases. Add sliced onion to the bacon. Stir well, and let the onions cook slowly with the bacon, about 3–5 minutes. They should become translucent, not brown.

2. Add the pork shoulder and brown it on each side for 5 minutes. Add carrots and stir well. Pour in the water, and bring to a boil over high heat.

3. Take the remaining peeled onion and nail the cloves in it. Add to the water. Add the bay leaf, thyme, salt, and pepper. When it reaches a boil, cover and reduce to low. Simmer for 90 minutes.

4. Add the lentils and stir well. Bring to a boil over high heat, then cover again and put back on low heat. Simmer for another 30 minutes.

5. Remove bay leaf. Serve dish warm, with a pot of Dijon mustard on the table.

Navarin d'Agneau (Spring Lamb Stew)

Spring in France is definitely the month of lamb. It's often what's cooked at Easter, for example. This navarin is even better with legumes nouveaux, the first crop of carrots, green onions, and peas.

INGREDIENTS | SERVES 4

2 tablespoons butter, divided

1 tablespoon sunflower oil

1 pound lamb shoulder, cut in 1½" cubes

5 medium carrots, 1 diced, and 4 cut in 2" sticks

1 medium onion, diced

1 tomato, diced

1 celery stalk, diced

1 cup white wine

4 cups chicken stock

5 teaspoons salt, divided

4 black peppercorns

1 tablespoon rosemary

4 leeks, green parts trimmed off, each cut in 3

4 small green onions, peeled

4 ounces fresh peas

1. Heat a medium French oven or pot over medium-high heat.

2. Melt 1 tablespoon butter and add the oil. Brown the cubes of lamb shoulder on each side, for 5 minutes total. Then add the diced carrot, onion, tomato, and celery. Stir well. Pour in the white wine, bring to a boil over high heat, and wait for it to reduce to half its volume before pouring in the chicken stock. Add 1 teaspoon of salt, the peppercorns, and the rosemary; cover and reduce the heat to low. Simmer for 1 hour.

3. Fill a saucepan with water, and bring to a boil over high heat. Add 1 teaspoon of salt, then add the carrot sticks when the water boils. Prepare a bowl of ice cold water. After 5 minutes, drain the carrots and put them immediately in the cold water. Then dry and reserve. Use the same method to cook the leeks, the peeled green onions, and the peas, all separately.

4. About 10 minutes before serving, melt 1 tablespoon of butter in a skillet over low heat. Pour all the vegetables in. Take 1 ladleful of cooking broth from the lamb pot and pour on the vegetables. Add 1 teaspoon of salt. Bring to a boil, then reduce to medium heat for 3 minutes. Put the lamb shoulder cubes in a serving dish. Bring the broth remaining in the pot to a boil over high heat, and let it reduce by half.

5. Add the vegetables to the lamb and pour the reduced sauce over everything. Serve immediately.

Poulet Marengo (Slow-Cooked Chicken with Tomatoes in White Wine)

Poulet Marengo is chicken slow-cooked in white wine and tomatoes. It's very common to cook it with veal, but the original recipe is with chicken.

INGREDIENTS | SERVES 4

2 tablespoons olive oil
2 medium onions, peeled and diced
4 chicken legs, cut in two
1 garlic clove, peeled and diced
½ pound mushrooms, diced
1 cup white wine
1 cup chicken stock
1 (28-ounce) can diced tomatoes
1 bay leaf
1 tablespoon thyme
1 tablespoon parsley, chopped
2 cloves
1 orange peel (organic)
1 teaspoon salt
1 teaspoon ground black pepper

1. Heat a medium French oven or pot over medium heat.

2. Add the olive oil, and add the diced onions. Add the chicken legs, making sure they get brown on each side, about 1–2 minutes. Cook slowly for another 3 minutes, stirring well.

3. Add the diced garlic, stir again, then add the diced mushrooms. Cook for another 3 minutes. Pour in the white wine and chicken stock and bring to a boil over high heat. When it starts boiling, add the diced tomatoes and their juice. Add the bay leaf, thyme, parsley, and cloves. Stir well, then reduce the heat to a simmer. Add a 2" strip of organic orange peel, sprinkle in the salt and pepper, cover, and simmer for 1 hour.

4. Remove bay leaf. Serve dish with a bowl of white rice.

A Chicken That Made History!

Legend has it that this recipe was invented by Napoleon's chef at the battle of Marengo in in 1800. The troops were extremely hungry, and the cook decided to feed them with whatever he could find around him: chicken, tomatoes, mushrooms, and white wine.

Poulet à la Normande (Normandy Chicken)

In France, Normandy is synonymous with apples, cider, calvados, great butter, and cream. This "Normandy style" chicken is a good example.

INGREDIENTS | SERVES 4

1 tablespoon butter

4 ounces bacon, sliced into ½" matchsticks

4 chicken thighs

4 chicken drumsticks

2 apples, peeled, halved, cored, then each divided in 4

½ cup calvados (apple brandy)

½ pound mushrooms, diced

10 tiny spring onions, peeled

1 (25-ounce) bottle of cider

1 teaspoon salt

1 teaspoon ground black pepper

¾ cup *crème fraîche* or crema Mexicana

1. Heat a medium French oven or pot over medium heat.

2. Add the butter, and cook the bacon for 3 minutes. Add the chicken thighs and drumsticks, making sure they get brown on each side, about 1–2 minutes. Cook slowly for 5 more minutes, stirring well.

3. Add apples to the pot and brown them on each side, about 1–2 minutes, stirring well. Pour in the calvados (be careful, it can flame). Add the diced mushrooms, onions, cider, salt, and pepper, and stir well.

4. Bring to a boil over high heat, then reduce to low and simmer for 45 minutes. Then add the cream, stir well, and simmer for another 15 minutes.

5. Serve immediately.

You Say Cider, the French Say *Cidre*

The cider culture is very important in Normandy and Brittany, where France's main ciders are made. You could never eat crêpes or *galette* there without a bowl of *cidre*. They come mainly in two different forms: *brut* and *doux*. *Doux* is sweeter and very low in alcohol, if there's any at all. *Brut* is stronger in alcohol and dryer to taste, and better to cook with for this recipe, for instance.

Poulet Basquaise (Basque Chicken)

Basque chicken is based on one of the main ingredients of the cuisine of this region in the southwest of France: Espelette pepper. This mild red pepper can be found in the United States, but most of the time at a high price. If you can't find it, paprika is a good substitute.

INGREDIENTS | SERVES 4

1 tablespoon olive oil

2 onions, sliced and minced

4 chicken legs

1 tablespoon Espelette pepper

1 red bell pepper, chopped

1 garlic clove, peeled and diced

1 (28-ounce) can of diced tomatoes

1 teaspoon salt

1 teaspoon ground black pepper

1 cup white wine

Red Pepper Land

Espelette pepper can only be grown in a very small part of the French Basque region, around the village of Espelette. There, you can see the walls of the traditional red and white Basque houses covered with red peppers that are hung outside to dry. A beautiful sight, even more when you go there for the *Fête du piment*, a huge festival each year where they celebrate their dear red Espelette pepper.

1. Heat a medium French oven or pot over medium-high heat. Add the oil, and cook the onions slowly in it, stirring often, for 2 minutes. They should become translucent, not brown.

2. Add the chicken legs, making sure they get brown on each side. Cook slowly for 5 minutes, stirring well. Add the Espelette pepper.

3. Add the chopped red pepper to the pot, and stir well. Cook for 3 minutes. The red peppers must also be slightly browned on each side. Add garlic. Pour in the diced tomatoes and their juice, add the salt and pepper, and stir well. Bring to a boil over high heat. Pour in the white wine. When the mixture starts boiling, stir well, then cover. Reduce the heat to its lowest and simmer for 1 hour.

4. Serve with a bowl of white rice, or small boiled potatoes.

Coq au Vin (Hen in Wine)

The traditional way to cook chicken, in wine, is mostly due to the fact that farmers would cook it when it was very old, and its flesh was less tender. Slow cooking in red wine makes everything better!

INGREDIENTS | SERVES 4

4 pounds of rooster or hen, cut in chunks

1 tablespoon butter

2 tablespoons sunflower oil

4 ounces bacon, cut in ½"-wide matchsticks

2 onions (1 peeled and sliced, 1 peeled)

¼ cup Cognac (or brandy)

1 (25-ounce) bottle of red wine

2 garlic cloves, peeled and diced

1 bay leaf

1 tablespoon thyme

1 teaspoon salt

1 teaspoon ground black pepper

4 cloves

½ pound mushrooms, diced

Hen or Chicken?

Unless you have your own henhouse, it's pretty rare to find a rooster to cook. Most of the time, it's actually hen that is used in this recipe. Just make sure it's not a chicken: An animal that is too young won't cook or taste the same.

1. Have your butcher cut the hen or the rooster in big parts.

2. Put a large French oven or pot over medium heat. Melt the butter and the oil in it, combine them, then raise the heat to medium-high and add the bacon pieces. Let them melt; the fat should be released. Add the sliced onion. Stir well, and let it cook slowly with the bacon; they should become translucent, not brown, about 3–5 minutes.

3. Add the rooster/hen parts and get them to brown on each side for 5 minutes, turning halfway. Pour in the Cognac (be careful, it may flame!). Stir well, and slowly pour in the red wine. Add the garlic, bay leaf, thyme, salt, and pepper. Take the unpeeled onion and nail the cloves in it. Add to pot.

4. Add as much water as is needed to make sure that all the ingredients are covered by liquid. Bring to a boil, then cover and reduce to the lowest heat. Simmer for an hour and a half, stirring from time to time.

5. About 30 minutes before serving, add the diced mushrooms, and keep simmering.

6. Remove bay leaf. Serve dish warm, with small boiled potatoes.

Poule au Pot (Hen Stew)

This recipe calls for a large, fat hen. It's been a traditional Sunday family meal for centuries.

INGREDIENTS | SERVES 4

1 hen (at least 10 pounds)

1 onion

4 cloves

6 carrots, peeled and cut in two

4 turnips, peeled and cut in 1" chunks

2 leeks, green part cut off, each cut in 2 chunks

2 cups chicken stock

1 teaspoon salt

1 teaspoon ground black pepper

1 tablespoon thyme

1 bay leaf

2 tablespoons butter

2 tablespoons flour

A King's Meal

Henri IV is supposed to have said, "Every French man should be able to have a hen in his pot on every Sunday." This was at a time when a meatless day was almost every day for a poor farmer. From the seventeenth century up to now, the *poule au pot*, the hen in a pot, reminds the French that a good meal can be simple and good, but cheap and rich at the same time.

1. Fill a very large stove pot (big enough to contain a whole hen!) with cold water, and add the hen. Peel the onion, and nail the cloves in it, then add it to the water. Bring to a boil, and regularly skim the foam.

2. Add the carrots, turnips, and leeks to the pot.

3. Add the chicken stock, salt, pepper, thyme, and bay leaf. Reduce the heat to low, skim the foam once again, then cover and simmer for 3 hours (4 hours is even better).

4. About 15 minutes before serving, take a small saucepan and put it over medium-low heat. Melt the butter in it, then add the flour and stir well. Remove bay leaf from broth. Take out 1 cup of broth from the pot. Pour it slowly over the butter and the flour when they have turned into a kind of paste. Stir well over low heat for 10 minutes, until it turns into a hearty and thick white sauce.

5. Take the hen out and put all its parts in a serving dish; it should have cooked for so long that parts are falling apart naturally. Add the vegetables around the hen. Pour the white sauce on it.

6. Serve immediately, with white rice.

Lapin Chasseur (Rabbit Stew)

Rabbit is a very common meal in France. It's full of flavor, easy to cook, and is very lean, making it one of the healthiest meats to eat. This classic recipe is called "hunter-style rabbit" surely because it could easily be made by hunters coming back from a day in the woods, with mushrooms picked in the forest.

INGREDIENTS | SERVES 4

1 rabbit (about 3 pounds) cut in chunks
7 tablespoons flour
4 tablespoons salted butter, divided
2 medium shallots, thinly sliced
½ pound mushrooms, thinly sliced
1 cup white wine
2 cups chicken stock
1 tablespoon tomato paste
3 tablespoons cilantro
1 tablespoon thyme
1 bay leaf
1 teaspoon salt
1 teaspoon ground black pepper

1. Have your butcher cut the rabbit in big pieces. If you cut it yourself, be careful to take out the head, the lungs and the heart. Discard them.

2. Pour the flour on the rabbit pieces, making sure they are all evenly powdered.

3. Take a French oven (or any pot that can go into the oven and has a cover), and put it on medium-high heat. Melt 2 tablespoons of salted butter, and brown the rabbit pieces on each side. Then take them out and put them on the plate. Reserve.

4. Preheat your oven to 350°F.

5. Melt 2 tablespoons of salted butter in the pot, and add the thin slices of shallots and mushrooms in it, cooking slowly for around 5 minutes. The shallots should be translucent, and the water from the mushrooms should release. Then reduce the heat to low.

6. Pour in the wine and the chicken stock, stir well, then add the tomato paste, the cilantro, thyme, bay leaf, salt, and pepper. Cover and simmer for 15 minutes. Add the rabbit, cover, and put in the oven for 30 minutes.

7. Remove bay leaf. Serve dish warm with fresh pasta.

CHAPTER 11

Family-Style Dishes

Endives au Jambon (Endives with Ham)

Baked endives in ham and Béchamel (see recipe in Chapter 22) is a typical family-style dish, and can be considered French comfort food.

INGREDIENTS | SERVES 4

1 tablespoon butter

8 endives, trimmed

½ cup *Béchamel* sauce (see recipe in Chapter 22)

8 slices of *jambon blanc* or thin slices of cooked ham

2 ounces grated cheese (Gruyère is better, but you can use grated mozzarella)

1. Preheat the oven to 450°F.

2. In a medium nonstick skillet, melt the butter over medium-high heat and cook the endives in it for about 3 minutes, making sure they get brown on each side. Add water to a depth of 1" and cover the skillet. Reduce the heat to its lowest and simmer for 20 minutes.

3. Meanwhile, prepare the *Béchamel*.

4. Drain the endives and wrap each of them in a slice of ham. Layer them in a rectangular baking dish. Pour the *Béchamel* on the endives, and sprinkle the grated cheese all over them. Put in the oven for 20 minutes.

5. Serve warm.

Hachis Parmentier (Shepherd's Pie)

This French version of shepherd's pie is also the best way to recycle leftovers of Bœuf Bourguignon or Bœuf Carottes (see recipes in Chapter 10)!

INGREDIENTS | SERVES 4

1 tablespoon kosher salt

2 pounds potatoes, peeled

1½ pounds braised beef

1 tablespoon olive oil

2 medium onions, peeled and sliced

1 cup beef stock

2 ounces butter, diced, at room temperature

1½ cups whole milk

1 teaspoon salt

1 teaspoon ground black pepper

2 ounces grated cheese (Gruyère or mozzarella)

Don't Have Braised Beef?

You can still make an *hachis* from scratch by cooking a sliced medium onion in a skillet with 1 tablespoon of butter over medium heat. Add two diced tomatoes, a pound of ground beef, a diced and peeled garlic clove, and stir well. Add ½ cup of beef stock, season with 1 teaspoon of salt and 1 tablespoon of pepper. Add 1 tablespoon of thyme, and cook for 5 minutes.

1. Fill a large saucepan with water, add a tablespoon of kosher salt, and boil the potatoes for 20 minutes. Grind the beef, and reserve.

2. In a nonstick skillet over medium-high heat, add oil, and cook the sliced onions for 2 minutes, stirring well. Add the ground meat and stir well. Pour in the beef stock, stir well again, and cook for 15 minutes over low heat. Remove from heat and reserve.

3. Preheat the oven to 350°F. When the potatoes are boiled, drain them and mash them in a medium bowl. Mash the diced butter with the potatoes, then pour in the milk slowly, stirring steadily until you get a smooth texture. Add the salt and the pepper, and stir again.

4. Spread half of the mashed potatoes in a large casserole dish. Then spread the meat on top. Finally, spread the rest of the mashed potatoes on the meat. Sprinkle grated cheese all over, and cook for 45 minutes.

5. Serve warm, with a simple salad of lettuce and *Vinaigrette* (see recipe in Chapter 22).

Hachis Parmentier de Canard aux Cèpes
(Shepherd's Pie with Duck and Mushrooms)

This version of a parmentier, *from the southwest of France, is made with duck confit and* Boletus *mushrooms.*

INGREDIENTS | SERVES 4

1 tablespoon kosher salt

2 pounds potatoes, peeled

2 tablespoons dried bolete mushrooms (or porcini)

4 duck legs *en confit*, drained

2 medium onions, sliced

1 cup chicken stock

4 tablespoons butter, diced, at room temperature

1½ cups whole milk

1 teaspoon salt

1 teaspoon ground black pepper

2 ounces grated Gruyère

Merci, Mister Parmentier!

This dish is named after Antoine-Augustin Parmentier, who saved France from hunger by bringing potatoes to the Old World. To convince French consumers to try this new ingredient, he famously had a large field of potatoes guarded by royal soldiers in the outskirts of Paris. Parisians became curious about this crop, and sneaked into the field at night to steal and cook some.

1. Fill a large saucepan with water, add kosher salt and the potatoes, and bring to a boil over high heat. Boil for 20 minutes. Put the dried bolete mushrooms in a bowl of warm water for 15 minutes.

2. Remove the duck fat from the *confit* duck legs by warming them in a *bain-marie*: Put the legs in a small saucepan, and put it over a larger one that has been filled with water. Bring to a boil. Stop boiling when all the fat has melted. Take the legs out, peel off the skin, and shred the flesh. Reserve the melted duck fat.

3. Put a medium skillet over medium-high heat. Add 1 tablespoon of the melted duck fat and the sliced onion. Cook for 2 minutes. Add the mushrooms and the duck meat. Pour in the chicken stock, and cook for 15 minutes over low heat. Reserve.

4. Preheat the oven to 350°F. Drain the potatoes and mash them in a medium bowl. Mash the diced butter into the potatoes, then pour in the milk slowly, stirring steadily until you get a smooth texture. Add salt and pepper. Spread half of the mashed potatoes in a large casserole dish. Then spread the meat mixture on it. Finally, spread the rest of the mashed potatoes on the meat. Sprinkle the grated cheese on top, and cook for 45 minutes.

5. Serve warm.

Tomates Farcies (Stuffed Tomatoes)

Stuffed tomatoes are always a good idea to feed a hungry family! Although all very simple, there are as many recipes for this dish as there are families in France. The differences come from what type of meat is added.

INGREDIENTS | SERVES 4

8 large tomatoes

1 tablespoon kosher salt

1 cup milk

2 slices of bread, stale if possible

2 medium shallots, peeled and sliced

1 pound sausage meat

½ pound ground veal

2 tablespoons parsley, finely chopped

2 tablespoons thyme

1 teaspoon salt

1 teaspoon ground black pepper

3 tablespoons water

½ cup dry rice, uncooked

Try Other Vegetables

Stuffed tomatoes are the most common stuffed vegetable, but you can also make this recipe with carved potatoes or zucchini. Just don't forget to make *chapeaux*, or the tops of the vegetables. Those little hats are typical of the dish, and kids are fond of them.

1. Cut off the top ½" of each tomato: The French call it the *chapeau*, hat. Reserve the hats. With a spoon, scoop out the tomato flesh, removing the seeds and the innards. Do not pierce the tomato. Reserve the innards of the tomatoes in a separate bowl. Sprinkle kosher salt inside each tomato.

2. Preheat the oven to 350°F. Pour the milk in a bowl, add the bread slices, and allow to soak. Then cut them in very small pieces, or process in a blender.

3. In a large bowl, mix the shallots with the sausage meat and the ground veal. Add the pieces of bread soaked in milk. Add the parsley, thyme, salt, and pepper to the meat. Mix well with your hands.

4. Take the bowl of tomato innards. Mix it with the water, and pour into the bottom of a large baking dish. Add the rice. Stuff each tomato with the meat mixture. Cover each with a "tomato hat." Place the tomatoes on the dish, over the rice. Put in the oven and cook for 45 minutes.

5. Serve warm.

Gratins de Pâtes (Mac and Cheese)

Mac and cheese is also a French specialty! In France it's mostly a recipe for leftovers, where you use pasta that was previously cooked.

INGREDIENTS | SERVES 4

½ pound uncooked pasta, or 1 pound cooked pasta

2 cups whole milk

9 tablespoons butter, divided

⅓ cup flour

1 tablespoon ground nutmeg

1 teaspoon salt

1 teaspoon ground black pepper

½ pound mushrooms, minced thin

1 tablespoon fresh parsley, minced thin

2 slices of ham, cut in ½" squares

1 tomato, diced

1 cup *Béchamel* sauce (see recipe in Chapter 22)

4 ounces grated cheese (Gruyère or mozzarella)

1. If you don't have leftover pasta, cook a half-pound of macaroni in boiling salted water. Drain. Preheat the oven to 400°F.

2. Bring the milk to a boil in a small saucepan over medium heat. In a medium nonstick saucepan, melt 7 tablespoons of butter over medium heat. Add the flour, stir well, and cook for 1 minute until the mixture is smooth. Pour the boiling milk slowly on the flour and butter mixture, stirring firmly. Bring to a boil over medium heat, stirring continuously. Season with ground nutmeg, salt, and pepper.

3. In another small saucepan, melt 1 tablespoon butter over medium heat. Add the minced mushrooms and the parsley, and cook for 5 minutes, stirring well.

4. Grease a large casserole dish with the last tablespoon of butter. Pour the pasta in it, and mix with the mushrooms, the ham, and the tomato. Combine so that every ingredient is spread evenly. Pour the *Béchamel* sauce on the pasta. Spread well. Sprinkle the grated cheese on it. Put in the oven and cook for 25 minutes.

5. Serve warm.

Choucroute Garnie (Sauerkraut)

This Alsatian specialty is beloved all over France. Don't forget that sauerkraut is actually very healthy and low in calories!

INGREDIENTS | SERVES 6

2 pounds sauerkraut, rinsed and drained

1 tablespoon sunflower oil

1 pound pork belly, cut in ½" thick slices

1 large onion, minced

1 pound pork shoulder

2 cups white wine

8 juniper berries

1 teaspoon caraway seeds

4 peppercorns

4 garlic cloves, peeled and minced

8 small potatoes, peeled

4 smoked sausage (such as Polish kielbasa) whole

4 frankfurter sausages whole

1. Rinse the sauerkraut in water and drain it. Reserve.

2. Put a large French oven over medium heat and heat the oil. Add the pork belly slices to the pot. Brown them on each side, then add the onion. Stir well and brown the onions slightly with the pork belly, about 2–3 minutes. Add the pork shoulder, brown it on each side. Add the sauerkraut, stir again, and pour in the white wine. Add the juniper berries, caraway seeds, peppercorns, and garlic. Pour in enough water to cover everything, and bring to a boil over high heat. Cover and reduce the heat to low. Simmer for 90 minutes.

3. About 30 minutes before serving, add the potatoes to the pot, cover again, and keep simmering.

4. Fill a medium saucepan with water and bring to a simmer. Cook the meat, 15 minutes for the smoked sausages, 5 minutes for the frankfurters.

5. Add the sausages to the pot and serve warm, with a pot of Dijon mustard on the table.

Choucroute de la Mer (Sauerkraut of the Sea)

This is a great way to enjoy French sauerkraut without the guilt of the sausage-related calories. This recipe was invented in Paris by restaurants who wanted to please guests who were trying to watch their figures.

INGREDIENTS | SERVES 6

2 pounds sauerkraut, rinsed and drained
1 tablespoon sunflower oil
1 large onion, minced
3⅔ cups white wine, divided
8 juniper berries
1 teaspoon caraway seeds
4 peppercorns
4 garlic cloves, peeled and minced
8 small potatoes, peeled
1 pound monkfish fillet, cut in 4 pieces
1 pound salmon steak, cut in 4 pieces
1 pound sea bass fillet, cut in 4 pieces
⅓ cup wine vinegar
2 medium shallots, peeled and minced
4 egg yolks
½ cup *crème fraîche* or crema Mexicana

1. Rinse the sauerkraut under water and drain it. Reserve.

2. Put a large French oven over medium heat and heat the oil. Add the minced onion, stir well, and cook slowly for 2 minutes. Add the sauerkraut, and slowly pour in 3 cups of wine, stirring continuously. Add the juniper berries, caraway seeds, peppercorns, and garlic. Pour in enough water to cover everything, and bring to a boil over high heat. Cover, reduce the heat to low, and simmer for 90 minutes.

3. About 30 minutes before serving, add the potatoes to the pot, cover again, and keep simmering. About 15 minutes later, put half of the sauerkraut on a plate, and place the monkfish, salmon, and sea bass over the sauerkraut left in the pot. Cover the fish with the other half of the sauerkraut. Simmer for another 15 minutes.

4. In a small saucepan, pour the vinegar, ⅔ cup wine, and the shallots. Bring to a boil over medium heat. Remove from heat when the liquid has reduced by half. In a medium bowl, whisk the egg yolks and the cream, and add the wine reduction. Then put back in the saucepan on simmer.

5. Serve a piece of each fish on each plate, add the sauerkraut, and gently pour the sauce on the fish.

Couscous Royal

Of course, couscous is originally from Northern Africa, but North Africans' emmigration to France and the return of French settlers who had lived there for many generations before coming back in the 1960s have made couscous a national dish.

INGREDIENTS | SERVES 4

3 tablespoons olive oil

2 large onions, minced

3 pounds lamb shoulder, cut in 2" cubes

4 chicken legs

2 tablespoons Ras el Hanout spices

2 tablespoons thyme

1 bay leaf

4 carrots, cut in 1" slices

1 tablespoon tomato paste

1 teaspoon salt

1 teaspoon ground black pepper

12 cups water

4 turnips, peeled and cut in 1" chunks

4 zucchini, cut in 1" slices

1 (15-ounce) can garbanzo beans, drained

4 merguez sausages (or any spicy lamb or beef sausage)

3 cups dry couscous

Make Your Own Ras el Hanout Spice Mix

This spice mix is essential in North African cuisine. You can find it everywhere in France. To make your own, grind together the following spices: coriander seeds (5 teaspoons), fennel seeds (2 teaspoons), turmeric (3 teaspoons), cumin seeds (1 teaspoon), 3 cloves, ground black pepper (2 teaspoons), ground ginger (2 teaspoons), cinnamon (1 teaspoon), and paprika (5 teaspoons).

1. In a very large pot, heat the olive oil over medium-high heat. Add the minced onions and cook for 1 minute. Add the lamb shoulders. Brown them on each side for 3 minutes. Add the chicken legs, and brown them on each side for 3 minutes. Add Ras-el-Hanout, thyme, and the bay leaf.

2. Add the carrots and tomato paste, season with the salt and the pepper, and stir. Cover with 12 cups of water. Bring to a boil over high heat, then cover the pot and simmer for 1 hour. Add turnips and simmer for 30 minutes. Add the zucchini and the drained garbanzo beans. Simmer for 15 minutes. Remove bay leaf.

3. In a nonstick skillet, cook the whole merguez sausages for 7 minutes.

4. Prepare the couscous as instructed on the box, using broth taken from the simmering meat to cook it.

5. Serve warm with the meats, vegetables, and couscous on the same plate.

Cassoulet de Toulouse (Sausage and White Bean Casserole)

This sausage and white bean casserole has been a favorite of French cooks for a long time.

1 tablespoon duck fat

3 medium onions, thinly minced

2 medium carrots, thinly sliced

3 garlic cloves, peeled and minced

½ pound pork belly, cut in ½"- thick slices

1 pound lamb shoulder, cut in 2" cubes

2 pounds pork spare ribs

2 tablespoons thyme

1 teaspoon salt

1 teaspoon ground black pepper

1 bay leaf

3 tablespoons tomato paste

2 pork sausages (mild Italian, for example)

4 duck legs *confit* (purchased, or see recipe in Chapter 22)

2 (15-ounce) cans of Great Northern beans, drained

½ cup bread crumbs

A Big Tradition

Cassoulet comes from the south of France, and there are different recipes depending on where you come from: For example, *cassoulet* from Castelnaudary is cooked with only pork, whereas in Carcassonne, you can also add lamb. This casserole is inspired by the Toulouse *cassoulet*, but as it's made with products you can find in the United States, you can call it *Cassoulet de Los Angeles!*

1. Heat a French oven over medium-high heat. Cook the duck fat and the minced onions for 2 minutes. Add the carrots, garlic, and the pork belly, and cook for 5 minutes. Add the lamb and the pork spare ribs, brown them on each side for about 5 minutes, then take them out. Reserve.

2. Add the thyme, salt, pepper, bay leaf, and the tomato paste, stir well, then add the sausages. Brown them on each side, about 2 minutes total, and cover. Reduce the heat to low and simmer for 1 hour.

3. Preheat the oven to 350°F. Remove the duck fat from the *confit* by warming the ducks legs in a *bain-marie*: Put the legs in a small saucepan, and put it over a larger one that has been filled with water. Bring to a boil. Stop boiling when all the fat has melted.

4. In a large baking dish, layer the pork belly slices at the bottom, then add the meats. Remove bay leaf. Cover with the drained Great Northern beans and tomato sauce. Add the duck legs on top. Cover with the bread crumbs. Cook for 2 hours.

5. Serve warm.

Brandade de Morue (Fish Pie)

Brandade could be called a fisherman's pie! It's kind of a shepherd's pie, but with salt cod in it.

INGREDIENTS | SERVES 4

2 pounds salt cod

2 pounds potatoes, peeled

2 tablespoons olive oil

2 medium onions, peeled and minced

2 garlic cloves, peeled and minced

½ cup whole milk

1 teaspoon ground black pepper

Morue: Salt Cod

Salt cod has been used a lot in south European cuisine, because it is a great way to preserve the fish for a long time. The only problem with this recipe is that you have to think of it in advance: Salt cod must be desalted 24 hours before it can be used.

1. Fill a large bowl with fresh water, and put the salt cod in it. Leave the cod in the water for a minimum of 24 hours, changing the water every three hours.

2. The next day, fill a medium saucepan with water, add the desalted cod, and bring to a boil over high heat. Cook for 8 minutes. Take the fish out with a slotted spoon and put it on a plate. Fill the saucepan with fresh water again, put the cod back in it, bring it to a boil, and poach for another 8 minutes. Take the fish out with a slotted spoon, and shred it. Take out all the remaining fish bones.

3. Fill another medium saucepan with cold water, add potatoes, and bring to a boil over high heat. Cook for 20 minutes.

4. In a nonstick skillet, heat the olive oil, and cook the sliced onions slowly over medium heat for 3–5 minutes. Add the garlic. Stir for 2 minutes, making sure the onion and the garlic don't get brown. Add the shredded cod, and mix it with the onion and the garlic over very low heat.

5. Preheat the oven to 350°F.

6. Lay potatoes on a plate and mash them with a fork. Add them to the skillet. Mix the cod and the potatoes well, add the milk, and stir again. Pour everything in a casserole dish. Use a wooden spatula to even it all. Season with pepper. Put in the oven and cook for 15 minutes.

7. Serve in the casserole, very warm, with a simple salad of green lettuce and *Vinaigrette* (see recipe in Chapter 22).

Croque-Monsieur Maison (Homestyle Croque-Monsieur)

This one is the home-cook version. Much easier, and a little less dangerous in terms of calorie count!

INGREDIENTS | SERVES 4

8 slices of bread, crusts removed

4 teaspoons Dijon mustard

4 ounces grated cheese (preferably Gruyère, or a tasty cheese like Mimolette or Comté)

4 slices of *jambon blanc*, or thin cooked ham

2 tablespoons butter

1. Preheat the oven at 400°F.

2. Lay out 4 slices of bread; spread with mustard. Add 2 tablespoons of cheese, then ham. Put another slice of bread on top, then spread a teaspoon of butter on the cover bread. Repeat for the other 3 sandwiches, and put in the oven over a parchment paper–lined baking sheet. Cook for 10 minutes. Serve warm, with a salad of lettuce and *Vinaigrette* (see recipe in Chapter 22).

Croque-Monsieur Béchamel
(Croque-Monsieur with Béchamel Sauce)

This version, with Béchamel, is often served in French bistrots.

INGREDIENTS | SERVES 4

2 cups whole milk

2 tablespoons butter

2 tablespoons flour

1 teaspoon salt

1 teaspoon ground black pepper

1 teaspoon ground nutmeg

8 slices of bread, crusts removed

4 ounces grated cheese (preferably Gruyère, or mozzarella)

4 slices of jambon blanc, or thin sliced cooked ham

1. In a small saucepan, bring the milk to a boil.

2. In a medium saucepan, melt the butter. Add flour. Cook together until they form a paste. Remove from heat and add the boiling milk, stirring firmly. Add the salt, pepper, and nutmeg. When the mixture is smooth, return it to the stove over medium heat. Bring to a boil, stirring for 5 minutes. Remove from heat; let cool.

3. Preheat oven to 350°F. On a plate, lay a slice of bread; spread *Béchamel* on top. Add 2 tablespoons of cheese, then ham; spread on another 2 tablespoons of *Béchamel*. Put another slice of bread on top; cover with 1 tablespoon of *Béchamel* and 1 tablespoon of cheese. Repeat for the other 3 sandwiches; put them in the oven on a parchment paper–lined baking sheet. Cook for 10 minutes. Serve warm with lettuce and *Vinaigrette* (see recipe in Chapter 22).

Croque-Chèvre (Croque-Monsieur with Goat Cheese)

A goat-cheese version of the classic recipe!

INGREDIENTS | SERVES 4

½ pound bacon, cut in ½" slices

2 *crottins* of goat cheese, or 4 ounces of goat cheese

8 slices of bread

4 ounces grated cheese (preferably Gruyère)

4 slices of *jambon blanc*, or thin cooked ham

1. Cook bacon in a medium nonstick skillet over high heat for 3 minutes. Slice the *crottins* into two, or cut the goat cheese in ½" slices.

2. Preheat the oven to 400°F. Lay out 4 slices of bread, cover with 2 tablespoons of grated cheese, then a folded slice of ham. Put another slice of bread on top, then top with half a *crottin* (or a ½" slice of goat cheese), and slice of bacon. Proceed this way for the other three sandwiches and put in the oven over a parchment paper–lined baking sheet. Cook for 10 minutes.

3. Serve warm, with a simple salad of green lettuce and *Vinaigrette* (see recipe in Chapter 22).

Cordon Bleu

This specialty has traveled all over the world, and is still a favorite of French kids. Here is an easy adapted recipe you can make at home.

INGREDIENTS | SERVES 4

8 slices of rotisserie chicken breast

8 slices of bacon

4 slices of cheese

⅓ cup flour

⅓ cup bread crumbs

2 eggs

1 teaspoon salt

1 teaspoon ground black pepper

1 tablespoon butter

1 tablespoon sunflower oil

1. On a plate, lay two slices of chicken breast on top of each other. Top with two slices of bacon. Add a slice of cheese on top of the bacon, and fold the chicken slices over in half.

2. Add the flour to a bowl. Add bread crumbs to another bowl. Beat the eggs in a third bowl, and season with salt and pepper.

3. Soak the chicken breasts in the eggs, then in the flour, and finish with the bread crumbs, flipping the chicken stack to coat each side.

4. In a nonstick skillet, melt the butter slowly over medium-high heat. Add the oil, combine in the skillet, then cook the *cordon bleu* for 2 minutes on each side, or until the bread crumbs are golden.

5. Serve warm, with a simple salad.

Tartiflette (Potato, Bacon, and Cheese Casserole)

This potato/bacon/cheese casserole was developed in the Alps, with the traditional milk cheese Reblochon. This creamy (and quite stinky!) raw-milk cheese is hard to find in the United States, but you can try the recipe with other strong flavored cheeses, like raclette cheese, for example.

INGREDIENTS | SERVES 4

2 pounds potatoes, boiled

½ pound bacon, cut in ½" slices

2 medium onions, peeled and sliced

⅔ cup *crème fraîche* or crema Mexicana

1 pound Reblochon (or equivalent)

1 teaspoon salt

1 teaspoon ground black pepper

Ski Gastronomy

Tartiflette used to be a home-cooked tradition only in the small villages of Savoie in the Alps. But like raclette or fondue, it has become nationally famous and cooked all over the country thanks to winter tourism. Since the 1960s, winter vacationing and skiing in the Alps has become very popular, unveiling a whole previously unknown culinary tradition.

1. Fill a large saucepan with cold water, add the potatoes, and bring to a boil over high heat. Boil for 20 minutes and drain.

2. Preheat the oven to 350°F. In a medium nonstick skillet, cook the bacon over medium-high heat. After 1 minute, add the slices of onions and cook for 5 minutes, stirring often with a wooden spatula.

3. Cut cooked potatoes in thin slices. Layer half of them at the bottom of a large baking dish. Add a layer of onion slices and bacon. Pour the cream on everything, then add a last layer of sliced potatoes on top.

4. If you have a whole Reblochon, slice it in two round, thinner cheeses. Put them on top of the dish, rind facing the top of the oven. If you're cooking with slices of cheese, spread them all over the potatoes. Season with salt and pepper. Put in the oven and bake for 20 minutes.

5. Serve warm, with a simple salad of green lettuce and *Vinaigrette* (see recipe in Chapter 22).

CHAPTER 12

Traditional Meals to Share

Pâte à Crêpes (Crêpe Batter)

The French love to make savory crêpes for a dinner party where the host only prepares the batter and makes the crêpes. The host provides the filling options, and the guests decide what they want to include in their own crêpes and reheat it on the spot.

INGREDIENTS | SERVES 6

1½ cups flour

2 large eggs

1 teaspoon salt

4 cups whole milk

2 tablespoons plus 1 teaspoon butter

The Crêpe Secret

The French all have their family secret to make the best crêpe batter they know. But the real secret is not a tablespoon of beer, or egg whites and yolks beaten separately. It's much more simple: It's time. Try and make the batter at least 1 hour in advance. Cover it and leave at room temperature.

1. Sieve the flour and pour it in a large bowl. Make a small well at the center of the flour (like a volcano crater), break the eggs into it, and add the salt. Whisk slowly. When the eggs and the flour are well combined, start adding the milk, very slowly. Never stop whisking.

2. Melt 2 tablespoons of butter in a small saucepan over very low heat, then add it to the flour and milk mixture. Whisk again. Cover with a damp cloth. Leave at room temperature for 1 hour.

3. In a medium nonstick skillet (preferably a crêpe pan), melt 1 teaspoon butter over medium-high heat. Wipe it out with a paper towel. Then take a small ladleful of batter, pour it in the center of the pan, and immediately swirl the pan so that the batter spreads all over it. Cook until the rim of the crêpe detaches itself from the pan, then use a wooden spatula to flip it on the other side. Cook for about 1 minute total.

4. Pile up the crêpes on a large plate, cover with aluminum wrap, and put the plate over a small saucepan filled with water that you put on a low heat. This will make sure they stay warm.

Pâte à Galettes (Buckwheat Crêpe Batter)

This savory buckwheat crêpe, called a galette, is typical of the Brittany region, and is the best batter to use for savory crêpes. Be careful, though, never to say crêpe in Brittany when you're talking about the buckwheat version; they are very proud of their difference, and a galette is a galette!

INGREDIENTS | SERVES 6

1½ cups buckwheat flour
½ cup regular flour
2 teaspoons salt
2 tablespoons plus 1 teaspoon butter
4 eggs
2 cups water

1. Sift the buckwheat flour and the regular flour and pour them in a large bowl. Add the salt, and stir well.

2. In a small saucepan, melt 2 tablespoons butter over very low heat. Take another large bowl, beat the eggs firmly, then slowly add the water and melted butter. Make a well in the flour. Slowly pour in the egg and water mixture, and whisk very firmly. Cover with a damp cloth and leave at room temperature for one hour.

3. In a medium nonstick skillet (preferably a crêpe pan), melt 1 teaspoon butter over medium-high heat. Wipe out the pan with a paper towel. Then take a small ladleful of batter, pour it in the center of the pan, and immediately swirl the pan so that the batter spreads all over it. Cook until the rim of the *galette* detaches itself from the pan, then use a wooden spatula to flip it on the other side. Cook for about 1 minute.

4. Pile up the *galettes* on a large plate, cover with aluminum wrap, and put the plate over a small saucepan filled with water. Place over low heat to keep them warm.

Crêpe ou Galette Complète (Ham, Cheese, and Egg Crêpe)

This is the most common savory crêpe or galette recipe. Complète means it's wholesome: Eggs, ham, and cheese make it a meal in itself.

INGREDIENTS | SERVES 4

1 teaspoon salted butter

8 cooked savory *Crêpes* or *Galettes* (see recipes in this chapter)

7 ounces grated cheese (Gruyère or mozzarella)

8 thin slices of *jambon blanc* or thinly sliced cooked ham

8 eggs

1 teaspoon salt

1 teaspoon ground black pepper

1. Heat a medium nonstick skillet (or a crêpe pan) over medium-high heat. Melt 1 teaspoon butter in it, then wipe out the pan with a paper towel.

2. Lay the already cooked crêpe in the skillet. Take 3 tablespoons of grated cheese and put it in the middle of the crêpe. Fold the ham slice in two and put it on the cheese.

3. Fold the crêpe like an envelope: Fold the right edge in toward the center, then the left, then the top, and the bottom. Once it's closed, break an egg on the top, sunny side up. Reduce the heat to low and simmer for 3 minutes. Sprinkle salt and pepper on it.

4. Serve warm, and use the same process to cook the other crêpes.

Crêpe ou Galette Nordique (Nordic Crêpes)

Smoked salmon and crème fraîche are a perfect combination with crêpes or galettes. And they don't need much time to cook!

INGREDIENTS | SERVES 4

1 cup *crème fraîche* or sour cream

2 tablespoons chives, chopped

1 teaspoon salt

1 teaspoon ground black pepper

1 teaspoon butter

8 cooked savory Crêpes or *Galettes* (see recipes in this chapter)

8 slices of smoked salmon

1 lemon

1. In a medium bowl, combine the cream with the chives, then add salt and pepper, and stir well.

2. Heat a medium nonstick skillet (or a crêpe pan) over medium-high heat. Melt 1 teaspoon butter in it, then wipe out the pan with a paper towel. Lay the already cooked crêpe in the skillet.

3. Take 2 tablespoons of cream mixture and put it in the middle of the crêpe. Fold the salmon slice in two and put it on the cream. Squeeze the lemon over the salmon. Fold the crêpe like an envelope: Fold the right edge in toward the center, then the left, then the top, and the bottom. Reduce the heat to its lowest and simmer for 3 minutes.

4. Serve warm.

Galettes de Monsieur Seguin (Goat Cheese and Bacon Buckwheat Crêpes)

This goat cheese and bacon buckwheat crêpe is named after a famous story that all French kids learn, about Monsieur Seguin's goat, a goat that dreamed too much.

INGREDIENTS | SERVES 4

½ pound bacon, cut in ½" slices

1 medium onion, thinly sliced

½ cup *crème fraîche* or sour cream

½ teaspoon salt

1¼ teaspoons ground black pepper, divided

1 teaspoon salted butter

8 cooked savory *Galettes* (see recipe in this chapter)

1 (8-ounce) goat cheese, cut in ½"-thick slices

1. Put a medium nonstick saucepan over medium-high heat. Start cooking the bacon in it, then add the sliced onion. Stir well and cook them together for 3 minutes. Then pour in the cream, stir again, add salt and 1 teaspoon black pepper, stir again, and reduce the heat to low. Simmer for 1 minute. Remove from heat and reserve.

2. Heat a medium nonstick skillet (preferably a crêpe pan) over medium-high heat. Melt the salted butter in it, then wipe out the pan with a paper towel. Lay the already cooked *galette* in the skillet.

3. Take 2 tablespoons of the bacon and cream mixture and put it in the middle of the *galette*. Lay 2 goat cheese slices on it. Sprinkle ¼ teaspoon of pepper on it. Fold the *galette* like an envelope: Fold the right edge in toward the center, then the left, then the top, and the bottom. Reduce the heat to its lowest and simmer for 3 minutes.

4. Serve immediately while warm, and use the same process to cook the other *galettes*.

Galettes Erquy (Scallop and Leek *Galette*)

This scallop and leek galette is named after the beautiful town of Erquy in Brittany, where the best scallops in France are fished. They love scallops so much there that they celebrate them with a special festival every year.

INGREDIENTS | SERVES 4

2 tablespoons plus 1 teaspoon butter, divided

4 leeks, green part cut off, julienned

1 cup *crème fraîche* or sour cream

2 medium shallots, peeled and diced

24 fresh scallops

8 cooked savory *Galettes* (recipe in this chapter)

1 lemon

1 teaspoon salt

1 teaspoon ground black pepper (and ¼ teaspoon on top of each *galette*)

1. In a small saucepan over medium heat, melt 1 tablespoon of butter, then add the julienned leeks. Stir them well in the butter, and let them cook for 5 minutes. Add the cream, and cook for 1 minute on low heat. Stir well, remove from the heat, and reserve.

2. In a medium nonstick pan, melt 1 tablespoon butter over medium-high heat. Add the diced shallot and cook for 1 minute, then add the scallops and brown on each side for 1 minute.

3. Heat a medium nonstick skillet (preferably a crêpe pan) over medium-high heat. Melt 1 teaspoon butter in it, then wipe out the pan with a paper towel. Lay the already cooked *galette* in the skillet.

4. Take 2 tablespoons of leeks and put them in the middle of the *galette*. Lay three scallops on top of them. Sprinkle ¼ teaspoon pepper, and squeeze the lemon on it. Fold the *galette* like an envelope: Fold the right edge in toward the center, then the left, then the top, and the bottom. Reduce the heat to its lowest and simmer for 2 minutes.

5. Serve warm, and use the same process to cook the other *galettes*.

Fondue Savoyarde

*The French think the cheese fondue was first created in Savoie
as a way for farmers to use the leftover cheese.*

INGREDIENTS | SERVES 8

1 baguette

2 garlic cloves, peeled

1 teaspoon potato starch

½ cup kirsch

1 pound Emmental, without the rind, cut in 1" cubes

1 pound Comté, without the rind, cut in 1" cubes

1 pound Beaufort, without the rind, cut in 1" cubes

1 bottle of white wine (any light, dry wine)

1 teaspoon ground black pepper

1 teaspoon ground nutmeg

1. At least 12 hours before the meal, cut the baguette into 1" cubes. Store at room temperature. Rub the garlic cloves inside the fondue pot. In a small bowl, combine the potato starch with the kirsch, stir well, and reserve. Put the cheese cubes in the pot; pour in the white wine.

2. About 15 minutes before serving, put the pot over low heat; stir constantly. Add the pepper, nutmeg, and the potato starch mixture. Stir for 1 minute; remove from heat. Put the fondue pot on the table, on a burner set to medium heat. Bring the bread cubes to the table and share with your guests.

Fondue aux Cèpes (Fondue with Mushrooms)

*The cèpe mushroom adds perfume and smoothness to the traditional
recipe. Dry porcini can be used as a substitute.*

INGREDIENTS | SERVES 8

1 baguette

1½ cups whole milk

3 ounces dry cèpes

2 garlic cloves, peeled

1 teaspoon potato starch

½ cup kirsch

1 tablespoon butter

1 tablespoon rosemary

1 pound Emmental, without the rind, cut in 1" cubes

1 pound Comté, without the rind, cut in 1" cubes

1 pound Beaufort, without the rind, cut in 1" cubes

1 bottle of white wine (any light, dry wine)

1 teaspoon ground black pepper

1. At least 12 hours before the meal, cut the baguette into 1" cubes. Store at room temperature. In a medium saucepan, heat the milk over low heat for 2 minutes. Turn off the heat, add the mushrooms; leave at room temperature for 2 hours. Put the saucepan back on medium-low heat; cook for 10 minutes.

2. Rub the garlic cloves inside the caquelon. In a bowl, combine the potato starch with the kirsch. About 20 minutes before serving, place the fondue pot over medium-low heat, melt the butter, and add the rosemary and the mushrooms. Cook for 5 minutes, reduce heat to low; add the cheeses and the wine. Stir constantly. Add the pepper, the kirsch, and the starch. Stir for 1 minute; remove from heat. Put the fondue pot on the table, on a burner set to medium heat. Bring the bread cubes to the table and share with your guests.

Fondue Bourguignonne (Burgundy Fondue)

Try to buy the best-quality meat you can. This recipe also relies on good sauces. You should serve at least three on the table: béarnaise, mayonnaise, and hollandaise are the most classic.

INGREDIENTS | SERVES 6

3 pounds beef fillet or tenderloin, cut in 1" cubes

3 cups peanut oil (or more, depending on the size of your *caquelon*)

1 cup French Mayonnaise (see recipe in Chapter 22)

1 cup *Béarnaise Sauce* (see recipe in Chapter 22)

1 cup Hollandaise Sauce (see recipe in Chapter 22)

A Fondue Essential

Fondue is often cooked in and eaten from a special pot called a caquelon. It can be ceramic or cast iron, and its bottom has to be thick enough to prevent the cheese from burning. A layer of cheese, called *la religieuse* ("the nun"), always forms on the bottom; it is usually shared at the end of the dinner.

1. Place the cut beef in a serving dish and bring to the table.

2. Fill the *caquelon* halfway with the peanut oil. Put on medium-high heat and heat up the oil. Stop before it boils. Then put the *caquelon* on its burner, at the center of the table.

3. Serve the three sauces on the table.

4. Your guests can all help themselves to meat and cook it in the oil for as long as they want, dipping it afterwards in the sauces.

Fondue au Vin Rouge (Red Wine Fondue)

Of course there's a French fondue recipe with red wine!

INGREDIENTS | SERVES 6

4 cups red wine (pinot noir)

1 medium onion, peeled and diced

1 medium shallot, peeled and diced

2 garlic cloves, peeled

3 cloves

1 tablespoon thyme

1 bay leaf

3 pounds beef fillet or tenderloin, cut in 1" cubes

1 cup French Mayonnaise (see recipe in Chapter 22)

1 cup *Béarnaise Sauce* (see recipe in Chapter 22)

1 cup Hollandaise Sauce (see recipe in Chapter 22)

1. Pour the red wine in the *caquelon,* add the diced onion, shallot, garlic, cloves, thyme, and the bay leaf. Stir well, and bring to a boil over high heat. At the boiling point, reduce the heat to low and simmer for 20 minutes before serving. Remove bay leaf.

2. Put the meat in a serving dish and bring to the table.

3. Put the *caquelon* on its burner, on high heat, at the center of the table. Serve the three sauces alongside. Your guests can all help themselves to meat and cook it for as long as they want, dipping it afterwards in the sauces.

Fondue Bressane (Bressane Fondue)

This recipe is named after a region of France famous for its chickens, le Pays de Bresse. It's exactly like the Fondue Bourguignonne, except you do not use beef, but chicken. A sort of do-it-yourself French-fried chicken!

INGREDIENTS | SERVES 6

3 pounds chicken breasts

1 cup white wine

3 garlic cloves, peeled

1 tablespoon thyme

3 cups peanut oil (or more, depending on the size of your *caquelon*)

1 cup crema Mexicana or half and half

1 cup bread crumbs

1 cup French Mayonnaise (see recipe in Chapter 22)

1 cup *Béarnaise Sauce* (see recipe in Chapter 22)

1 cup Hollandaise Sauce (see recipe in Chapter 22)

1. Cut the chicken breasts in 1" cubes. Put them in a medium bowl. Pour the white wine in, add the peeled garlic and the thyme, and put in the refrigerator for 12 hours.

2. The next day, take the chicken cubes out of the wine, dry them with a cloth, and put in a serving bowl on the table.

3. Fill the *caquelon* halfway with the peanut oil. Put on a medium-high heat and heat up the oil, removing it before it boils. Then put the *caquelon* on its burner, at the center of the table.

4. Add the cream to a medium bowl, and put the bread crumbs in another serving bowl. Bring to the table with the three sauces.

5. Your guests can all help themselves to chicken: They should dip it first in the cream, then in the bread crumbs, and cook it for as long as they want, dipping it afterwards in sauces.

Fondue Gitane (Gipsy Fondue)

This fondue is referred to as Gipsy fondue and is much healthier than the other versions. No oil, cream, or cheese; it's all about the meat!

INGREDIENTS | SERVES 4

1 pound beef fillet or tenderloin, cut in 1" cubes

1 pound chicken breast, cut in 1" cubes

4 cups chicken stock

1 tablespoon thyme

1 bay leaf

1 tablespoon rosemary

1 teaspoon salt

1 teaspoon ground black pepper

6 medium carrots, each cut in 3 chunks

4 turnips, peeled and cut in half

4 parsnips, each peeled and cut in 3 chunks

4 leeks, greens cut off

1. Reserve the cubed beef and chicken in a bowl.

2. In a large saucepan, bring the chicken stock to a boil over high heat. Add the thyme, the rosemary, the bay leaf, and the salt and pepper. When the broth is boiling, add the vegetables, reduce the heat to medium-high, cover, and cook for 25 minutes.

3. Using a slotted spoon, take the vegetables out and put them on a serving dish. Strain the broth into the *caquelon*. Remove bay leaf. Place on the burner, and turn to high.

4. Serve the meat in two separate bowls. Bring the steamed vegetables to the table as well.

5. Each guest will dip their meat in the boiling stew to cook it. Serve with a jar of Dijon mustard.

Raclette

This recipe calls for some equipment: you have to buy a raclette maker, but it's a great investment you can use a lot for fun nights with friends and family.

INGREDIENTS | SERVES 6

2 pounds potatoes

2 pounds raclette cheese from Savoie

1 small shallot, peeled and diced

1 tablespoon red wine vinegar

1 teaspoon salt

1 teaspoon ground black pepper

2 tablespoons olive oil

1 head of romaine lettuce

½ pound prosciutto

½ pound Bresaola (dried salt beef)

½ pound rotisserie chicken or ham

1 jar of *cornichons* (gherkins)

Party Recipe!

Raclette is easy to prepare at the last minute, and always a good excuse to spend time chatting with the ones you love. As French *charcuterie* is hard to find in America, use what is the most similar: Italian *charcuterie*.

1. Fill a large saucepan with cold water, add the unpeeled potatoes, and bring to a boil over high heat. Cook for 20 minutes.

2. With a slotted spoon, take the potatoes out of the water. Put them in a serving dish and place on the table.

3. Cut the raclette cheese in slices about 2" wide. Place them in another serving dish, and put on the table. In a large salad bowl, combine the diced shallots with the vinegar, salt, and pepper. Add the olive oil slowly, stirring well until you get a smooth texture. Then add the romaine lettuce leaves, toss well, and put on the table.

4. Put the raclette maker at the center of the table, and turn it on. Put the *charcuterie* on a big serving plate, and put on the table. Each guest will melt their own slice of raclette cheese in the raclette maker, then pour on a potato and *charcuterie*.

5. Serve with the green salad and small *cornichon* pickles.

CHAPTER 13

Viandes (Meat)

Gigot de Sept Heures (Leg of Lamb)

This leg of lamb recipe is also called gigot à la cuillère, *spoon leg of lamb, because the meat is so tender that you use a spoon, not a knife, to help yourself. It's cooked for 7 hours, and is very often served for Easter.*

INGREDIENTS | SERVES 8

1 (4-pound) leg of lamb
4 tablespoons kosher salt
2 tablespoons ground black pepper
10 garlic cloves
4 tablespoons sunflower or vegetable oil
2 bay leaves
1 tablespoon thyme
1 tablespoon rosemary
6 peppercorns
1 (14.5-ounce) can of diced tomatoes
1 (25-ounce) bottle of white wine (sauvignon blanc)

1. Preheat the oven to 250°F. Rub the leg of lamb with kosher salt and pepper. Cover it with a cloth, and let rest for 1–2 hours at room temperature.

2. Rinse the leg of lamb under fresh water and dry it. Peel 4 garlic cloves and stick them in the flesh of the lamb, near the bone.

3. In a large French oven, heat the oil over medium-high heat. Brown the leg of lamb on each side for about 4 minutes. Then take out the lamb and discard the oil. Put the lamb back in the pot; place the 6 unpeeled garlic cloves in the bottom, and add the bay leaves, thyme, rosemary, and peppercorns. Pour the can of diced tomatoes and their juice over the lamb. Then pour in the bottle of wine. Cover the French oven and put it in the oven for 7 hours.

4. At halftime, grab the leg of lamb slowly, using a fork, and flip.

5. When the 7 hours are done, use a ladle to remove the juices and the tomatoes from the French oven. Pour in a small saucepan, and put on high heat. The sauce should reduce to ¼, and take on a brown color.

6. Pour the sauce over the lamb and serve with mashed potatoes or steamed French beans.

Gigot Haricots (Leg of Lamb with White Beans)

This recipe of leg of lamb with white beans is also called Gigot à la Bretonne, *from Brittany, possibly because many lambs are raised in the west of France.*

INGREDIENTS | SERVES 8

2 pounds navy beans, dry

2 tablespoons thyme

1 bay leaf

2 tablespoons fresh parsley, chopped

3 medium onions, peeled

3 tomatoes, unpeeled

2 teaspoons salt, divided

4 garlic cloves, peeled

1 (4-pound) leg of lamb

2 teaspoons ground black pepper, divided

½ cup butter, divided

2 small shallots, peeled and diced

1. Put the navy beans in a large bowl and cover them with boiling water. Let them soak for 1 hour. Then drain and wash them under cold water.

2. Fill a French oven with cold water. Pour in the beans with the thyme, bay leaf, and parsley. Peel the onions and add them whole to the pot with the whole tomatoes. Stir well, then cover and put on low heat. Add 1 teaspoon salt. Simmer for 90 minutes.

3. Preheat the oven to 450°F. Stick the garlic cloves in the lamb around the bone. Take a large ovenproof dish and put the lamb on it. Sprinkle 1 teaspoon salt and pepper on it. Cut ¼ cup butter in cubes, and sprinkle all over the lamb. Put the lamb in the oven.

4. After 20 minutes, reduce the heat to 400°F. Try to spoon up some of the cooking liquid and pour it back on the lamb every so often. Calculate the length the lamb should stay in depending on its weight: Cook for 10 minutes per pound.

5. About 10 minutes before the beans are done cooking, take the tomatoes and the onions out of the French oven, and chop them.

6. In a nonstick skillet, melt the remaining butter on medium heat, and brown the diced shallots in it, about 2–3 minutes. Add the chopped tomatoes and onions and cook slowly for 5 minutes. Then with a slotted spoon, add the beans into the skillet. Add 2 ladlefuls of the water the beans were cooked in. Remove bay leaf. Stir well, add a teaspoon pepper, and put on the lowest heat possible.

7. Take the lamb out of the oven and let it rest 15 minutes before serving. Serve the lamb and the white beans together.

Côtes de Porc à la Moutarde (Pork Ribs with Mustard)

Dijon mustard is a great cooking ingredient, and a great complement to pork. When combined with crème fraîche, *they give tenderness and moisture to the pork chops.*

INGREDIENTS | SERVES 4

1 cup *crème fraîche* or sour cream

8 tablespoons Dijon mustard

½ cup grated cheese (preferably Gruyère, or grated Cheddar)

1 teaspoon salt

1 teaspoon ground black pepper

4 pork ribs

1 teaspoon butter

2 medium onions, diced

½ cup white wine (sauvignon blanc)

Choose Your Mustard

You can also make this recipe with whole-grain and ancient-recipe Dijon mustard, or any flavored mustard you might have, like Savora, a sweeter kind of French mustard.

1. In a medium bowl, combine the *crème fraîche* with the Dijon mustard, stir well, then add the grated cheese, salt, and pepper, and stir again.

2. Spread the mixture on the pork chops on each side. You can then cook them at once, or reserve and wait for the mustard to soak in a little more (1 hour).

3. Preheat the oven to 400°F. Take a large ovenproof dish and grease it with the butter. Lay the diced onions in the bottom of the dish. Put the pork chops on the onions.

4. Pour the white wine into the bottom of the dish, then put the dish in the oven. Cook for 45 minutes.

5. Serve with mashed potatoes and butter.

Escalopes de Veau à la Normande
(Veal Scaloppini in Cream and Cider)

These veal scaloppini in cream and cider are named after the Normandy region, where most of the main ingredients come from good beef and veal, good butter, good crème fraîche, and, of course, good cider!

INGREDIENTS | SERVES 4

2 tablespoons butter

1 medium onion, sliced

4 (8-ounce) veal scaloppini

½ pound mushrooms, trimmed at the feet, then quartered

1 cup cider

1 cup *crème fraîche* or sour cream

1 teaspoon salt

1 teaspoon ground black pepper

The Chicken Solution

You can also make this recipe with chicken breasts that have been pounded very thin. Turkey is also a very popular option.

1. In a nonstick skillet, melt the butter over medium-high heat. Add the sliced onion, stir well, and cook it slowly for 5 minutes. The onion slices should become translucent, not brown. Reduce the heat to its lowest, and put the veal scaloppini in the skillet. Cook them for 5 minutes on each side. Then use a wooden spatula to take them out of the skillet, put them on a plate, cover with aluminum wrap, and reserve.

2. Put the skillet back on the burner over medium-high heat, and add the mushrooms. Cook them slowly for 5 minutes, stirring well; the mushrooms will release their liquid and get slightly brown. When the mushrooms are done, pour in the cider and reduce the heat to low. When the sauce has reduced to half its level, add the cream, salt, and pepper. Stir well. Put the scaloppini back in the skillet for 1 minute.

3. Serve warm, with steamed French beans or potatoes.

Rôti de Veau à la Sauge (Roast Veal with Sage)

Sage and veal are a very refined combination. Veal is very common in France, and is also perfect for diners who want to watch their figure; it's one of the leanest and lowest-calorie meats.

INGREDIENTS | SERVES 4

1 teaspoon salt

1 teaspoon ground black pepper

1 (2-pound) veal roast

1 tablespoon salted butter

1 tablespoon vegetable oil

2 tablespoons fresh sage leaves

1 tablespoon thyme

1 bay leaf

6 small green onions, green parts cut off, peeled

2 garlic cloves, peeled and crushed

½ cup white wine

1. Sprinkle salt and pepper on all sides of the veal roast, and reserve. Preheat the oven to 350°F.

2. Put a medium French oven over medium-high heat. Melt the salted butter in it, and combine with the vegetable oil. Then add the veal roast, and brown it on each side, for about 5 minutes in total.

3. Add the sage leaves, the thyme, the bay leaf, the green onions, and the crushed garlic to the pot. Stir. Cook slowly for 3 minutes, then pour in the white wine and turn off the heat.

4. When the oven is hot, put the pot in the oven for around 30 minutes, without the cover. The cooking time depends on the weight of the meat: You should count 15 minutes for each pound of veal. When cooked, take the veal roast out of the pot and cut it in thin slices.

5. Serve warm, with steamed French beans or white beans.

Steak Tartare

Raw beef steak is a great French classic. There's only one rule about this recipe (but it's very important): The meat should be ground only a few minutes before it's served.

INGREDIENTS | SERVES 4

1½ pounds trimmed center-cut beef tenderloin

6 green onions, peeled and diced

3 tablespoons fresh parsley, diced

2 tablespoons *cornichons*

4 eggs, very fresh

2 tablespoons capers, drained

Dijon mustard

Ketchup

Worcestershire sauce

Tabasco sauce

Olive oil

Red wine vinegar

Kosher salt

Ground black pepper

A DIY Recipe

The principle of the recipe is that the diner creates the mixture him or herself. Ingredients and spices should be at the table for the guests to try and taste their best combination. You usually first combine the egg yolk, then add capers, *cornichons*, ketchup, and/or Dijon mustard to your taste.

1. Take the meat out of the refrigerator at the last minute.

2. Make sure all fat and nerves have been cut out, and put it in the grinder. (You can also chop it yourself with a butcher knife. It's called *tartare au couteau* and it is served this way in the best restaurants.)

3. Put green onions in a small serving bowl. Put parsley in a separate serving bowl. Drain the *cornichons* and cut them in thin slices. Take the meat out of the grinder and form 4 patties. Put each patty on a serving plate.

4. Break the eggs carefully. Reserve egg whites for another recipe. Leave the yolk in half a shell. Put the egg yolk in its shell next to the beef patty, and add a full teaspoon of capers and a full teaspoon of *cornichons* on the plate, next to the meat.

5. Serve immediately, with the bowls of onions and parsley, Dijon mustard, ketchup, Worcestershire, Tabasco, olive oil, vinegar, salt, and pepper on the table. And hot french fries!

Tartare Aller-Retour (Two-Way Tartare)

This reinvention of the tartare steak was created in the 1990s and has since been considered as a new classic. Aller-retour means two-way trip: It's basically an already combined Steak Tartare that is cooked for only a few seconds on each side.

INGREDIENTS | SERVES 4

2 shallots, peeled and diced

2 tablespoons capers, drained

1½ pounds trimmed center-cut beef tenderloin

6 cornichons, thinly sliced

2 tablespoons fresh parsley, diced

1 lemon

3 tablespoons olive oil

1 tablespoon ketchup

2 tablespoons Dijon mustard

A few drops of hot sauce

1 teaspoon salt

1 teaspoon ground black pepper

1 tablespoon vegetable oil

1. Grind the shallots and the capers together. Grind the beef. In a large bowl, combine the meat, the shallots, and the capers. Use a fork to mix everything, and add the *cornichons*, parsley, the lemon and juice, and olive oil. Add ketchup, Dijon mustard, and a few drops of hot sauce, then stir again with the fork. Season with salt and pepper.

2. Divide the meat mixture in two halves, and each half in two, to form 4 patties. In a nonstick skillet, heat a tablespoon of vegetable oil over medium-high heat. Put the patties in it for 30 seconds on one side, then flip immediately, cook the other side for 30 seconds, and take them out to put them on a serving plate.

3. Serve immediately, with a salad, and/or french fries.

Lapin à la Moutarde (Rabbit with Mustard)

Dijon mustard is a great way to add more flavor to rabbit meat, which can be a bit bland. And remember, rabbit meat is very lean, and good for your health! Ask your butcher to cut it for you.

INGREDIENTS | SERVES 4

1 tablespoon butter

1 tablespoon sunflower oil or olive oil

3 mediums shallots, peeled and diced

1 rabbit, cut in parts

4 tablespoons Dijon mustard

1 tablespoon rosemary

1 teaspoon salt

1 teaspoon ground black pepper

1 cup white wine

½ cup *crème fraîche* or crema Mexicana

1. Put a French oven or any cast-iron pot over medium-high heat. Melt the butter, then add the oil and combine them, using a wooden spoon. Add the shallots, and brown them slightly for 2 minutes. Then add the rabbit parts and brown them on each side, cooking for 5 minutes, then reduce the heat to low. Add the Dijon mustard, rosemary, salt, and the pepper. Stir well. Cover the pot and simmer for 10 minutes.

2. After 10 minutes, take the cover off, add the white wine and the cream, and stir well. Cover again and cook slowly for 45 minutes.

3. Serve warm with *pappardelle* pasta or steamed French beans.

Rôti de Porc au Lait (Pork Roast in Milk)

A pork roast cooked in milk is more tender and moist. And if you're using a frozen pork roast, milk is a great way to thaw it while keeping the flavor. If this is the case, thaw in the milk then take the roast out, dry it, and use the milk later in the recipe.

INGREDIENTS | SERVES 4

1 tablespoon butter

1 tablespoon sunflower or vegetable oil

2 medium onions, peeled and minced

1 (3-pound) pork roast

1 garlic clove, peeled

10 fresh sage leaves

4 cups milk

1 teaspoon salt

1 teaspoon ground black pepper

1. Take a medium French oven or any cast-iron pot in which the pork roast would fit, and put it on the burner over medium-high heat. Melt the butter in it. Add the oil, combine, and brown the diced onions and cook them slowly, stirring often with a wooden spoon, for 3 minutes. Then add the pork roast. Brown it on each side, about 1–2 minutes total. Add the garlic.

2. Wash the sage leaves, and add them to the pot. Pour the milk all over the pork roast, then add the salt and the pepper. Heat for 2–3 minutes until the milk starts to bubble, then reduce the heat at once to low.

3. Put the cover on, and simmer for 1 hour.

4. Take the pork roast out, cut it in thin slices, and serve with mashed potatoes or salad.

Saucisses au Chou (Pork Sausage with Green Cabbage)

Pork sausages slow cooked in green cabbage make a great winter dish. For a French-Cajun adaptation, you can use smoked (and spicy) andouille.

INGREDIENTS | SERVES 4

1 cabbage head
1 tablespoon baking soda
1 tablespoon butter
1 tablespoon sunflower or vegetable oil
½ pound bacon, cut in ½"-wide strips
8 (4-ounce) pork sausages
1 cup white wine
1 teaspoon salt
1 teaspoon ground black pepper

1. Wash the cabbage and cut off the leaves, discarding the first ones. Fill a large saucepan with water and bring to a boil over high heat. When the water reaches the boiling point, add the baking soda and cabbage leaves, and cook for 5 minutes. Then use a colander to drain them, and reserve.

2. Take a French oven or any cast-iron pot, and melt the butter in it over medium-high heat. Combine with the oil. Add the bacon and cook for 2 minutes, stirring often with a wooden spoon. Using a fork, make small holes in the sausages, then add them to the pot and brown them on each side, for about 5 minutes total.

3. Add the cabbage leaves to the pot, stir well, then pour in the white wine and reduce the heat to low. Add salt and pepper, and cover the pot. Simmer for 1 hour.

4. Serve as is, or with boiled potatoes.

Magret de Canard aux Pommes (Duck Breast with Apples)

Duck breast has been a classic in France for the last 50 years. It's always better to use a fattened duck, especially free-range: more meat, more fat, and more flavor!

INGREDIENTS | SERVES 4

4 duck breasts

1 teaspoon salt

1 teaspoon ground black pepper

1 teaspoon Espelette pepper
(or paprika)

2 apples, peeled, cored, and cut in slices

1. Lay the duck breasts on a cutting board with the fat facing you. With a cutting knife, cut slits in a diamond pattern in the fat. Make sure you never reach the meat. Flip the duck breasts, and season with salt, pepper, and Espelette pepper.

2. Heat a nonstick skillet on high heat, then put the breasts in it, fat side on the skillet. Cook them for 2 minutes, then reduce the heat to medium.

3. After 5 minutes of cooking the duck breasts, slowly pour out a large amount of the duck fat. Then put the skillet back on heat, and add the apple slices. Stir well. After a total of 10 minutes of cooking, flip the duck breasts to the meat side, and cook for one last minute. Then take the duck breasts out and turn off the heat.

4. Let them cool for 5 minutes and serve with the sliced apples.

Tournedos Rossini
(Beef Fillets with Foie Gras and Black Truffle)

This is surely the most nouveau riche and over-the-top French recipe: a combination of three deluxe ingredients, beef fillet, foie gras, and black truffle! Perfect for Christmas or New Year's Eve.

INGREDIENTS | SERVES 4

4 (6-ounce) tournedos or beef fillets

1 teaspoon salt

1 teaspoon ground black pepper

2 tablespoons butter

4 slices of bread, preferably stale

¼ cup Cognac or brandy

4 slices of foie gras (¼" thick and 2" in diameter)

20 thin slices of black truffles (about 1 ounce in total)

A Lyrical Invention!

Tournedos Rossini was invented in the nineteenth century by a very famous Parisian chef at the time, Marie-Antoine Carème. It's traditionally served with a cream and Madeira sauce, but this recipe is leaner and more focused on the amazing flavors of the three main ingredients.

1. Season the beef on each side with salt and pepper, and reserve on a plate.

2. Melt the butter slowly in a nonstick skillet on medium-high heat. As soon as it is liquid, gently brown the slices of bread in the butter, flipping them often, for around 3 minutes.

3. Take the bread slices out, reserve, and put the meat in the skillet. Increase the heat to high and cook for 3–5 minutes, flipping the fillet very often. Flambé with the Cognac and take the skillet off of the heat.

4. Put a slice of buttered bread on each plate, then put a slice of beef on it. Add a slice of foie gras on top, then add 5 slices of black truffle on top of each.

5. Serve immediately with mashed potatoes or mushrooms.

Chapon Farci (Stuffed Capon)

Stuffed capon is a great option for a small holiday party. A smaller bird, but definitely full of flavor!

INGREDIENTS | SERVES 4

1 tablespoon kosher salt

1 (6-pound) capon

⅓ cup milk

2 slices of stale bread

3 medium shallots, peeled and diced

4 garlic cloves, divided (1 peeled and diced for the stuffing, 3 unpeeled)

7 ounces ground veal

3 ounces sausage meat

2½ pounds precooked chestnuts, divided

2 tablespoons parsley, chopped

1 egg

1 teaspoon salt

2 teaspoons ground black pepper

¼ cup water

1. Sprinkle kosher salt all over the capon. Put a cloth on it and leave at room temperature while preparing the stuffing.

2. Pour the milk in a small bowl, and soak the bread slices in it. Put shallots and one garlic clove in a blender with the milk bread slices and the ground veal, and process for 1 minute. Put the mixture in a large bowl, use a fork to incorporate the sausage meat, and add ½ pound chestnuts. Add the parsley, egg, salt, and pepper. Toss well until the mixture seems combined.

3. Stuff the stuffing in the bird, then truss the bird. Put the capon in a roasting pan. Pour ¼ cup water at the bottom, and add the three unpeeled garlic cloves. Put the capon in a cold oven, then set the heat at 400°F. With a spoon, regularly sprinkle the capon with the cooking juices. Cook for 3 hours.

4. About 30 minutes before the end of the cooking time, add the remaining 2 pounds of chestnuts to the bottom of the dish.

5. When the cooking time is up, remove the chestnuts with a slotted spoon and put them on a serving dish. Put the capon in it. Serve warm.

Pintade au Chou (Guinea Fowl with Green Cabbage)

This guinea fowl with green cabbage recipe is a family reunion classic dish for winter.

INGREDIENTS | SERVES 4

2 teaspoons salt, divided

2 teaspoons ground black pepper, divided

1 guinea fowl (about three pounds)

1 head of green cabbage

½ pound bacon, cut in ½"-wide slices

2 tablespoons butter

1 cup chicken stock

A French-African Bird!

Guinea fowl are originally from Africa, but they have been domesticated for centuries in France. France is actually the biggest producer and consumer of this strange, beautiful (and delicious!) bird.

1. Sprinkle salt and pepper inside the guinea fowl and on its skin. Reserve.

2. Fill a large saucepan with water and bring it to a boil. Cut the cabbage in 4 parts, and put them in the boiling water for 10 minutes. Prepare a large bowl full of ice water, and put the cabbage in it as soon as it has been boiled. Then pour into a colander to dry.

3. Put a large French oven (or any cast-iron pot that will fit the guinea fowl) over medium-high heat. Melt the butter in it slowly, then add the bacon slices. Stir well for 5 minutes, then add the guinea fowl and brown it on each side, for around 10 minutes total. Add the cooked cabbage and stir with a wooden spoon so that all sides can also get slightly brown. Pour in the chicken stock, and reduce the heat to its lowest. Cover the pot and simmer for 45 minutes.

4. Using a slotted spoon, take out the cabbage and put it in a serving dish. Put the guinea fowl in another serving dish, and carve. Strain the juices and broth that are left into a gravy boat.

5. Serve with the cabbage, the sauce, and the bird.

Dinde de Noël (Christmas Turkey)

Turkey is also a holiday bird in France, but of course, it's not eaten in November: There were no Pilgrims landing in France, and therefore no American Thanksgiving! However, Christmas turkey is a great tradition. It's usually cooked with chestnuts or more fancy, with black truffles.

INGREDIENTS | SERVES 4

2 teaspoons salt, divided

2 teaspoons ground black pepper, divided

1 small black truffle

1 (10-pound) turkey (with liver, heart, and gizzard reserved)

4 slices stale bread

¼ cup milk

2 medium onions, minced

3 tablespoons minced parsley

3 ounces ground veal

3 ounces sausage meat

1 egg

¼ cup Cognac

2 pounds small potatoes

Evolution of Turkey

The first turkey said to have been eaten in France was at the wedding of King Charles IX in 1570, half a century before the Pilgrims had their historic meal in America. The French name recalls what people then thought of America: *Dinde* means "from India," where Christopher Columbus was supposed to have landed.

1. Sprinkle 1 teaspoon salt and 1 teaspoon pepper inside the turkey and on its skin.

2. Cut the truffle in very thin slices. Reserve a teaspoon of the truffle for the stuffing. Put the rest of the slices under the skin of the turkey.

3. Preheat the oven to 350°F. In a bowl, soak the stale slices of bread in milk. Put them in a blender with the minced onions, parsley, the liver, the heart, and the gizzard. Process for 30 seconds. In a large bowl, combine the ground veal and sausage meat, using a fork. Add the egg and the Cognac, then add the bread mixture. Stuff the turkey and truss it.

4. Put the turkey in a roasting pan, and pour water in to a depth of ½". Put in the oven and cook. Cooking time will depend on the weight of the turkey: Cook it for 18 minutes per pound. About 30 minutes before serving, add the potatoes in their skin to the bottom of the pan.

5. When the cooking time is up, take out the potatoes, put them on a serving dish, then carve the turkey and serve.

Oie Rôtie aux Navets (Roast Goose with Turnips)

Goose is also a traditional Christmas bird in France. Its size makes it more convenient for big families than capon. It's such a fat and flavorful bird that no stuffing is needed, but turnips are perfect cooking companions!

INGREDIENTS | SERVES 8

1 (10-pound) goose
2 teaspoons salt
2 teaspoons black ground black pepper
2 medium onions, peeled
3 tablespoons parsley, chopped
2 tablespoons thyme or rosemary
8 garlic cloves, unpeeled, divided
8 medium turnips, peeled

1. Take the goose out of the refrigerator at least 1 hour before cooking it. Season it with salt and pepper inside the bird and on its skin. Keep at room temperature.

2. Preheat the oven to 400°F. Put 1 whole peeled onion in the goose. Stuff parsley in the goose. Add the thyme or the rosemary, and 4 garlic cloves.

3. Slice the remaining onion and layer the slices in a roasting pan. Put the goose on them. Pour water into the pan to a depth of ½". Put 4 unpeeled garlic cloves in the pan.

4. Put the goose in the oven. After 30 minutes, reduce the heat to 300°F. Cook for 3½ hours. The time might depend on the weight of your goose and the oven, so watch carefully. Count around 15 minutes per pound of flesh. Every 15 minutes, baste the goose with the fat that comes out of it.

5. About 30 minutes before serving, add the turnips at the bottom of the pan.

6. Once cooked, take the turnips out of the pan, put them on a serving dish, then carve the goose and serve it warm.

CHAPTER 14

Poisson (Fish)

Saumon à l'Oseille (Salmon in Sorrel Sauce)

Salmon in sorrel sauce is now a classic of French cuisine. It was first invented in the 1960s by the two Troisgros brothers. Their son and nephew still serve it in the family's Michelin three-star restaurant. Here is an adaptation.

INGREDIENTS | SERVES 4

4 (7-ounce) salmon fillets, about 1" thick
1 teaspoon salt
1 teaspoon ground black pepper
1 cup white wine
1 bay leaf
3 black peppercorns
3 small shallots, minced
2 cups *crème fraîche* or crema Mexicana
1 pound fresh sorrel, minced
1 teaspoon butter
1 teaspoon sunflower or olive oil

A Culinary Revolution

Saumon à l'Oseille is as big a symbol for French cooking as the Bastille was for the French Revolution. When the brothers Troisgros first served it in their Michelin three-star restaurant, classic food critics were outraged. The way the salmon was cut, the fact that it was undercooked by contemporary standards, and the combination of sorrel and lemon were unthinkable at the time. But the Troisgros did it, contributing to the invention of *nouvelle cuisine*.

1. Season the salmon fillets with salt and pepper. Reserve.

2. In a medium saucepan, pour the white wine and add the bay leaf, peppercorns, and minced shallots. Bring to a boil over medium-high heat, then reduce to medium heat for 15 minutes. Take the bay leaf out, add the cream, stir well, then add the sorrel, and stir for 5 minutes. Reduce the heat to low.

3. In a large nonstick skillet, melt butter and oil over medium-high heat. Add the salmon fillets, and cook them 2 minutes on each side. The edges will be cooked, and the center almost raw.

4. Pour the sorrel sauce over dinner plates, and quickly put the salmon on them.

5. Serve immediately.

Thon Basquaise (Tuna Steaks with Tomatoes and Peppers)

Tuna steaks prepared with tomatoes and green bell peppers is a traditional dish in the French Basque country, which is in the southwest of France.

INGREDIENTS | SERVES 4

4 (1-pound) tuna steaks (about 1¾" thick)

2 teaspoons Espelette pepper (or paprika), divided

2 teaspoons salt, divided

2 teaspoons ground black pepper, divided

3 tablespoons olive oil, divided

2 green bell peppers, peeled, seeded, and cut in 1" cubes

1 large onion, peeled and minced

4 garlic cloves, peeled and diced

1 (28-ounce) can diced tomatoes

Straight from Pays Basque

French Basque country is a small heaven for food-lovers. This recipe was invented in Saint-Jean-de-Luz, where tuna has been fished for generations. Each year in July, tuna is celebrated in this beautiful town with a big festival.

1. Season the tuna steaks with 1 teaspoon Espelette pepper, 1 teaspoon salt, and 1 teaspoon black pepper. Reserve.

2. In a large nonstick skillet, heat 2 tablespoons olive oil over medium-high heat. Add the cubes of green pepper, stir well, and cook for 5 minutes, stirring again from time to time. Add the minced onion and diced garlic, and cook again for 5 minutes, stirring very often. Add the tomatoes and their juice, 1 teaspoon salt, 1 teaspoon pepper, and 1 teaspoon Espelette pepper; stir again, then reduce the heat to low and simmer for 15 minutes.

3. Heat another skillet over high heat. Add 1 tablespoon olive oil, then add the tuna steaks and cook for 2 minutes on each side.

4. Using a wooden spatula, take the tuna steaks out of the second skillet, and put them in the tomato sauce. Simmer for 10 minutes.

5. Serve warm with a bowl of white rice.

Sole Meunière (Salmon with Butter and Lemon)

Sole fillets à la meunière *means they are cooked with flour, butter, and lemon. This recipe is usually served in bistrots.*

INGREDIENTS | SERVES 4

4 (½-pound) sole fillets

1 teaspoon salt

1 teaspoon ground black pepper

¾ cup flour

7 tablespoons butter, divided

3 lemons, 2 squeezed and 1 sliced for garnish

A King's Fish

Sole is one of the most noble fish of French gastronomy. Louis XIV, the Sun King, loved it, and it was very often served in his palace of Versailles. This recipe is the most famous. *Meunière* means "miller," and is a reference to the use of flour in the recipe. You can also use the *meunière* technique to cook other white fishes.

1. Season the sole fillets with salt and pepper.

2. Pour the flour in a large dish. Coat sole fillets with flour.

3. In a large nonstick skillet, melt 4 tablespoons butter over medium-high heat. Let it slightly brown to a hazelnut color.

4. Put the sole fillets in the skillet and cook for 2 minutes on one side, then flip to the other side and cook for 1 minute. Be careful not to overcook it. Using a wooden spatula, take the sole fillets out of the skillet and put them on four plates. Don't turn off the heat. Add 3 tablespoons butter to the skillet, let it turn slightly brown, then add the lemon juice. Stir well, and pour on the sole fillets.

5. Serve warm with a bowl of white rice, and garnish with lemon slices.

Truite aux Amandes (Trout with Almonds)

Trout used to be a very common river fish in France. It's been farmed there since the fifteenth century. Here is the most popular recipe.

INGREDIENTS | SERVES 4

1 cup whole milk
½ cup flour
4 (½-pound) trout, cleaned out
1 teaspoon salt
1 teaspoon ground black pepper
3 tablespoons butter, divided
1 tablespoon olive oil
4 ounces slivered almonds
1 lemon, thinly sliced
2 tablespoons fresh parsley, minced

1. Pour the milk in a soup plate, and the flour in another soup plate.

2. Clean the trout well under cold water and dry them. Season the trout with salt and pepper inside of the fish, and put them in the milk. Flip them, then put them in the flour and flip them again, making sure they are coated with flour on each side.

3. In a large nonstick skillet, melt 2 tablespoons butter over medium-high heat, then add the oil and stir to combine. Put the trout in the skillet, and cook for 5 minutes on each side.

4. Heat a serving dish in a 150°F heated oven. With a wooden spatula, put the trout in the warm dish.

5. Add 1 tablespoon butter to the hot skillet and brown the slivered almonds in it for about 2 minutes, stirring all the time.

6. Remove the trout from the oven. Pour the almonds and the butter on the fish. Add the slices of lemon and the minced parsley.

7. Serve immediately with small boiled potatoes.

Truite à la Normande (Normandy-Style Trout)

Truites à la Normande are actually cooked in a mussel sauce. Of course, as every classic dish from Normandy does, it calls for the local specialty: crème fraîche!

INGREDIENTS | SERVES 4

2 tablespoons butter

3 medium shallots, peeled and minced

3 pounds mussels, scrubbed and beards removed

2 cups white wine

1 teaspoon salt

1 teaspoon ground black pepper

2 cups *crème fraîche* or crema Mexicana

4 (½-pound) trout, cleaned out

2 medium onions, peeled and thinly sliced

1 tablespoon fresh parsley, minced

1. In a large saucepan, melt the butter over medium-high heat. Add the shallots, stir well, and cook them slowly for 3 minutes, stirring often with a wooden spoon so that the shallots cook but do not get brown. Add the mussels and white wine and cook for 5 minutes, stirring constantly. The mussels should all be opened by now. Discard those that do not open. Season with salt and pepper, stir again for 1 minute, then turn off the heat.

2. Strain the cooking juice into a medium saucepan. Add the cream, stir to combine altogether, and put over medium heat for 5 minutes.

3. Preheat the oven to 350°F. Put the trout in a large cooking dish, one next to each other. Lay the onion slices on top of them. Add the mussels, then cover it all with the cream sauce. Bake for 15 minutes.

4. Add minced parsley on top, and serve with small boiled potatoes.

Aioli de Poissons (Steamed Fish)

This steamed fish recipe is typical of Provençal *cuisine.*

INGREDIENTS | SERVES 4

4 salted cod fillets

4 eggs

8 medium potatoes, unpeeled

1 pound carrots, peeled

1 small cauliflower

1 pound organic zucchini, unpeeled, cut in 1" slices

2 medium leeks, green part discarded

1 pound French beans, trimmed at the ends

1 cup Aioli Sauce (see recipe in Chapter 22)

History of Aioli

Aioli was generally served on Friday, following the Catholic Church's mandate that no meat should be eaten on this day. The sauce was traditionally served in the mortar, a household essential; every bride was offered a marble mortar and an olive wood pestle on the day of her wedding.

1. One day before cooking, put the salted cod fillets in a large bowl of fresh water for 24 hours. Try to change the water at least 5 times.

2. The next day, fill a large saucepan with water and bring to a boil over high heat. When the water starts boiling, add the salted cod, reduce the heat to low, and cook for 10 minutes. Using a slotted spoon, take the fish out, place on a serving plate, cover, and reserve.

3. Fill a medium saucepan with water, bring to a boil, then carefully put the eggs in it, and boil them for 10 minutes. Prepare a bowl of ice water. Remove the eggs using a slotted spoon and put the eggs in the ice water. Peel the eggs when they are cool.

4. Fill a large saucepan with water, put the potatoes in, bring to a boil, and cook for 20 minutes. Do the same for the carrots, cauliflower, zucchinis, leeks, and the French beans. Cook them all around 15 minutes, in separate saucepans.

5. Serve the drained vegetables in a serving dish, and the fish in another one. Put the Aioli Sauce on the table. Guests should help themselves to as much Aioli Sauce as they want on their plate!

Bouillabaisse de Marseille (Fish Stew)

This fish stew was invented in Marseille, the second biggest city in France, and a big port town. It's traditionally made with local Mediterranean fish (people would cook with what the fishermen brought back), but they are hard to find in America. Try using sea bass, monkfish, red snapper, or turbot.

INGREDIENTS | SERVES 4

1 cup plus 2 tablespoons olive oil, divided

2 medium onions, diced

1 (14-ounce) can of diced tomatoes

4 garlic cloves, divided (1 minced, 3 whole)

1 fennel, chopped in ½" cubes

1 bay leaf

1 tablespoon thyme

½ teaspoon saffron threads

1 teaspoon salt

1 teaspoon ground black pepper

8 cups white fish stock

1 pound mussels, scrubbed and beards removed.

4 pounds white fish fillets

1 slice of bread

1 egg yolk

Rouille

The *rouille* is a typical sauce that is served with fish dishes, like bouillabaisse or fish soup. It is traditionally made with monkfish liver, and has a distinct orange color. That's why it's called *rouille*, is the French word for "rust."

1. In a large soup pot, heat 2 tablespoons of olive oil over medium-high heat. Add the diced onions, stir well for 2 minutes, and then add the diced tomatoes and the minced garlic. Reduce the heat to medium and cook for 5 minutes, stirring occasionally. Add the fennel, bay leaf, thyme, saffron, salt, and pepper. Pour in the white fish stock, bring to a boil over high heat, then reduce to low, cover, and simmer for 5 minutes.

2. Add the mussels, cover, and simmer for another 5 minutes, then add the fish fillets. Cover again and cook for 15 minutes. Remove bay leaf.

3. Meanwhile prepare the *rouille*: Using a ladle, take ⅓ cup broth from the pot. Pour it in a soup plate, and soak the bread in it. Put in a blender with 3 garlic cloves until smooth and process. Pour the mixture into a medium bowl, stir in an egg yolk, and slowly whisk in 1 cup of olive oil until you get a thick sauce.

4. Serve the mussels and the fish in a large bowl. Pour the broth in a separate bowl, and bring the *rouille* to the table. Guest should help themselves.

5. Fill a large saucepan with water. Add the small potatoes, bring to a boil over high heat, then reduce the heat to medium-low and cook for 25 minutes. Drain potatoes and put them in a serving dish.

6. Bring the fish to the table and break the crust with a knife. Serve each guest with a piece of sea bass, and small potatoes.

Sardines à l'Escabèche (Marinated Sardines)

*Escabèche is a traditional way of cooking and preserving the fish, by taking
the head and the guts out of the fish before marinating it.*

INGREDIENTS | SERVES 4

2 tablespoons olive oil

2 medium onions, peeled and
thinly sliced

1 carrot, peeled and thinly sliced

1 celery stalk, cut in ½" chunks

2 garlic cloves, peeled and minced

1 bay leaf

1 tablespoon rosemary

1 tablespoon thyme

2 cups white wine

1 teaspoon salt

1 teaspoon ground black pepper

8 fresh sardines, cleaned out,
heads removed

1. Put a medium saucepan over medium-high heat. Add the olive oil, then add the onions, carrot, and celery. Stir well with a wooden spoon and cook for 3 minutes. Add the garlic, the bay leaf, rosemary, and thyme. Stir well and cook for 1 minute. Add the white wine. Add salt and pepper, reduce the heat to medium-low, and simmer for 10 minutes.

2. Put a nonstick skillet over high heat, wait until it's warm, then add the sardines and cook for 2 minutes on each side. Remove to serving dish. Using a slotted spoon, take the vegetables out of the saucepan and lay them on the fishes. Pour the broth on the fish, cover, and put in the refrigerator for at least 48 hours.

3. Remove bay leaf. Serve dish cold with toasted bread.

Moules Marinières (Mussels in White Wine)

*This recipe for mussels cooked in white wine is now famous all over
the world. But the great thing is, it is so easy to make!*

INGREDIENTS | SERVES 4

3 pounds mussels, scrubbed and
beards removed

⅓ cup butter

1 tablespoon sunflower oil

4 medium shallots, peeled and minced

2 garlic cloves, peeled and crushed

1 tablespoon thyme

1 bay leaf

1 teaspoon salt

1 teaspoon ground black pepper

2 cups white wine (sauvignon blanc)

3 tablespoons fresh parsley,
chopped roughly

1. Scrub and clean the mussels. Reserve.

2. In a large pot, melt the butter over medium heat, and combine with the oil. Add the minced shallots, stir well, and cook for 2 minutes. Add garlic and stir well for another 4 minutes, then add the thyme, bay leaf, salt, and pepper.

3. Pour in the white wine, and add the mussels. Cook over high heat, until the mussels are all opened. Discard the unopened ones. Stir well and then remove from the heat. Add the fresh parsley leaves and stir again. Remove bay leaf.

4. Serve immediately, with french fries.

Bar en Croûte de Sel (Sea Bass with Salt Crust)

A sea bass cooked in a salt crust is always impressive, but it is also one of the best ways to bake a fish slowly. And don't worry, it doesn't make the fish too salty.

INGREDIENTS | SERVES 4

1 (3-pound) sea bass, cleaned out
1 tablespoon thyme
1 tablespoon rosemary
1 fennel stalk
3 pounds kosher salt
3 egg whites
12 small potatoes, unpeeled

1. Preheat the oven to 400°F. Clean the fish, dry it, and stuff the inside with thyme and rosemary. Add a fennel stalk.

2. In a large bowl, combine the salt with the egg whites. Stir well, then pour ⅓ of it in a large baking dish. Put the fish on the salt bed, then pour the rest of the salt over the fish. It should be about ½" thick above the fish. Put in the oven and cook for 45 minutes.

3. Fill a large saucepan with water, add the small potatoes, bring to a boil over high heat, then reduce the heat to medium-low and cook for 25 minutes. Drain potatoes and put them in a serving dish.

Moules à la Plancha (Grilled Mussels)

Mussels à la Plancha are all the rage in France in summer. This is a healthy and easy barbecue recipe.

INGREDIENTS | SERVES 6

4 pounds mussels, scrubbed and
  beards removed
2 tablespoons olive oil
4 medium shallots, peeled and minced
2 pounds tomatoes, cut in 1" chunks
3 garlic cloves, peeled and minced
3 tablespoons fresh parsley,
  chopped roughly
1 teaspoon ground black pepper

1. Scrub and clean the mussels. Run them twice through clean water, and then put them in a colander. Reserve.

2. Preheat the *plancha* by putting it over high heat on the barbecue or on your stove. Add the olive oil. When it is warm, add the minced shallots, stir for 1 minute, then add the tomatoes. Stir again for 1 minute, and add the mussels. Stir constantly.

3. As soon as the mussels start to open, sprinkle in the minced garlic, stir for 1 minute, then remove mussels from the pan and put them in a large serving bowl. Add the parsley and stir one last time. Season with pepper.

4. Serve immediately.

Cuisses de Grenouilles (Frog Legs)

Oui oui! The French eat frogs. A common British insult for the French people was "frogs" because of the habit. This is the traditional frog legs recipe, with persillade, a parsley butter.

INGREDIENTS | SERVES 4

30 frog legs

1 teaspoon salt

2 teaspoons ground black pepper

½ cup flour

⅔ cup butter, cut in ½" cubes

3 garlic cloves, peeled and minced

4 tablespoons fresh parsley,
  thinly minced

American Frogs for a Typical French Recipe

Frog legs used to be fished near the Alps, in the Dombes, not far from Lyon. But they are more and more scarce, and most of them are imported now—more than 2,000 tons a year! And where do these imported frog legs come from? Some are from Asia, and the rest from America!

1. Clean the frog legs under fresh water, then dry them and season them with salt and pepper.

2. Pour the flour in a large dish and put the frog legs in the flour, flipping them to the other side, and making sure they are totally covered with flour.

3. Put a large nonstick skillet on medium heat, and melt the butter in it. Stir constantly, and add the frog legs. Watch for the moment when the butter turns lightly brown: This is called *beurre noisette*, hazelnut butter. When that happens, flip the legs to the other side, and stir well for 1 minute.

4. Add the garlic and the parsley, stir again, then cover the skillet and cook slowly for 5 minutes on low heat.

5. Serve immediately, with paper napkins (you can only eat frog legs with your hands!).

Maquereaux Grillés Sauce Moutarde
(Mackerel with Mustard Sauce)

Mackerel is a very common fish in Europe, and therefore in France.
Here is a recipe for grilled mackerel with a mustard sauce.

INGREDIENTS | SERVES 4

8 mackerel, cleaned out
1 teaspoon salt
1 teaspoon ground black pepper
1 tablespoon turmeric
4 bay leaves, halved
1 tablespoon olive oil
½ cup *crème fraîche* or crema Mexicana
3 tablespoons butter
2 tablespoons Dijon mustard
Juice of 1 lemon

1. Clean the mackerel and season the insides with salt, pepper, and turmeric. Place half a bay leaf inside each mackerel. Using a pastry brush, cover the fishes with olive oil.

2. Preheat your oven to broil, then wrap the mackerels in aluminum foil, on the grill rack. Cook for 5 minutes on each side.

3. In a small saucepan, slowly bring the cream to a boil over medium heat. Then reduce the heat to low, and add the butter. Whisk well. When butter and cream are well combined, take the saucepan off the heat, add the Dijon mustard and lemon juice, and stir well.

4. Remove bay leaf halves. Serve the grilled mackerel and pour the mustard sauce on them. Serve with small boiled potatoes.

Pain de Saumon (Salmon Loaf)

This "salmon bread" could be nicknamed "fishloaf," as it is a fish version
of meatloaf. It's great to serve at banquets or potluck dinners.

INGREDIENTS | SERVES 4

2 pounds salmon fillets
½ lemon
1¼ teaspoons salt, divided
1½ teaspoons ground black pepper
10 ounces Greek yogurt
3 large eggs
2 tablespoons chives, minced
2 tablespoons fresh parsley, minced
1 tablespoon butter

1. Preheat the oven to 400°F. Put the salmon fillets on a large piece of aluminum foil. Squeeze half a lemon over them, and season with 1 teaspoon salt and 1 teaspoon pepper. Fold the aluminum over and put in the oven. Bake for 10 minutes.

2. When done, immediately add fish to the blender along with the Greek yogurt, the eggs, ¼ teaspoon of salt, and ½ teaspoon pepper. Process for 30 seconds. Add the chives and the parsley, and process for 20 seconds.

3. Butter a medium nonstick meatloaf pan. Pour the fish mixture in it. Heat the oven to 350°F. Take a larger baking dish, pour in cold water to a depth of 1", and put the meatloaf pan in it. Bake in the oven for 45 minutes.

4. Put in the refrigerator for 12 hours, and serve cold.

CHAPTER 15

Side Dishes

Ratatouille

This dish is very representative of Provençal *cuisine. And don't let the Pixar movie fool you; it's actually pretty easy to prepare!*

INGREDIENTS | SERVES 4

1 tablespoon olive oil

7 ounces bacon, cut in ½"-wide slices

2 medium onions, peeled and diced

1 medium bell pepper, cut in ½" cubes

4 medium zucchini, cut in ½" cubes

1 large eggplant, cut in ½" cubes

1 teaspoon salt

1 teaspoon ground black pepper

1 garlic clove, peeled and minced

1 tablespoon thyme

1 bay leaf

1 (48-ounce) can diced peeled tomatoes

1. Put a medium French oven or any cast-iron pot over medium-high heat. Heat the olive oil, and add the bacon slices. Stir well, cook for 1 minute, then add the onion. Cook for 2 minutes together, stirring well, then add the bell pepper. Cook together for 2 minutes, then add the zucchini cubes. Stir well, and add the eggplant cubes.

2. Season with salt and pepper, add the minced garlic, thyme, and the bay leaf. Stir well, reduce the heat to low, cover, and cook for 10 minutes. Then add the diced tomatoes with their juice, cover again, and simmer for 45 minutes, stirring often.

3. Remove bay leaf. Serve dish warm, or cold the next day.

Piperade

Piperade is in some ways the ratatouille of the southwest of France cuisine. It's great with eggs, ham, or roasted meats.

INGREDIENTS | SERVES 4

1 tablespoon olive oil

3 medium onions, peeled and minced

1 green bell pepper (or if you are lucky, 10 ounces *piments doux*)

4 garlic cloves, peeled and minced

1 teaspoon salt

1 teaspoon ground black pepper

1 teaspoon Espelette pepper (or paprika)

1 pound tomatoes, peeled and diced

1 tablespoon tomato paste

½ teaspoon sugar

1. Heat a nonstick skillet over medium-high heat. Add the olive oil, and then the onions and the pepper. Stir well for 5 minutes, then add the garlic, salt, pepper, and Espelette pepper, and cook for 5 minutes, still stirring often. Add the tomatoes, the tomato paste, and the sugar. Stir well, reduce the heat to low, and simmer for 45 minutes.

2. Serve warm, with Bayonne ham, prosciutto, or a poached egg.

Purée Saint-Germain (Puréed Peas)

This is the purée version of Petits pois à la française. Recommended for babies after 12 months!

INGREDIENTS | SERVES 4

1 teaspoon salt
1 pound shelled fresh peas
1 cup Bibb lettuce leaves, minced
1 tablespoon fresh parsley, minced
4 tablespoons butter, diced and at room temperature
1 teaspoon black ground black pepper

Use the Pods!

You can make this recipe with frozen peas, of course (and in that case, reduce the cooking time by about 2 minutes), but it's always better with fresh peas. You can use the pods to make a delicious soup. Trim them on each side, brown them in 1 tablespoon butter over medium heat with a sliced onion, add 2 cups of chicken stock and 3 peeled potatoes, cook for 20 minutes, and process in a blender.

1. Fill a large saucepan with water and bring to a boil over high heat. Add salt and pour in the fresh peas.

2. Add the lettuce leaves and parsley. Cook for 7 minutes.

3. Put a strainer over a large bowl. Pour the contents of the saucepan into the strainer. Put the peas, lettuce, and parsley into a blender and process for 30 seconds. Put the cooking liquid back into the saucepan, bring to a boil over high heat, and reduce up to the point where its depth is 1".

4. In a medium serving bowl, pour the puréed peas and slowly add the cubes of butter, stirring well with a wooden spoon. Season with pepper, and add the reduced cooking liquid to the peas, tablespoon by tablespoon, stirring. Stop when the purée is smooth and thick.

5. Serve immediately.

Petits Pois à la Française (French Peas)

The French love their green peas, particularly served with a good red meat. And these are much healthier than french fries!

INGREDIENTS | SERVES 4

2 tablespoons butter
1 pound shelled fresh peas
1 cup Bibb lettuce leaves, minced
1 teaspoon salt
1 teaspoon sugar
1 teaspoon ground black pepper
8 small pearl onions, peeled
2 tablespoons fresh chervil, minced

1. Fill a small saucepan with water and bring to a boil over high heat.

2. In a medium saucepan, melt the butter over medium heat. Add peas and the lettuce, and stir with a wooden spoon. Add salt and sugar, stir well, then add the pearl onions, and stir again. Cook slowly for 3 minutes, constantly stirring. Add the chervil, stir again, then pour about ½ cup of the boiling water on the peas. Stir well, reduce the heat to low, and cook for 7 minutes. The peas should stay vibrantly green, and not get mushy.

3. Serve immediately.

Petits Pois Lardons (Peas with Bacon)

The perfect marriage of pork and vegetables, great with a nice entrecôte (rib steak)!

INGREDIENTS | SERVES 4

6 ounces bacon, cut in ½" slices
1 medium onion, peeled and minced
1 pound shelled fresh peas
1 teaspoon ground black pepper
2 cups chicken stock

1. Heat a medium nonstick saucepan over medium-high heat. Add the bacon slices, cook for 1 minute, stirring constantly, and then add the onion slices. Cook for 3 minutes, stirring constantly. Add the peas and pepper.

2. Pour in the chicken stock, bring to a boil over high heat, then reduce to low and simmer for 25 minutes.

3. Serve immediately.

Petits Pois Carottes (Peas and Carrots)

The most classic fresh peas side dish in France! Fresh peas and carrots is one of the bestselling canned vegetables. It is, of course, better made with fresh spring vegetables.

INGREDIENTS | SERVES 4

1 tablespoon butter
1 pound shelled fresh peas
1 cup lettuce, thinly sliced
3 small carrots, peeled and diced
4 pearl onions, peeled
1 teaspoon salt
1 teaspoon ground black pepper
1½ cups chicken broth

1. In a medium saucepan, melt the butter over medium heat. Add the peas, the sliced lettuce, carrots, and onions. Stir well, and add salt and pepper.

2. Pour in the chicken broth, bring to a boil over high heat, then reduce to low and simmer for 25 minutes.

3. Serve with meat (poultry, for example).

Carottes Vichy (Vichy Carrots)

The best way to rediscover the sweet taste of carrots! In this recipe, they are traditionally cooked in Vichy mineral water. You can also use any type of mineral water.

INGREDIENTS | SERVES 4

3 tablespoons butter, diced
2 pounds medium carrots, peeled and bevel-cut
1 tablespoon raw sugar
1 teaspoon salt, divided
3 cups Vichy water or mineral water
1 teaspoon ground black pepper
1 tablespoon fresh parsley, minced

1. Put a large saucepan over medium heat, and melt the butter in it. Add the sliced carrots, use a wooden spoon to stir well, then add the raw sugar. Stir often for 4 minutes. Add ¼ teaspoon salt, then pour the water over the carrots. Reduce the heat to low, and simmer for 20 minutes.

2. Add ¾ teaspoon salt and ground pepper to the carrots, put in a serving bowl, and sprinkle the parsley on top.

3. Serve warm.

Purée de Pois Cassés (Split Peas Purée)

Split peas purée is a great side dish for a simple roasted chicken or steamed fish. This is how peas were eaten in France in the Middle Ages.

INGREDIENTS | SERVES 4

1 pound dried split peas

5 cups water

4 carrots, peeled and thinly sliced

2 leeks, green part discarded, minced

4 lettuce leaves, thinly sliced

1 medium onion

4 cloves

1 tablespoon fresh parsley, minced

1 bay leaf

1 teaspoon salt

1 teaspoon ground black pepper

A Great Source of Protein

Split peas were cooked a lot in France back in the days when eating meat only happened on rare occasions. They are a great source of protein: Half a pound of cooked split peas provides half the protein a woman needs in a day. They are also rich in magnesium, calcium, and iron.

1. Fill a large bowl with cold water, and put the dried split peas in it for 90 minutes. Then pour in a colander and dry them.

2. Fill a large saucepan with 5 cups of water. Put the dried peas in it and bring to a boil over high heat. When boiling, add the carrots, leeks, and lettuce leaves. Peel the onion, and nail the cloves in it. Add it to the saucepan, with the minced parsley and the bay leaf. Add salt and pepper and reduce the heat to low. Simmer for 2 hours.

3. Once the split peas are cooked, take the bay leaf and the onion out of the saucepan and discard. Use a ladle to take out ½ cup of broth from the saucepan and reserve. Drain the peas in a colander, and put them in a blender. Process until smooth. Pour them in a serving bowl and stir in the reserved broth tablespoon by tablespoon, until you reach the thickness you want.

4. Serve as is, or with some diced chervil on top.

Carottes Glacées (Glazed Carrots)

Carottes glacées *are carrots glazed in sugar, a great way to add some sweetness to your dinner.*

INGREDIENTS | SERVES 4

2 tablespoons butter, diced

8 medium carrots, peeled and sliced in half

½ teaspoon salt

1 tablespoon raw sugar

1 cup chicken stock

½ teaspoon ground black pepper

1 tablespoon fresh chives, minced

1. Melt the butter in a large nonstick skillet over medium-low heat, and lay the carrots in the butter next to each other. Add the salt and sugar, and pour the stock over the carrots. Add water if the stock doesn't cover the carrots.

2. Take a sheet of parchment paper, and cut to about the same size as the skillet. Make three small holes in it, and lay it on the carrots in the skillet. Bring to a boil over high heat, then reduce the heat to low and simmer for 25 minutes. Remove the parchment paper and wait for the liquid to have almost disappeared. Season with pepper, and top with the minced chives.

3. Serve warm.

Epinards à la Crème (Creamed Spinach)

Crème fraîche *and spinach make a great side dish with red meat or pork roast.*

INGREDIENTS | SERVES 4

1 tablespoon kosher salt

4 cups fresh spinach leaves

1 tablespoon butter

1 cup *crème fraîche*

1 teaspoon salt

1 teaspoon ground black pepper

1 teaspoon ground nutmeg

1. Fill a large saucepan with water, add kosher salt, and bring to a boil over high heat. Add the spinach. Cook for 10 minutes, then drain and put in a blender. Process for 30 seconds.

2. Melt the butter in a nonstick skillet over medium heat. Add the spinach. Pour in half of the cream, all the salt, pepper, and nutmeg, and stir. Cover, reduce the heat to low, and simmer for 7 minutes.

3. Put a small saucepan on low heat, and pour the rest of the cream in it.

4. Pour the spinach in a serving plate, pour the warmed cream on it, stir, and serve.

Haricots Verts à l'Ail
(French Beans with Garlic and Parsley)

The French way to serve French beans: with garlic and parsley!

INGREDIENTS | SERVES 4

1 tablespoon kosher salt

2 pounds fresh French beans, trimmed at the ends

2 garlic cloves, peeled and minced

1 tablespoon butter, diced

½ teaspoon salt

1 teaspoon ground black pepper

1 tablespoon fresh parsley, finely minced

1. Fill a large saucepan with water, add 1 tablespoon kosher salt, and bring to a boil over high heat. Add the French beans. Cook for 8 minutes, then drain in a colander.

2. Put the beans in a serving dish, add the minced garlic and the butter, salt, and pepper, and stir well until the butter melts.

3. Add the minced parsley, stir again, and serve.

Tomates Provençales (Tomatoes Provençale)

An ideal side dish for barbecue, these roasted tomatoes from Provence call for a glass of iced rosé and some great grilled meat.

INGREDIENTS | SERVES 4

8 medium round tomatoes, halved

1 teaspoon kosher salt

4 garlic cloves, peeled and minced

4 tablespoons bread crumbs

4 tablespoons fresh parsley, minced

2 tablespoons thyme

1 tablespoon oil

1. Season tomatoes with kosher salt. Take a large plate and put the tomatoes on it, face down so that their water drains out. Reserve for 15 minutes.

2. In a small bowl, combine the minced garlic cloves with the bread crumbs, parsley, and thyme.

3. Preheat the oven to 400°F.

4. Place the tomatoes in a large baking dish. Using a teaspoon, top each tomato with the garlic, bread crumbs, and herbs mixture. Top with a few drops of olive oil on each tomato. Put in the oven and bake for 15 minutes.

5. Serve immediately.

Tian Provençal

A great vegetable dish straight from the south of France. You're supposed to make it with all the vegetables you can find at the farmers' market in summer.

INGREDIENTS | SERVES 4

2 medium onions, peeled and minced
2 tablespoons olive oil, divided
4 tomatoes, thinly sliced
3 medium zucchini, thinly sliced
1 small eggplant, thinly sliced
2 tablespoons thyme
1 tablespoon rosemary
1 teaspoon salt
1 teaspoon ground black pepper
5 garlic cloves, unpeeled

Do You Have Your Tian?

Tian is also the name of the dish this recipe is cooked in. *Provençale* women invented this easy recipe to be able to leave the vegetables slowly cooking while they ran errands or washed clothes.

1. Preheat the oven to 350°F.

2. Place onions in a large baking dish. Add a tablespoon of olive oil and stir the onion, spreading them all over the bottom of the dish so that they cover it completely. Put in the oven for 10 minutes.

3. Take the dish out of the oven (don't turn off the oven, though). Let the dish cool a little, then start layering the slices of vegetables on the onions: one slice tomato, one slice zucchini, one slice eggplant, then another slice of tomato, etc. Once the vegetables cover the whole dish, sprinkle on the thyme, rosemary, salt, and pepper, and add the garlic cloves in different places around the dish. Pour 1 tablespoon of olive oil over the vegetables and put in the oven for 90 minutes.

4. Serve immediately.

CHAPTER 16

Pommes de Terre (Potatoes)

Gratin Dauphinois (Potatoes au Gratin)

Potatoes au gratin are a very typical family dish in France, especially in winter. They are great with a roast beef, a nice roasted chicken, or just on their own with a green salad of lettuce in garlicky vinaigrette.

INGREDIENTS | SERVES 4

1 garlic clove, peeled

3 tablespoons plus 1 teaspoon butter, diced

1 cup whole milk

3 cups whipping cream

1 teaspoon ground nutmeg

3 pounds potatoes, peeled and thinly sliced

1 teaspoon salt

1 teaspoon ground black pepper

Gratin Secrets

Contrary to popular belief, there's no cheese in the "real" *Gratin Dauphinois*. If you add *fromage*, it turns into a *Gratin Savoyard* (which is also very good). Never wash the potatoes after peeling them: It would take the starch out, and you need it for the milk, eggs, and the potatoes to stick well together. If you want to reheat it, add some cream and milk to the plate to keep everything moist.

1. Peel the garlic clove, and rub it inside a large baking dish. Butter the dish with 1 teaspoon of butter. Preheat the oven to 350°F.

2. In a medium saucepan, pour the milk and the cream and add nutmeg. Bring to a boil over high heat, stir well, and add the potato slices. Reduce the heat to low, and simmer for 10 minutes.

3. Using a slotted spoon, take the potato slices out of the saucepan and lay them in the buttered baking dish. Season with salt and pepper. Raise the heat of the stove to medium to reduce the milk and cream combination by half. Pour on the potatoes and add 3 tablespoons of diced butter on top. Put in the oven and cook for 20 minutes.

4. Serve lukewarm.

Les Vraies Frites (Thin Fries)

Did the French or the Belgians invent them? The controversy seems to be impossible to solve. But fries are for sure a big part of French culture. Here is the perfect recipe. In northern France, they are fried using a combination of ¾ beef tallow and ¼ lard.

INGREDIENTS | SERVES 4

2 pounds starchy potatoes (Idaho, Russet), peeled and cut in ⅛" sticks

Peanut oil

Salt

Size Matters

There are actually different kinds of *frites*, depending on their thickness. What Americans call french fries are called *Pommes Allumettes* (matchsticks) in France, and are about ⅛" thick. But the historic recipe is *Pommes Pont-Neuf*, like the famous Parisian *Pont Neuf* bridge where they are supposed to have first been sold, a few weeks before the French Revolution in 1789. They are thicker than the *Pommes Allumettes* (more than ½") and are fried twice.

1. Add potatoes to a bowl of water. Cover and reserve for 1 hour.

2. Pour in a colander, and dry the potatoes thoroughly with a cotton cloth. Divide them into three batches of equal size. Fill a large saucepan with oil and bring to 300°F. Put ⅓ of the potatoes in a frying basket and plunge them in the saucepan for 7 minutes. Then take them out, put them back in the dried colander, and do the same for the two other batches. Let them cool down for about 30 minutes.

3. Prepare 2 large bowls lined with paper towels in the bottom. Bring the oil or the fat to 350°F. Plunge the first batch into the heated oil and cook for around 3 minutes (they must be perfectly golden), then put the fries in the first bowl. Transfer them to the second bowl, and replace the paper towel of the first bowl before frying the second batch of potatoes. Repeat the draining process, and cook the third batch the same way.

4. Serve immediately, with salt on the table.

Pommes Gaufrettes (Waffle Fries)

Waffle fries are not only elegant and fun to make, they are delicious!

INGREDIENTS | SERVES 4

2 pounds starchy potatoes (Idaho, Russet), peeled

Peanut oil

Salt

About Fat

As in the French fries recipe, you can fry these with a combination of ¾ beef tallow and ¼ lard as they do in the north of France. At the beginning of the century, the French even used horse fat from the horses that were used to work in the coalmines.

1. Peel the potatoes. Using a mandoline equipped with the zigzag blade (and good rubber gloves; this is a dangerous operation!), slice the potato once, then turn it ¼ turn after each cut. The slices must be just the right thickness so that you are able to see through the holes this creates. Add potatoes to a large bowl of fresh water. Cover and reserve for 1 hour.

2. Drain in a colander. Prepare a large bowl with paper towels at the bottom, put the waffle fries in it, and dry them carefully with another paper towel on top. They are very thin and can shred easily. Divide them into three batches of equal size. Put the first batch in the frying basket.

3. Fill a large saucepan with oil (or the beef tallow and lard combination if you can!), and bring to 340°F. Plunge the fry basket into the hot oil, and use a long fork to make sure the potatoes don't stick together. Cook until golden, about 3 minutes.

4. Prepare 2 large bowls with paper towels lining the bottom. When the *gaufrettes* are golden, put them in the first bowl. Transfer them to the second and change the paper towels in the first bowl before frying the second batch of the potatoes. Repeat the draining process, and cook the third batch the same way.

5. Serve immediately, with salt on the table.

Pommes Dauphines (Potato Puff Balls)

Kids love potato puff balls . . . and adults do, too!

INGREDIENTS | SERVES 4

1 pound potatoes, peeled and diced
1 tablespoon kosher salt
⅓ cup water
⅓ cup butter, diced
1 cup flour
4 large eggs
2 teaspoons salt, divided
1 teaspoon ground black pepper
Peanut oil

1. Fill a large saucepan with water. Add kosher salt. Put the diced potatoes in the water and bring to a boil over high heat. Reduce to medium and cook for 25 minutes.

2. Fill a medium saucepan with ⅓ cup water, add the butter, and bring to a boil. When the butter is melted and well combined, pour in the flour, and stir steadily. Take the saucepan off the heat and stir continuously until the combination doesn't stick to the saucepan anymore. Add the eggs, one at a time. Stir again continuously until you get a smooth combination.

3. Pour the potatoes in a colander, dry them with a clean cloth, and mash them finely. Add the mashed potatoes to the egg, butter, and flour combination. Season with 1 teaspoon salt and pepper, stir well, and let it cool for 10 minutes.

4. Flour your hands slightly, and use a tablespoon to make small balls (the size of a walnut). Fill a large saucepan with oil, and bring to 350°F. Carefully pour the potato balls one after another in the oil, and take them out with a slotted spoon once they are puffed and golden. Dry them all on paper towels and put in a large serving bowl. Season with remaining salt.

5. Serve immediately.

Pommes Duchesses (Duchess Potatoes)

This potato dish may not have been invented by a duchess, but it's still delicious!

INGREDIENTS | SERVES 4

1 tablespoon kosher salt

1 pound potatoes, peeled and diced

3 tablespoons butter, diced

2 large egg yolks

1 teaspoon salt

1 teaspoon ground black pepper

1 teaspoon ground nutmeg

Other Possibilities

You can also cook the *Pommes Duchesses* in a skillet. Melt 1 tablespoon butter over medium-high heat; add the potato (you don't need to brush them with butter, as in the recipe) for a few minutes.

1. Fill a large saucepan with water, add kosher salt, put the diced potatoes in it and bring to a boil over high heat. Reduce to moderate heat and cook for 25 minutes.

2. Pour the potatoes in a colander, dry them with a clean cloth, and mash them. Add 2 tablespoons diced butter, and put back in the saucepan. Put over medium heat and stir for 5 minutes, drying the mashed potatoes. Take the saucepan off the heat, let it cool for a moment, then add the egg yolks and stir. Season with salt, pepper, and ground nutmeg, and stir again until the combination is smooth.

3. Preheat the oven to 400°F. Put a large parchment paper sheet on a baking sheet. In a small saucepan, melt 1 tablespoon of butter. Transfer the mashed potatoes to a piping bag fitted with a ½" star tip. Use the pipe to make small circles on the paper, about 2" wide. Using a pastry brush, brush with the melted butter. Put in the oven for a few minutes until golden brown.

4. Serve immediately.

Pommes de Terre Boulangères (Onion and Potato Casserole)

In French, this recipe means "baker's potatoes," because it used to be cooked in a baker's oven. This onion and potato casserole is perfect with lamb or beef.

INGREDIENTS | SERVES 4

2 tablespoons plus 1 teaspoon butter, divided

2 tablespoons olive oil, divided

1 pound potatoes, peeled and thinly sliced

1 teaspoon salt

1 teaspoon ground black pepper

2 medium onions, peeled and thinly sliced

2 cups chicken stock

1 tablespoon thyme

1. In a medium nonstick skillet, melt 1 tablespoon butter over medium-high heat. Add 1 tablespoon oil, combine well, then add the potato slices. Season with salt and pepper and cook slowly for 10 minutes, stirring often. Pour the contents of the saucepan in a colander. Let the potatoes dry, and reserve.

2. Melt 1 tablespoon of butter in the skillet, over medium-high heat. Combine with 1 tablespoon of oil. Add the onion slices, stir well, and cook slowly for 10 minutes, stirring often. Turn off the heat.

3. Preheat the oven to 350°F. In a medium saucepan, bring the chicken stock to a boil over high heat. Butter a medium baking dish with remaining butter. Put a layer of onions on the bottom, season with half the thyme. Add a layer of potatoes and sprinkle on the rest of the thyme. Pour the boiling chicken broth over the potatoes and the onions, and put in the oven for 40 minutes.

4. Serve with grilled meat.

Galettes de Pommes de Terre Alsaciennes (Potato Pancakes)

A tradition in Alsace, in the east of France, these potato pancakes are actually called Grumbeerekiechle *in the local language.*

INGREDIENTS | SERVES 4

2 pound potatoes, peeled
2 large eggs
1 tablespoon flour
1 tablespoon fresh parsley, minced
1 medium onion, peeled and minced
1 teaspoon salt
1 teaspoon ground black pepper
1 teaspoon ground nutmeg
½ cup sunflower oil

1. Grate potatoes with a box grater (not too thin). Use a paper towel to blot them dry (the drier they are, the easier they are to mix and cook).

2. Place the grated potatoes in a large bowl, and break the eggs over them. Combine well, and add the flour, parsley, and onion, stirring constantly. Season with salt, pepper, and ground nutmeg. Stir again until you get a combined mixture.

3. Take a spoonful of potato mixture and create 3"-wide pancakes. Press them flat with your hands. Heat a large nonstick skillet over medium-high heat, add the oil to a depth of about ½", and fry the potato pancakes for 5–7 minutes. Flip the potato pancakes over to cook the other side for 5–7 minutes. They must be golden and crunchy outside, but soft inside. Use a paper towel to blot the grease.

4. Serve with smoked salmon or ham.

Crique Ardéchoise (Large Potato Pancake)

This very large potato pancake, the size of the skillet you're making it in, is a traditional recipe of Ardèche in south central France, where most potatoes eaten in France used to be produced.

INGREDIENTS | SERVES 4

2 pound potatoes, peeled

1 large egg

1 tablespoon fresh parsley, minced

1 garlic clove, minced

1 teaspoon salt

1 teaspoon ground black pepper

1 tablespoon butter

1 tablespoon sunflower oil

1. Peel the potatoes and grate them with a box grater (not too thin). Use a paper towel to blot them dry (the drier they are, the easier they are to mix and cook).

2. Place the potatoes in a large bowl and break the egg over them. Combine well, then add the parsley and the garlic, stirring constantly. Season with salt and pepper. Stir until combined.

3. Heat a large nonstick skillet (or a large crêpe pan) over medium-high heat. Melt the butter, and add the oil. Combine the two, and when the skillet is very hot, pour all the potato mix in the skillet and spread well. Reduce the heat to medium-low and cook for 10 minutes. Then flip it as you would flip an omelet, sliding it gently out of the skillet and using a wooden spatula. Cook the other side for another 10 minutes. When the pancake is golden, slide it onto a plate.

4. Serve immediately, with roasted chicken, grilled red meat, or just a simple salad.

Pommes de Terre Sarladaises
(Potatoes Cooked in Duck Fat)

These potatoes cooked in duck fat are simply a touch of heaven on earth!

INGREDIENTS | SERVES 4

2 pounds potatoes, peeled

4 tablespoons duck fat

2 garlic cloves, minced

1 tablespoon fresh parsley, minced

1 teaspoon ground nutmeg

1 teaspoon ground black pepper

Duck Fat Culture

These potatoes are named after the small town of Sarlat, in southwest France, more precisely in the *Périgord Noir*. This region is home to the biggest concentration of prehistoric caves in the world, but is also known for its duck fat culture. Every winter, people go to the *marché au gras,* literally the fat market, where you can buy foie gras, fat ducks and geese, and of course, duck fat, used daily for cooking there.

1. Fill a large bowl with water, and put the potatoes in it for 1 hour. Drain them in a colander, and dry them well with a clean cotton cloth.

2. Heat a large nonstick skillet over medium-high heat. Melt the duck fat in it, then pour in the potato slices. Cook for 10 minutes on high heat, stirring from time to time, then reduce to low and simmer for 20 minutes. Add the garlic, nutmeg, and the parsley, and season with salt and pepper.

3. If you can wait, remove the skillet from the heat and cover. Reserve for 10 minutes before serving. If you can't wait, you can serve them immediately.

Truffade Auvergnate

No truffle in this truffade, but it's a little gem in itself: a marvelous potato, bacon, and cheese cake, eaten in Auvergne, in the southern center of France.

INGREDIENTS | SERVES 4

2 pound potatoes, peeled and diced

8 thick slices of bacon cut into ½" matchsticks

1 teaspoon salt

1 teaspoon ground black pepper

1 pound young Cantal cheese (or a very young Cheddar), diced

1 garlic clove, peeled and minced

1 tablespoon fresh parsley

Shepherd Cake

This recipe was invented by shepherds from Auvergne who would spend weeks without seeing anybody when the sheep had to be taken to green distant places. They didn't have many ingredients to bring with them to cook, and created this dish with potatoes and the young cheese they had just made.

1. Rinse potatoes under water and dry them well in a clean cotton cloth.

2. Heat a large nonstick skillet over medium-low heat. Put the bacon slices in the skillet, and cook them slowly, stirring often, about 3 minutes. When done, remove the bacon from the pan, but leave the fat. Add the potato to the skillet. Increase the heat to medium-high and stir often. Cook for around 7 minutes, until golden. Season with salt and pepper.

3. Pour in a large bowl, mash the potatoes with a fork, then add the bacon sticks. Add the cheese cubes and stir constantly with a wooden spoon until it sticks together. Pour it back in the skillet, spreading it out with the wooden spoon. Cover and reduce the heat to low. Simmer for 5 minutes, then add the garlic and the parsley on top. Put the cover back on for 2 minutes, then raise the heat to medium-high and take off the cover. Remove the skillet from the heat when edges are golden, about 3 minutes.

4. Flip onto plate and serve with a simple green salad.

Purée de Pommes de Terre (Mashed Potatoes)

Mashed potatoes à la française call for a utensil that is in every French kitchen cupboard: a food mill.

INGREDIENTS | SERVES 6

1 tablespoon kosher salt

2 pound potatoes (Russet or Yukon Gold), peeled, cut in big chunks

1 cup whole milk

2 tablespoons butter, diced

1 teaspoon ground nutmeg

1 teaspoon salt

1 teaspoon ground black pepper

1. Fill a large saucepan with water, add kosher salt and the potatoes, and bring to a boil over high heat. Boil for 25 minutes. A knife blade should be able to pierce the potatoes easily. Drain the potatoes in a colander, and mash them with the food mill.

2. In a medium saucepan, warm the milk over medium heat. Stop before the boiling point, then pour slowly over the potatoes, stirring constantly with a wooden spoon. Add the butter, nutmeg, salt, and pepper, and stir till smooth.

3. Serve immediately.

Purée de Pommes de Terre aux Truffes (Mashed Potatoes with Truffles)

A decadent version of the classic mashed potatoes, with black truffles and butter.

INGREDIENTS | SERVES 6

1 tablespoon kosher salt

2 pound small potatoes (Russet or Yukon Gold), with their skins on

⅔ cup butter, diced

1 cup whole milk

1 teaspoon salt

1 teaspoon ground black pepper

1 small (1.5-ounce) black truffle, very thinly sliced

1. Fill a large saucepan with water, add kosher salt and the potatoes, and bring to a boil over high heat. Boil for 25 minutes. A knife blade should be able to pierce the potatoes easily. Drain and peel them, and mash them with the food mill.

2. Add potatoes to a medium saucepan over low heat. Add the butter slowly to the potatoes. Stirring continuously, add the milk little by little, then add the salt and pepper. Stop when smooth, then add the truffle slices and stir again.

3. Pour in a large bowl and serve.

Patates en Robe des Champs (Boiled Potatoes in Jackets)

A potato in a country dress! That's one of the strange names for this basic French recipe, along with another weirder name: Pommes de Terre en robe de chambre, *or "potatoes in a bathrobe"!*

INGREDIENTS | SERVES 4

4 large potatoes (Bintje or Russet)
1 tablespoon kosher salt
1 cup *crème fraîche* or Greek yogurt
1 tablespoon chives, minced
1 teaspoon salt
1 teaspoon ground black pepper

Big vs. Small Potatoes

The *Patates en Robe des Champs* uses generally big potatoes, but the recipe has a more subtle taste when using small potatoes. Cook them a little less time (around 15 minutes). You can also just add a teaspoon of salted butter on each cooked half. A great simple dinner.

1. Wash the potatoes and jab them with a fork to prevent them from splitting.

2. Fill a large saucepan with water, add the kosher salt and the potatoes, and bring to a boil over high heat. Cook for 20 minutes.

3. In a medium bowl, combine the cream or the yogurt with the chives, salt, and pepper. Drain the potatoes, and slice them in half.

4. Serve the potatoes immediately, with the skin, and add sauce on them.

Patates en Robe des Champs au Four (Baked Potatoes in Jackets)

Almost the same name as the previous recipe, but still very different.
This is how you cook these potatoes in the oven.

INGREDIENTS | SERVES 4

4 large potatoes (Bintje or Russet)
6 tablespoons *crème fraîche*
2 tablespoons Dijon mustard
1 teaspoon salt
1 teaspoon ground black pepper

1. Preheat the oven to 350°F. Wash the potatoes, and dry them thoroughly with a clean tablecloth. Wrap them in aluminum foil and cook for 30 minutes.

2. In a medium bowl, combine the cream with the Dijon mustard. As soon as you take the potatoes out of the oven, slice them and add 1 tablespoon of sauce on each half. Season with salt and pepper.

3. Serve immediately.

CHAPTER 17

Le Goûter (Snacks)

Quatre Quarts (French Pound Cake)

The first recipe French kids learn how to bake is the French version of the pound cake!
The weight of the ingredients depends on the weight of the first one, the eggs.

INGREDIENTS | SERVES 4

3 large eggs

Same weight of flour, plus one
  tablespoon to flour the dish

Same weight of sugar

Same weight of butter, diced, at room
  temperature, plus 1 tablespoon to
  butter the dish

1 teaspoon of baking powder

1. Weigh your 3 eggs, then weigh out the same amount of flour, sugar, and butter.

2. In a large bowl, work the butter by stirring it with a wooden spatula. It should become smooth, and turn into a *beurre pommade*. Add the sugar and flour, and whisk firmly with an electric beater, until the mixture whitens and gets creamy. Add the flour and the baking powder, and whisk until the mixture is combined.

3. Preheat the oven to 350°F. Butter an 8" round baking dish, pour 1 tablespoon flour in it, and shake the dish so that the flour gets everywhere in the dish. Pour the mixture in the dish and bake for 45 minutes.

4. Serve lukewarm or cold.

Gâteau au Yaourt (Yogurt Cake)

Yogurt Cake is another very easy recipe that kids learn to bake early: They use a yogurt container as a scale to determine the amount of the other ingredients. Very easy, with a very smooth texture.

INGREDIENTS | SERVES 4

⅔ cup yogurt, plain

3 eggs

1⅔ cups flour

⅔ cup plus 1 tablespoon sugar, divided

⅓ cup sunflower oil

¼ teaspoon salt

2 tablespoons baking powder

1 organic lemon

1 tablespoon butter

1. Preheat the oven to 400°F.

2. In a large bowl, combine the yogurt and the eggs, and beat firmly with a wooden spatula. Add the flour, ⅔ cup sugar, the oil, the salt, and the baking powder, and beat again until combined. Using a box grater, grate the peel of the lemon over the bowl, and stir it into the mixture.

3. Butter an 8" round baking dish, pour one tablespoon sugar in it, and shake the dish so that the sugar gets everywhere in the dish. Pour the mixture in the dish and bake for 25 minutes. The cake is cooked when a knife blade put in the center comes back out clean.

4. Serve lukewarm or cold.

Gâteau au Yaourt de Pommes (Apple Yogurt Cake)

Yogurt cake is so easy to make that you can invent as many recipes as your imagination allows. The apple yogurt cake is the most popular.

INGREDIENTS | SERVES 4

2 tablespoons plus 1 tablespoon butter, divided

4 medium apples, thinly sliced

2 tablespoons vanilla raw sugar

⅔ cup yogurt, plain

3 eggs

1⅔ cups flour

⅔ cup plus 1 tablespoon sugar, divided

⅓ cup sunflower oil

1 teaspoon baking powder

¼ teaspoon salt

Skin to Skin

Try to choose organic apples. This way you can keep the skin on the apples instead of peeling them. It adds flavor and crunch to the cake.

1. Preheat the oven to 350°F.

2. Heat a nonstick skillet over medium-high heat. Melt 2 tablespoons butter, and add the apple slices. Brown them on each side, about 2–3 minutes total, and then sprinkle vanilla sugar on them so that they caramelize slightly, for about 1 minute. Remove from heat and reserve.

3. In a large bowl, combine the yogurt and eggs, and beat firmly. Add the flour, sugar, oil, baking powder, and the salt, and beat again, until the mixture is combined.

4. Butter an 8" round baking dish with 1 tablespoon butter, pour 1 tablespoon sugar in it, and shake the dish so that the sugar gets everywhere in the dish. Spread the slices of apple at the bottom, then add the batter. Bake for 40 minutes. The cake is cooked when a knife blade put in the center comes back out clean.

5. Serve lukewarm or cold.

Tartine au Cacao (Chocolate Sandwich)

This is the French peanut butter sandwich! It's the snack every French kid loves to have at 4 P.M. sharp.

INGREDIENTS | SERVES 4

2 tablespoons butter

½ fresh baguette, cut in 2 and sliced down the middle

2 tablespoons pure cocoa powder

1. Spread butter on the 4 pieces of bread. Using a teaspoon, sprinkle powdered chocolate on the butter.

2. Serve immediately.

Le Quatre-Heures

Quatre-heures, as in 4 P.M., is what French parents and kids call snack time. Snack time is very ritualized in the traditional French upbringing: You snack at a certain time, not earlier, not later.

Trempée au Lait (Cold Milk and Bread)

Surely this is one of the most popular snacks at the beginning of the twentieth century and up to the 1960s in rural France. Chilled cold milk and bread is very refreshing in the summer. In a way, this is the ancestor of a bowl of cereal and milk.

INGREDIENTS | SERVES 4

4 cups whole milk

½ baguette, cut into 1" cubes

1. In a medium bowl, pour the milk on the bread cubes, then cover and put in the refrigerator for at least 30 minutes.

2. Serve in individual bowls with a spoon.

Pain d'Épices (Gingerbread)

Gingerbread is as great a tradition in France as it is in America, but is much milder in taste. At snacktime, the French like to cut it in ½" slices and spread it with good butter.

INGREDIENTS | SERVES 6

½ cup whole milk
½ cup honey
½ cup sugar
2 cups flour
1 teaspoon baking soda
1 tablespoon butter

"Spice Cake" in Alsace

Pain d'épice means "spice cake" in French, although the traditional recipe doesn't call for any spice: The quality of the honey you choose makes all the difference. In Alsace, in the east of France, cinnamon, ginger, and clove are added. Gingerbread is a great tradition there, especially during the holidays.

1. Preheat the oven to 250°F.

2. In a small saucepan, warm the milk slowly over medium heat. Add the honey and the sugar. Stir with a wooden spatula until melted and combined.

3. Pour the flour in a large bowl, add the baking soda, mix it in the flour, then make a small well in the middle, and slowly pour in half of the warm milk and honey combination. Stir, and then slowly add the rest of the milk, stirring continuously. Stop when the mixture is perfectly smooth.

4. Butter a loaf pan and pour in the mixture. Use a wooden spoon to smooth the surface. Cook in the oven for 1 hour.

5. You can serve warm, but it's better the next day, and even the following days.

Gaufre Légère (Light Waffles)

This light waffle is perfect for a Sunday snack. The French love to serve it with jam, crème de marrons, melted chocolate, or much more simply, with just raw sugar sprinkled on top.

INGREDIENTS | SERVES 4

5 tablespoons butter
3 large eggs
½ cup sugar
2 cups whole milk
2 cups regular flour
1 teaspoon salt
1 tablespoon orange blossom water

1. Melt the butter in a small saucepan over very low heat. Remove from heat and reserve.

2. In a large bowl, break the eggs and whisk them. Add the sugar, and whisk firmly until the mixture whitens. Whisk continuously as you add ½ cup of the milk, then ½ cup of flour, and so on until you've used all the milk and flour. The batter should be smooth, with no lumps.

3. Add the melted butter and the salt, and whisk again. Add the orange blossom water and stir one last time, then cover with a cloth. Wait for at least 1 hour before using batter. Cook the waffles in a waffle maker for about 3–4 minutes.

4. Serve immediately.

Gaufre à la Crème (Waffles with Cream)

This waffle recipe includes a French favorite: crème fraîche.

INGREDIENTS | SERVES 6

⅔ cup butter
4 cups flour
½ teaspoon salt
2 teaspoons baking powder
4 large eggs, egg whites and yolks separated
3 tablespoons sugar
1 cup water
1 cup *crème fraîche* or crema Mexicana

1. Melt the butter in a small saucepan over very low heat. Remove from heat and reserve.

2. In a large bowl, whisk the flour, salt, baking powder, egg yolks, and sugar. Then add the water slowly, whisking continuously. Once it's well combined, add the melted butter and then the cream.

3. In another bowl, whisk the egg whites until they are very firm. Add them slowly to the batter. When it's smooth, with no lumps, cover it and wait for at least 1 hour before cooking using a standard waffle iron.

4. Serve immediately, with powdered sugar on top.

Crêpe Sucrée (Basic Crêpes with Powdered Sugar)

Cheap, quick, and easy, crêpes have been the perfect goûter for years in France!
The most common is crêpe au sucre, with just plain sugar on top.

INGREDIENTS | SERVES 6

2 tablespoons plus 1 teaspoon butter
1½ cups flour
2 large eggs
¼ teaspoon salt
4 cups whole milk
1 tablespoon orange blossom water
Powdered sugar for garnish

February 2 Is Crêpe Day!

On this date every year, the French celebrate *La Chandeleur*. It used to be a religious day, celebrating the presentation of Jesus Christ at the Temple, but now it's mostly a national crêpe day. You're supposed to cook your crêpes with a coin in your left hand. If you manage to flip it with just one hand, you will have money all year long!

1. Melt 2 tablespoons butter in a small saucepan over very low heat. Remove from heat and reserve.

2. Sift the flour into a large bowl. Make a small hole at the center (like a volcano crater), break the eggs into it, and add the salt. Whisk slowly and continuously. Add the milk slowly, then the orange blossom water, and the melted butter. Whisk again. Cover with a damp cloth. Leave at room temperature.

3. In a medium nonstick skillet (preferably a crêpe pan), melt 1 teaspoon butter over medium-high heat. Wipe it out with a paper towel. Then take a small ladleful of batter, pour it in the center of the pan, and immediately swirl the pan so that the batter spreads all over the bottom of the pan. Cook until the rim of the crêpe detaches itself from the pan, and then use a wooden spatula to flip it on the other side. Cook for about 1 minute.

4. Pile up the crêpes on a large plate, cover with aluminum foil, and put the plate on a small saucepan filled with water on a low heat. This will make sure they stay warm. Garnish with powdered sugar and serve.

Gaufre à la Limonade (Lemonade Waffles)

Limonade is a sparkling version of the American lemonade, a French soda that you can now find in the United States.

INGREDIENTS | SERVES 6

⅓ cup butter
4 cups flour
¼ teaspoon salt
4 large eggs
⅓ cup sugar
3 cups *limonade*
3 teaspoons baking powder

1. Melt the butter in a small saucepan over very low heat. Remove from heat and reserve.

2. In a large bowl, whisk the flour, salt, eggs, and the sugar. Slowly add the *limonade*, whisking continuously. Once it's well combined, add the melted butter and the baking powder. When it's smooth, with no lumps, cover it and wait for at least 1 hour before cooking them with a standard waffle iron.

3. Serve immediately with powdered sugar.

Crêpe Montblanc

This crêpe recipe is named after the highest mountain in Europe. Every French athlete dreams of standing on its white top, at the French and Italian border.

INGREDIENTS | SERVES 4

1 tablespoon butter
½ cup silvered almonds
8 sweet crêpes (see *Crêpe Sucrée* recipe in this chapter)
1 cup *Crème de Marrons* (see recipe in Chapter 2)
1 cup Chantilly Cream (see recipe in Chapter 22)

1. In a nonstick skillet, melt the butter over medium heat. Brown the almonds slightly on each side, stirring continuously for 1 minute. Reserve.

2. Reheat the crêpes slowly in a slightly buttered crêpe pan, over low heat. Spread 1 tablespoon *Crème de Marrons* at the center of each crêpe, then fold over and put on a dessert plate. Top with 2 tablespoons Chantilly Cream and sprinkle with almonds.

3. Repeat for all the crêpes. Serve immediately.

Gâteau de Crêpes (Crêpes Cake)

A Napoleon in crêpes! This cake consists of layered crêpes. Funny and easy!

INGREDIENTS | SERVES 4

1 pound strawberries, mashed (reserve 8 whole strawberries)

2 tablespoons mint leaves, minced, plus 4 whole leaves

12 crêpes (see *Crêpe Sucrée* recipe in this chapter)

1 cup Chantilly Cream (see recipe in Chapter 22

1. Put all the strawberries but 8 in a medium bowl, and mash them with a wooden spoon. Add the minced mint leaves, and stir.

2. Spread one crêpe with Chantilly Cream. Put it on a large serving plate. Then top with another crêpe, and spread mashed strawberries on it. Spread Chantilly on another crêpe, put it on top of the strawberries, and continue as long as you have crêpes and strawberries.

3. Top with a last layer of Chantilly Cream, then add the 8 whole strawberries and 4 mint leaves to decorate.

Crêpes Suzette

This is a very vintage crêpe! There was a time when a good restaurant had to be able to flambé a Crêpe Suzette in front of the bewildered customer to show that it was a high-class establishment.

INGREDIENTS | SERVES 4

Juice of 3 peeled organic mandarins (reserve peels)

⅓ cup plus 1 tablespoon butter, diced, at room temperature, divided

⅓ cup sugar

2 tablespoons Cointreau or triple sec, and ½ cup for flambé

8 crêpes (see *Crêpe Sucrée* recipe in this chapter)

1. Slice the mandarin peels into strips. In a large bowl, stir ⅓ cup butter with the mandarin peels using a wooden spatula. Stir continuously as you add the sugar, then add 2 tablespoons of the mandarin juice and the Cointreau. Reserve 1 hour in the refrigerator.

2. Spread the mandarin butter on each crêpe. Fold them in 4. Melt 1 tablespoon butter in a crêpe pan and reheat the crêpes slowly in it. Heat ½ cup Cointreau in a small saucepan, over medium heat.

3. Pour some warm Cointreau on one *crêpe* at a time, and strike a match to *flambé*! The alcohol will burst into flames, caramelizing the crepe. Shake the pan for 30 seconds and serve immediately.

Beignets de Mardi Gras (Mardi Gras Doughnuts)

These doughnuts are usually made for Fat Tuesday, the day in the year where French kids dress up in costumes and eat sweet things, forty days before Easter.

INGREDIENTS | SERVES 4

2 (0.75-ounce) packets of baker's yeast

2 tablespoons lukewarm water

4 cups flour

4 tablespoons sugar

3 tablespoons whole milk

4 large eggs

4 tablespoons orange blossom water

⅔ cup butter, diced, at room temperature

Frying oil (peanut or sunflower)

Powdered or raw sugar for garnish

Rondiaux or Merveilles?

There are tons of recipes all over France for Fat Tuesday doughnuts, all with slightly different ingredients, and all with different names: *merveilles, crespèths, bugnes, bottereaux, faverolles, foutimassons, guenilles, roussettes.* This recipe here is for *rondiaux,* as they are made in the Loire Valley.

1. In a small bowl, mix the baker's yeast with the lukewarm water. Cover with a tepid cloth and put it in a warm room for 10 minutes.

2. In a large bowl, mix the flour and the sugar. Pour in the milk slowly, stir with a wooden spoon, then add the eggs, stir again, and add the orange blossom water. Add the diced butter, and knead with your hands for at least 10 minutes until the butter is totally incorporated in the dough. Cover with a damp cloth, and leave in a warm room for at least 1 hour (2–3 hours is better).

3. Add some flour to knead the dough again so that it doesn't stick to the bowl. Cover again and leave for 1 hour. Flatten the dough to ¼" thick and cut it in diamond shapes.

4. Fill a large saucepan with frying oil, bring to medium heat, and fry the *beignets* in it. When they are golden on each side (about 2 minutes), take them out with a slotted spoon.

5. Sprinkle powdered or raw sugar on the *beignets* immediately. Cover with a cloth and store at room temperature. Eat the next day.

Beignets aux Pommes (Apple Doughnuts)

*These apple doughnuts are easy to make and one of the first recipes
a French mom learns to make for her kids for goûter.*

INGREDIENTS | SERVES 4

1 pound apples, peeled, cored, and
  sliced into ½" rounds
3 tablespoons rum
1 tablespoon sugar
1 lemon peel, minced
1 cup flour
¼ cup whole milk
½ teaspoon salt
2 cups frying oil (peanut or sunflower)
Raw sugar for garnish

Alcohol-Free Recipe

For kids, leave out the rum and marinate
the apples in 3 tablespoons of orange blossom water and 1 tablespoon sugar. Cover
and leave at room temperature for 1 hour.

1. Put the apples in a medium bowl, and add rum, sugar,
    and the minced lemon peel. Cover with a cloth and
    marinate for 1 hour.

2. In a large bowl, pour the flour, milk, and salt, and stir
    well with a wooden spoon. Cover and leave at room
    temperature for 1 hour.

3. Strain the apples. Pour the oil in a saucepan and bring
    to 350°F. Soak the apples one after another in the
    batter, then put them in the frying oil. Once a side is
    golden, flip it to the other side. Use a slotted spoon to
    take them out when golden on each side, about
    2 minutes.

4. Sprinkle raw sugar on each. Eat (almost!) immediately.

CHAPTER 18

Petits Gâteaux (Cookies)

Petits Sablés (Butter Cookies)

Sablé means "sandy" in French, but don't worry, there's no sand in these butter cookies! It's all about the way the dough is made.

INGREDIENTS | SERVES 30 *SABLÉS*

1 large egg

1 teaspoon salt

1 tablespoon orange blossom water

1 cup sugar

2 cups flour

½ cup butter, diced, at room temperature

1 tablespoon coarse salt

No French Cookie Jar!

In France, cookies are not kept in a cookie jar, but in tin boxes. They are great for storage, above all because they are airtight. They also protect the cookies from being damaged by the sun.

1. Preheat your oven to 350°F.

2. In a large bowl, put the egg, salt, orange blossom water, and sugar, and beat well using a wooden spoon, until the mixture has doubled in size. Add the flour, and start kneading with your hands. Add the butter slowly. You should "sand" it into the dough (pinch it with your fingers, as you would crumble sand on the beach).

3. Once your dough is combined, shape it into a large ball. Roll it until it is ¼" thick. Then use cookie cutters to cut as many *sablés* as you can. Put them all on a baking sheet lined with parchment paper. Be careful to space them out enough, about ½" from each other. Sprinkle coarse salt on them and put in the oven. Bake for 8–9 minutes, until slightly brown.

4. Take them out immediately and put them in a metal box immediately. You can store them for two weeks.

Palets Bretons (Brittany Butter Cookies)

These butter cookies were created in Brittany by fishermen's wives who wanted their husbands to go to sea with nourishing sweets. They can be stored for a long time in a tin can. Their name, palet, means "puck."

INGREDIENTS | SERVES APPROXIMATIVELY 30

⅔ cup salted butter, diced, at room temperature

4 egg yolks

1 cup sugar

1¼ cups flour

½ teaspoon vanilla extract

1 tablespoon baking powder

Chocolate Version

You can also add ¼ cup dark chocolate chips to the mixture, and cook for the same amount of time. Serve with a *Crème Anglaise* (see recipe in Chapter 22).

1. In a medium bowl, stir the butter with a wooden spoon until it's soft and smooth.

2. Put the egg yolks and the sugar in the bowl of a stand mixer and whisk until the mixture whitens. Add the butter. Combine well. Then add the flour, the vanilla extract, and the baking powder.

3. Once the mixture is well combined, take it out of the bowl and roll it into a large cylinder, about 2" wide. Wrap it in plastic wrap, and put in the refrigerator for at least 2 hours, or as long as it needs for the cylinder to be really firm.

4. Take the cylinder out of the refrigerator and cut it in ½"-thick slices. *Palets Bretons* should not be too thin. Space them well on a parchment paper–lined baking sheet, then put them back in the refrigerator for 1 hour.

5. Preheat your oven to 325°F. Bake for around 15 minutes (the time might vary depending on how thick your *palets* are), or until they are slightly golden.

6. Take them out immediately, remove them to a cooling rack, and wait for them to cool down.

Langues de Chat

Ever tasted cat tongues? Don't worry, it's just the name of these cookies! Langues de Chat are part of the petit four tradition. They are called that because their size and shape make them look like cat's tongues.

INGREDIENTS | SERVES ABOUT 20 LANGUES DE CHAT

½ cup butter, melted
½ cup sugar
¾ cup flour
4 egg whites
1 teaspoon vanilla extract

Petits Fours

Langues de Chat belong to the *petit four* family. *Petits fours* are small pastries that you serve for tea or for celebrations, with Champagne, for example. You usually serve a variety of different small cookies or mini pastries.

1. Preheat your oven to 350°F.

2. In a small saucepan, melt the butter over very low heat. Remove from heat and pour in a large bowl. Add the sugar and stir firmly, until the sugar combines with the butter. Stir continuously while adding the flour.

3. In another bowl, whisk the egg whites until they are very firm. Add them to the first bowl, and fold them in slowly; you have to wrap the whites around the rest of the mixture until they combine together. Once it's combined, put it in the refrigerator for 30 minutes.

4. Pour the combination in a pastry bag, and pipe 2"-long lines (about ½" wide) on a parchment paper–lined baking sheet. Be careful to space them well, about ½" apart from each other. Cook for 10–12 minutes. The "tongues" are ready when they are slightly golden.

5. Wait for them to cool down and put in an airtight box.

Cigarettes Russes (Wafer Rolls)

These wafer rolls are great with tea, or a nice bowl of ice cream.

INGREDIENTS | SERVES ABOUT 20 WAFERS

½ cup butter

4 egg whites

¾ cup sugar

¾ cup flour

2 tablespoons almond flour

¼ teaspoon salt

Take Your Time!

Be careful of these wafers; they can burn you easily, because you have to roll them as soon as you take them out of the oven, when they are still pretty hot. Try not to cook big batches at the same time. By the time you get to the last ones, they will be too cool for you to roll.

1. In a small saucepan, melt the butter over very low heat. As soon as it is melted, take off the heat and reserve. Preheat the oven to 350°F.

2. In a large bowl, whisk the egg whites (you can use a fork, they don't have to be very firm). Add the sugar, whisking continuously, then slowly add the flour and the almond flour. Add the salt, whisk until well combined, add the melted butter. Stop whisking when the mixture is combined.

3. Put a parchment paper sheet on a baking sheet. Fill a pastry bag with the mixture, and make very thin 2" rounds (you can also drop the batter onto the sheet using a teaspoon). Space them well, about ½" apart from each other. Bake for 8 minutes. When they start getting golden, take them out of the oven. Remove each disc from the parchment paper and roll each disc around a pencil, then slide off the pencil extremely quickly and lay on another plate.

4. Let them cool down and put them in an airtight container.

Tuiles aux Amandes (Almond Tiles)

Tuile means "tile" in French, because these cookies are shaped like the clay tiles you can see on many roofs in France. They are very delicate and delicious with a mousse au chocolat, *for example.*

INGREDIENTS | SERVES 20 *TUILES*

¼ cup butter

8.5 ounces sliced almonds

¾ cup sugar

¼ cup flour

4 egg whites

2 empty wine bottles

Stay Close!

Depending on your oven and the thickness of your *tuiles*, they might be ready at a different time. Stay close to the oven, and take them out as soon as they are slightly golden on the top surface.

1. In a small saucepan, melt the butter over very low heat. As soon as it is melted, remove from heat and reserve.

2. In a large bowl, whisk the sliced almonds with the sugar and the flour. Whisking continuously, add the egg whites, and then the melted butter. Once everything is well mixed, put in the refrigerator for at least 1 hour.

3. Preheat the oven to 350°F. Put a parchment paper sheet on a baking sheet. Take one spoonful of batter and put it on the parchment paper. With a fork, flatten the dough into a thin oval. Repeat 5 times; never bake more than 6 *tuiles* at the same time. Put in the oven for 10 minutes.

4. Prepare two clean empty wine bottles. When the *tuiles* are all golden, take them out of the oven. Use a spatula to take them off of the parchment paper immediately, and put them on the bottles. They have to take the shape of the bottle so they are curved.

5. Take the *tuiles* off the bottles and let them cool down. Store them in an airtight container.

Palets Solognots (Butter and Raisin Cookies)

These butter and raisin cookies are a classic in the Loire Valley, where they are sometimes also called Palets Chambord, *in homage to the beautiful French castle. They are great petits fours to serve with Champagne, for instance.*

INGREDIENTS | SERVES 20 *PALETS*

3 ounces raisins

⅓ cup rum

½ cup butter, diced, at room temperature

2 large eggs

⅔ cup sugar

1¼ cups flour

Kid-Friendly Recipe

If you want to avoid alcohol in your recipe, you can marinate the raisins in pineapple juice with 1 teaspoon almond extract.

1. In a small bowl, marinate the raisins in the rum for about 1 hour at room temperature.

2. In a large bowl, work the butter by stirring it with a wooden spoon until it's really smooth and soft. Break the eggs into the butter, and stir with the wooden spoon until it's well mixed. Stirring continuously, adding the sugar, flour, and the raisins. If the batter is very liquid, place in the refrigerator to firm it up.

3. Preheat the oven to 400°F. Put a parchment paper sheet on a baking sheet. Take one tablespoonful of batter and put it on the parchment paper. Repeat until the entire rack is full (be careful to space them well, about 1" apart).

4. Bake for 10 minutes. Only the edges of the cookie should have changed color.

5. Let them cool down and store in an airtight container.

Financiers (Almond Cakes)

Also called visitandines, *these small almond cakes were invented by nuns in the Middle Ages. They are called* financiers *because they had a huge success in the nineteenth century among financiers, who loved the fact that they could always have some in their pocket at the stock exchange.*

INGREDIENTS | SERVES 12 *FINANCIERS*

1 vanilla pod
15 tablespoons butter, divided
6 egg whites
½ cup flour
7 tablespoons almond flour
⅓ cup powdered sugar

Gold Bars or Muffin Pan?

Financiers are usually rectangular (some people say they were shaped like that to make them look like gold bars!), but in the United States they are easier to make with a muffin pan.

1. Preheat the oven to 450°F. Slice the top outer layer of the vanilla pod in half lengthwise. In a small saucepan, heat 14 tablespoons butter and the sliced vanilla pod over low heat, and remove from heat when the butter has melted. Reserve.

2. Put the egg whites in the bowl of a stand mixer. Start whisking them slowly for 1 minute, then add the flour, almond flour, and sugar, and whisk steadily.

3. Take the vanilla pod out of the saucepan, open it, put it on a flat surface, and scrape the inside of the pod with a paring knife. Add to the batter, with the butter, and whisk until completely combined.

4. Butter the muffin pan with 1 tablespoon butter, and pour batter in each hole. Bake for 10 minutes.

5. Using a knife, take cakes out of the pan immediately, and let them cool down.

Madeleines (Butter Cakes)

Created in Lorraine, in the East of France, these small delicious cakes are now famous all over the world. No wonder! They are delicious.

INGREDIENTS | SERVES ABOUT A DOZEN MADELEINES

7 tablespoons butter, diced, at room temperature

2 large eggs

1 egg yolk

½ cup sugar

½ teaspoon baking powder

1 cup flour

1. In a small saucepan, melt the butter over very low heat. As soon as it melts, remove from heat and reserve. Preheat the oven to 350°F.

2. In a large bowl, whisk 2 eggs and the egg yolk with the sugar. You can use a fork or a whisk. Add the baking powder, whisking continuously, and add the flour very slowly. Add the butter, and whisk again until smooth. Put in the refrigerator for 2 hours.

3. Butter the Madeleine pan if you have the steel version (the modern silicone version is better), and pour the batter in each hole ¾ way up. Bake for 13 minutes.

4. Unmold them as soon as they are out of the oven. Cool on a rack. Serve alone, with tea, or applesauce.

Vrais Macarons (Almond Cookies)

Flavorful and colorful, Parisian macarons are all the rage, but they were at first very simple and delicious small almond cookies invented in the Basque country. Here is the authentic recipe.

INGREDIENTS | SERVES ABOUT 20 MACARONS

4 egg whites

¼ teaspoon salt

1¼ cups sugar

1 tablespoon orange blossom water

½ pound almond flour

1. Preheat your oven to 350°F.

2. Put the egg whites and the salt in the bowl of a stand mixer. First whisk at moderate speed for 1 minute, then add the sugar, orange blossom water, and the almond flour. Stop when the batter is combined.

3. Put a parchment paper sheet on a baking sheet. Using a spoon, take some of the batter (the size of a walnut), roll it with your hands, and press it on the parchment paper. They should be about 1¾" wide. Fill the pan, spacing the cookies well, and put in the oven for 15 minutes. Take the *macarons* out as soon as they start to get golden.

4. Let them cool down, and store in an airtight metallic box for at least one day before eating.

Cannelés

These wonderful, soft, and tasty tiny cakes were invented in Bordeaux, and only have two drawbacks: You need a cannelés pan, and the dough has to be prepared 24 hours in advance.

1. Slice top outer layer of the vanilla pod in half lengthwise. Put it in a small saucepan with the milk and 2 tablespoons butter. Bring to a boil slowly over medium-low heat. Turn off heat once it begins to boil.

2. Beat the eggs and the egg yolks in a small bowl very roughly with a fork. In a large bowl (or stand mixer) whisk the flour and the sugar, then add the eggs, whisking continuously. Take the vanilla pod out of the saucepan, open it, put it on a flat surface, and scrape the inside of the pod with a paring knife. Stir into the batter, and pour the milk slowly. Let it cool down, then add the rum. Cover and put in the refrigerator for 24 hours minimum (48 hours maximum).

3. Take the batter out of the refrigerator at least 1 hour before baking the *Cannelés*. Preheat the oven to 500°F. Butter the *Cannelé* molds if they are metallic (the silicone version is better). Pour the batter in each mold until each hole is ¾ full.

4. Bake for 11 minutes, then reduce the heat of the oven to 350°F, and bake for another hour. Wait for them to cool down before unmolding.

5. Serve with tea or Champagne.

Roses des Sables (Chocolate and Cornflake Cookies)

These "desert roses" look like the desert jewel, and they are delicious! A very easy recipe to make with kids.

INGREDIENTS | SERVES 6

¾ cup butter

7 ounces dark chocolate chips

½ cup powdered sugar

5 ounces cornflakes, unsweetened

1. Fill a small saucepan with the butter and the chocolate chips. Melt slowly over very low heat. Stir continuously with a wooden spoon until the chocolate and the butter are totally melted. Pour in the powdered sugar, stir until the mixture is perfectly smooth, and remove from heat.

2. In a large bowl, put the unsweetened cornflakes. Pour the chocolate sauce on them, and stir with the wooden spoon until all flakes are covered in chocolate. Put a parchment paper sheet on a baking sheet. Using 2 spoons, take a spoonful of chocolate flakes and make small mounds of about 2". Lay them on the parchment paper. Put in the refrigerator for 1 hour.

3. Serve with a glass of milk.

Croquants aux Amandes (Almond *Croquants*)

A traditional recipe from Provence, Almond Croquants can be stored for a very long time.

INGREDIENTS | SERVES 6

2 large eggs

¾ cup sugar

2 cups flour

¼ teaspoon salt

9 tablespoons almonds

1. In the bowl of a stand mixer, whisk the eggs and the sugar until the mixture whitens. Whisk continuously and add the flour and the salt. Add the almonds, stir with a spoon, and put in the refrigerator 1 hour.

2. Preheat your oven to 325°F. Put a parchment paper on a baking sheet and put the batter on it, shaped into a 2"-wide loaf. Bake for 35 minutes. Cut in ½" slices as soon as you take it out of the oven. Lay the slices on the paper, and bake again for 10 minutes on each side.

3. Cool down and store in a metallic box.

Meringues

Meringues made French pastry famous all over the world, and they are extremely easy to make! Be careful not to have any egg yolks mixed with the egg whites; it will prevent them from whipping up. Never use "fake" sweetener. This recipe calls for the real deal.

INGREDIENTS | SERVES 4

6 egg whites
½ teaspoon salt
1½ cups sugar
½ cup powdered sugar

Budget Friendly

Many pastry recipes call for only egg yolks, so this recipe is perfect to use the leftover egg whites. They are actually easier to use after one or two days. Store them in an airtight container in the refrigerator. Take them out of the refrigerator one hour before cooking, to bring them to room temperature.

1. Preheat your oven to 200°F.

2. Put the egg whites and the salt in the bowl of a stand mixer. First whisk at moderate speed for 1 minute. Then add the sugar, tablespoon by tablespoon, increasing the speed of the mixer, until the egg whites are very firm. They must be smooth and shiny.

3. Put a parchment paper sheet on a baking sheet. Fill a pastry bag with the egg whites, and pipe small round shapes onto the sheet. You can also use two spoons to shape them. Space them well so they can inflate easily. Sprinkle powdered sugar on them. Put in the oven and bake for 90 minutes. They should dry out, but not get brown.

4. Let them cool down before serving. You can store the meringues for a week in a metallic box.

CHAPTER 19

Gâteaux (Cakes)

Gâteau Basque (Basque Cake)

Basque Cake is a great traditional gâteau, and at the same time is very simple and delicious.

INGREDIENTS | SERVES 6

½ cup plus 1 tablespoon butter, diced and at room temperature

¾ cup plus ⅔ cup sugar, divided

2½ cups plus ⅓ cup flour, divided

1 tablespoon baking powder

5 large eggs, divided

1 teaspoon salt

4 tablespoons rum, divided

2 cups whole milk

1 egg yolk

Different Fillings

The other classical *Gâteau Basque* filling is black cherry jam. Of course you can try it with other jams, like apricot or blueberry.

1. In a large bowl, stir ½ cup butter with a wooden spoon until it's soft. Stir continuously as you add ¾ cup sugar, 2½ cups flour, the baking powder, 2 eggs, salt, and 2 tablespoons of rum. Stop when the dough is combined and can be shaped in a large ball. Refrigerate for 1 hour.

2. Meanwhile, prepare the cream. In a medium saucepan, bring the milk to a boil over medium-low heat. In a bowl, whisk 3 eggs and ⅔ cup sugar, then add ⅓ cup flour. When they are perfectly combined, add half of the warm milk. Whisk firmly together, then pour everything back in the saucepan, with the rest of the milk. Whisk continuously as you bring to a boil over medium heat, for 3–4 minutes. Add the rest of the rum, stir, and stop the heat. Let the cream cool down to room temperature.

3. Preheat the oven to 350°F. Butter a 9"-round springform pan. Put half of the dough at the bottom, and press it lightly onto the bottom and up the side of the pan. Pour the cream on it. Roll the rest of the dough into a 9" circle, and put it on top. Press gently to seal the edges. Using a fork, lightly score the top in a diamond pattern. Brush it with the egg yolk. Bake for 40 minutes.

4. Eat cold the next day.

Far Breton (Prune Cake)

This prune and egg cake is a classic in Brittany.

INGREDIENTS | SERVES 6

3 tablespoons rum
½ cup water
25 pitted prunes
1 vanilla pod
4 cups whole milk
6 large eggs
¾ cup sugar
2 cups flour
½ teaspoon salt
1 tablespoon butter

No Alcohol

If you want to avoid alcohol, you can marinate the prunes in 1 cup black tea. Some also make this recipe with raisins.

1. In a small bowl, combine the rum with ½ cup water, and marinate the prunes in it for at least 1 hour.

2. Slice the top outer layer of the vanilla pod in half lengthwise. In a medium saucepan, bring the milk and the vanilla pod to a boil over moderate heat. When it starts to boil, remove from the heat. Take the vanilla pod out, and scrape the inside with a paring knife. Put the seeds back in the warm milk. Let them infuse for 10 minutes.

3. In a medium bowl, beat the eggs and the sugar until the mixture whitens. In a large bowl, pour the flour and the salt, and add half of the egg and sugar mixture. Whisk, and slowly add the rest of the egg and sugar mixture. Once the batter is smooth, add the warm milk. Whisk continuously until it's combined.

4. Preheat the oven at 350°F. Butter a round 9" × 2" high baking dish. Drain the prunes. Pour the batter in the baking dish, then add the prunes, spreading them evenly. Put in the oven for 45 minutes, or until the top is golden. Let it cool down.

5. Serve in large 2" squares, lukewarm or cold.

Gâteau de Savoie (Savoie Cake)

This cake is a classic from Savoie, in the Alps. It's extremely light and airy, and is served in renowned restaurants like Le Grand Véfour in Paris.

INGREDIENTS | SERVES 6

3 large eggs, yolks and egg whites separated

7 tablespoons sugar

2 teaspoons baking powder

7 tablespoons cornstarch

½ teaspoon salt

1 tablespoon butter

1. Preheat the oven at 350°F. In a large bowl, whisk the egg yolks and the sugar until the mixture whitens. Stir continuously as you add the baking powder, and then the cornstarch, tablespoon by tablespoon.

2. In the bowl of a stand mixer, whisk the egg whites and the salt steadily, until they are very firm. Add ⅓ of the whites to the batter, folding them in slowly and gently. Add the other ⅔ the same way, very slowly.

3. Butter a 9" round baking dish. Pour the batter in it. Bake for 40 minutes.

4. Unmold immediately, and let it cool down. Sprinkle powdered sugar on top.

Gâteau de Savoie aux Framboises (Raspberry Savoie Cake)

Gâteau de Savoie is also a great basis for other French cakes, like this one, with Chantilly Cream (see recipe in Chapter 22) and raspberries.

INGREDIENTS | SERVES 6

½ pound fresh raspberries

1 Gâteau de Savoie (see recipe in this chapter)

1 cup Chantilly Cream (see recipe in Chapter 22)

1. Wash the raspberries and dry them softly.

2. Wait for the *Gâteau de Savoie* to be cold, and slice it lengthwise across the middle to make two layers. Spread half the Chantilly on the bottom half, and scatter ⅔ of the raspberries all over the cream. Put the other half back on top, and spread the rest of the cream all over the top. Decorate with the rest of the raspberries.

3. Put in the refrigerator for 3 hours before serving.

Gâteau Alexandra (Alexandra Cake)

This is a very simple and delicious chocolate cake filled with apricot jam.

INGREDIENTS | SERVES 6

11 tablespoons butter, divided

11 ounces dark chocolate, divided

⅔ cup cornstarch

2 tablespoons flour

½ cup plus ⅔ cup sugar, divided

1 teaspoon baking powder

½ cup almond flour

4 large eggs, beaten

½ jar of apricot jam (about 5 ounces)

1 tablespoon cold water

¾ cup icing sugar

No Alcohol

You can skip the rum if you want. Just melt the chocolate and the butter together. You can also skip the icing and just spread apricot jam on top.

1. Preheat the oven to 400°F. In a small saucepan over low heat, slowly melt 7 tablespoons of butter with 7 ounces chocolate, and add the rum. Using a wooden spoon, stir until smooth. Remove from the heat and reserve.

2. In a large bowl, whisk the cornstarch, flour, ½ cup sugar, baking powder, and almond flour. Beat the eggs in a smaller bowl, then add them to the large bowl. Whisk continuously, and add the melted chocolate. Use a wooden spoon to stir slowly until the batter is smooth. Butter a regular round 9" baking dish. Pour the mixture in it. Bake for 30 minutes.

3. Wait for the cake to cool, then cut it lengthwise across the middle into two layers. Spread apricot jam all over the inside. Then put the top on, and spread apricot jam on the top.

4. In a small saucepan over very low heat, melt 4 tablespoons butter with 4 ounces dark chocolate and 1 tablespoon of cold water. Stir continuously with a wooden spoon, and add the icing sugar slowly. When fully incorporated, spread it all over the top of the cake.

5. Refrigerate before serving.

Gâteau Chocomarron (Chocolate and Chestnut Cream Cake)

Chocolate and chestnut cream make a delicious combination. Great in winter, or all year long if you have jars of French Crème de Marrons. And it's gluten free!

INGREDIENTS | SERVES 8

½ cup plus 1 tablespoon butter, divided

3.5 ounces dark chocolate

¼ teaspoon salt

3 large eggs

1 pound *Crème de Marrons* (chestnut cream, in a jar or following the recipe in Chapter 2)

1. Preheat the oven to 350°F. In a small saucepan over low heat, slowly melt ½ cup butter with the chocolate (you can also melt it in a *bain-marie*, putting a larger saucepan of water under the small saucepan). Add the salt. Using a wooden spoon, stir until smooth. Remove from heat and reserve.

2. In a large bowl, whisk the eggs. Add the *Crème de Marrons*, then the chocolate and butter mixture, and use a wooden spoon to stir until smooth. Butter a meatloaf pan with 1 tablespoon butter. Pour the mixture in it. Bake for 45 minutes.

3. Unmold and serve in thin slices, plain or with a *Crème Anglaise* (see recipe in Chapter 22).

Fondant Au Chocolat (Almost Flourless Chocolate Cake)

This is an almost flourless chocolate cake that is as tasty as it is easy to bake.

INGREDIENTS | SERVES 8

⅔ cup salted butter

7 ounces dark chocolate, 60% cocoa minimum

3 large eggs

¾ cup sugar

½ cup flour

1. Preheat the oven to 350°F. In a small saucepan over low heat, slowly melt the butter with the chocolate (you can even make it in a *bain-marie* by putting a larger saucepan of water under the small saucepan). Using a wooden spoon, stir until smooth, then remove from heat and let it cool.

2. In a medium bowl, whisk the eggs, then pour them in a larger bowl. Add the sugar, whisk continuously, then add the melted chocolate and butter. Add the flour slowly, and whisk until smooth. Butter a 9" round springform pan. Pour the mixture in it. Bake for 25 minutes.

3. Serve plain or with a *Crème Anglaise* (see recipe in Chapter 22).

Choux à la Crème (Cream Puffs)

Who doesn't love cream puffs? They are delicious, and a classic French pastry. Mastering how to make the dough, the famous pâte à choux, *is essential to make a lot of French pastries.*

INGREDIENTS | SERVES 6

⅓ cup water

¼ cup whole milk

⅓ cup butter, diced, at room temperature

½ teaspoon salt

1 teaspoon sugar

¾ cup flour

3 large eggs

1 batch of *Crème Pâtissière* (see recipe in Chapter 22)

½ cup powdered sugar

A Renaissance Legacy

The first *petits choux*, pastry puffs, were created in France by Popelini, who was Queen Catherine de Medici's pastry chef. At the time, he served his puffs filled with jam.

1. Preheat the oven to 400°F. In a medium saucepan, add the water, milk, butter, salt, and sugar, and bring to a boil over medium-high heat. Stir constantly with a wooden spoon.

2. Remove saucepan from heat as soon as it boils. Stirring continuously, add the flour. Stir firmly until the dough is elastic and doesn't stick to the bottom of the saucepan anymore. Place the pan back on low heat for 2 minutes, and stir continuously. Remove from heat.

3. In a large bowl, pour the flour and milk mixture, and stir in the eggs one by one. Stir continuously until the dough is combined.

4. Put a parchment paper sheet on a baking sheet. Using a pastry bag, or just two teaspoons, shape small mounds of dough (about 1" wide) and space them well on the parchment paper, about ½" apart. Bake for 10 minutes, then reduce the temperature to 350°F and bake for another 10 minutes.

5. Once baked, and while they're still hot, cut off the top of each puff, one-third of the way down. Using a pastry bag or a teaspoon, fill the inside with *Crème Patissière*, and put the top back on.

6. Sprinkle with powdered sugar before serving.

Profiteroles au Chocolat (Chocolate Profiteroles)

This might be the best way to enjoy a pastry puff! Profiteroles au Chocolat combine the airy magic of puffs with chocolate and Chantilly Cream (see recipe in Chapter 22).

INGREDIENTS | SERVES 4

⅓ cup water

¼ cup whole milk

⅓ cup plus 3 tablespoon butter, diced, at room temperature

½ teaspoon salt

1 teaspoon sugar

¾ cup flour

3 large eggs

½ cup whipping cream

½ pound dark chocolate

1 pound *Crème Chantilly* (see recipe in Chapter 22)

Profiteroles à la Mode

You can also fill the *choux* with vanilla ice cream. Pour the hot chocolate sauce on the rolls at the last minute.

1. Preheat the oven to 400°F. In a medium saucepan, add water, milk, ⅓ cup butter, salt, and sugar, and bring to a boil over medium-high heat. Stir constantly with a wooden spoon.

2. Remove saucepan from heat as soon as it boils, stir continuously, and pour in all the flour. Stir firmly until it's elastic and doesn't stick to the bottom of the saucepan anymore. Put pan back on low heat for 2 minutes, stirring continuously. Then remove from heat. In a large bowl, pour the flour and milk mixture, and stir in the eggs, one by one. Stir continuously until the dough is combined.

3. Put a parchment paper sheet on a baking sheet. Using a pastry bag, or just two teaspoons, shape small mounds of dough (about 1" wide) and space them well on the parchment paper, at least ½" apart. Bake for 10 minutes, then reduce the temperature to 350°F and bake for another 10 minutes. Once baked, remove from the oven.

4. In a small saucepan, bring the whipping cream to a boil over medium-high heat. When it starts to boil, reduce the heat to low and add the chocolate. Stir until the chocolate has melted into the cream and remove from the heat.

5. Cut off the top of each puff one-third of the way down. Using a pastry bag or a teaspoon, fill the inside with *Crème Chantilly*, and put the top back on.

6. Pour chocolate sauce on each Chantilly puff. Serve immediately.

Paris-Brest (Cream Pastry Ring)

This large ring of choux pastry filled with cream was invented by a pastry chef who wanted to celebrate a famous bicycle race that ran from Paris to Brest. That's why it's shaped like a bicycle wheel.

INGREDIENTS | SERVES 6

⅓ cup water

¼ cup whole milk

⅓ cup plus 3 tablespoons butter, diced, at room temperature

½ teaspoon salt

1 teaspoon sugar

¾ cup flour

3 large eggs

3 tablespoons sliced almonds

1 cup *Crème Chantilly* (see recipe in Chapter 22)

1 cup *Crème Pâtissière* (see recipe in Chapter 22)

1 cup powdered sugar

Do Not Over-Bake

If the top of this cake turns golden too early, put aluminum foil on top of it to protect it until the cooking time is over.

1. In a medium saucepan over medium-high heat, put the water, the milk, ⅓ cup butter, salt, and sugar, and bring to a boil. Stir constantly with a wooden spoon. Remove saucepan from heat as soon as it boils, stir continuously, and pour in the flour. Stir firmly until it's elastic and doesn't stick to the bottom of the saucepan anymore. Put pan back on low heat for 2 minutes, and stir continuously. Remove from heat.

2. Preheat the oven to 350°F. In a large bowl, pour the flour and milk mixture, and add the eggs, one by one. Stir continuously until the dough is combined.

3. Put a parchment paper sheet over a baking sheet. Using a pencil, draw a 9"-diameter circle on the paper. Fill a pastry bag with the dough and pipe a circle, following the line you just drew; the line of pastry should be ½" wide. Pipe another circle inside the first one; they should touch one another. Then pipe another circle on top of the two others. Sprinkle the sliced almonds over the circles. Put in the oven for 30 minutes.

4. Let the pastry ring cool down, then slice it in half lengthwise through the middle to make two layers. In a medium bowl, slowly fold the *Crème Chantilly* into the cold *Crème Pâtissiere*. Fill a pastry bag fitted with star tip and pipe onto the bottom layer of the pastry. Carefully put back the other part of ring on top.

5. Sprinkle powdered sugar over the pastry before serving.

Gâteau Nantais (Almond and Rum Cake)

This almond and rum cake was invented at the beginning of the twentieth century in Nantes in the west of France, and was developed by the same company that created the famous cookies Petits Beurres.

INGREDIENTS | SERVES 6

½ pound plus 1 tablespoon
  salted butter, diced and at room
  temperature, divided
1½ cups sugar
⅔ cup flour
1⅓ cups almond flour
6 large eggs
¾ cup rum, divided
⅓ cup powdered sugar

Long Storage

The original recipe of *Gâteau Nantais* was famous for having a very long shelf life, of about three to four weeks. The present recipe calls for eggs, and can't be stored for as long, but it's tastier on the third or fourth day. The more you wait, the more you'll pick up the subtle taste of rum.

1. Preheat the oven to 350°F.

2. In a large bowl, stir the ½ pound butter using a wooden spoon until it's smooth, and slowly add the sugar, the flour, and the almond flour.

3. In a medium bowl, whisk the eggs steadily, then pour them in the large bowl. Stir continuously, then add ¼ cup rum. Whisk until the mixture is smooth and combined. Butter a 9"-round springform pan with 1 tablespoon butter. Pour the batter in it, and bake for 40 minutes.

4. As soon as you take the cake out of the oven, pour ¼ cup rum over it. Let it cool down, then prepare the icing.

5. In a small bowl, stir ¼ cup rum with the powdered sugar. Spread on top of the cake.

6. Serve cold, preferably the next day.

Bûche de Noël (Christmas Log)

There's no Christmas in France without the traditional Bûche de Noël. It means "Christmas log," and pastry chefs can spend hours making it look like a real wood log. It is a symbol of the burning fire that unites and warms everybody up during the holidays.

INGREDIENTS | SERVES 6

8 large eggs, divided
½ cup plus ⅔ cup sugar, divided
½ cup cornstarch
½ cup flour
4.5 ounces dark chocolate
½ pound butter, diced, at room temperature
2 egg yolks
⅔ cup powdered sugar

All Year Cake!

This recipe is great all year round. Substitute the buttercream with jam, like raspberry jam, for example, and roll your cake following the recipe. A kids' favorite to eat and to make!

1. Preheat the oven to 400°F.

2. Break 6 eggs and separate the yolks and whites. Put the egg yolks in a large bowl, and the egg whites in the bowl of a stand mixer. Whisk the whites steadily for 1 minute, then very slowly add the ½ cup sugar.

3. In the large bowl, whisk the 6 egg yolks, then slowly add the cornstarch and the flour. Add the egg whites slowly, folding them gently into the batter.

4. Prepare the cream: In a small saucepan, melt the chocolate by melting it in a *bain-marie*: Put the small saucepan over a larger saucepan filled with water, over low heat. Let it cool down. In another large bowl, stir ⅔ cup butter using a wooden spoon until smooth. Break two eggs in the bowl, add the 2 egg yolks, and whisk steadily. Add the powdered sugar and the melted chocolate. Whisk until smooth and combined. Reserve.

5. Put a parchment paper sheet on a rimmed baking sheet. Spread the batter all over the parchment paper, using a wooden spoon to make sure it is evenly spread. Bake for 5 minutes.

6. Put the cake, still on its parchment paper, on your kitchen counter. Cover it with plastic wrap so that it doesn't dry out. Let it cool down.

7. Take the plastic off, and spread ⅔ of the chocolate cream over the whole surface. Using your two hands, roll the cake over into a log shape. Spread the rest of the chocolate cream on the sides of the cake.

8. Refrigerate 24 hours before serving.

Galette des Rois (Kings Cake)

A tradition in France for Epiphany, Galette des Rois is eaten all over the country on the first Sunday of January and for the following weeks.

INGREDIENTS | SERVES 6

⅓ cup butter, diced and at room temperature

1 egg

½ cup almond flour

⅓ cup sugar

1 tablespoon orange blossom water

2 puff pastry sheets or 1 batch of *Pâte Feuilletée* (see recipe in Chapter 22)

1 egg yolk, beaten

Who Is the King?

You should traditionally add a *fève* to this cake. Once a dried bean, it is now a small ceramic figurine placed in the cake. Whoever gets the *fève* is crowned king or queen and must invite everybody for the next *galette*.

1. In the bowl of a stand mixer, whisk the butter and the egg until the mixture is smooth. Add the almond flour, the sugar, and the orange blossom water. Whisk until everything is smooth.

2. Roll out the pastry sheets. Cut out two large 10" circles from the pastry. Put a parchment paper sheet on a baking sheet. Put one puff pastry round on the parchment paper. Spread the almond mixture on it, making sure to leave 1 inch around the rim bare. Add the *fève*, if you have one.

3. Using a pastry brush, moisten the rim of the bottom pastry circle with cold water. Cover with the second round of puff pastry. Glue the two pastry sheets together by pressing them and folding the edge under. Using a pastry brush, brush the egg yolk all over the top of the cake. Use the tip of a knife to draw lines on it, in a diamond pattern. Put in the refrigerator for 1 hour (24 hours is best).

4. Preheat the oven to 400°F. Cook the *galette* for 30 minutes, then reduce the oven heat to 350°F for 10 minutes.

5. Serve warm, but the *galette* is also very good cold, the next day.

Gourmandise au Café (Coffee Cake)

This refreshing coffee cake is perfect if you don't have an oven. It doesn't require any baking! It calls for a very French cookie that can now be found in the United States called Petits Beurres. Note that this cake contains uncooked egg.

INGREDIENTS | SERVES 6

12 ounces *Petit Beurre* cookies

¾ cup butter, diced, at room temperature

1 egg

1 egg yolk

1⅓ cups powdered sugar

1½ cups black coffee, cooled

1 cup *Crème Chantilly*, for decoration (see recipe in Chapter 22)

A Very French Cookie

The *Petit Beurre* cookie was invented in 1886 in Nantes by a manufacturer, Louis Lefèvre-Utile, who has since managed to sell his butter cookies all over the world. One billion cookies are made each year. French connoisseurs will always eat it the same way: first the 4 "ears" (the 4 corners), then the rest of the cookie!

1. Put the *Petit Beurre* cookies in a blender, and process until they turn into a very fine powder.

2. In a medium bowl, use a wooden spoon to stir the butter until it is smooth. Reserve.

3. In a large bowl, pour the *Petit Beurre* powder and make a small well in the center, like a volcano crater. Break the egg into the hole, add the egg yolk, the sugar, and the softened butter. Stir continuously until smooth, then slowly pour in the coffee. Beat the entire mixture until it's completely combined.

4. Put a parchment paper inside a meatloaf pan, and pour the mixture into it. Put in the refrigerator for 24 hours.

5. Unmold 5 minutes before serving, and decorate with *Crème Chantilly*. Serve very cold.

Millefeuille (Napoleon Pastry)

Don't try to buy a Napoleon in a French pastry shop! The actual French name is millefeuille, which is much more poetic: it means a thousand layers.

INGREDIENTS | SERVES 6

2 puff pastry sheets or 1 batch of the *Pâte Feuilletée* (see recipe in Chapter 22)

2 tablespoons sugar

⅓ cup powdered sugar

½ cup *Crème Pâtissière* (see recipe in Chapter 22)

½ cup *Crème Chantilly* (see recipe in Chapter 22)

1. Roll out the pastry sheets, and cut them in 6 rectangles of 3" × 8". Put them in the fridge for 30 minutes. Preheat your oven to 450°F.

2. Put the pastry sheets on a parchment paper–lined baking sheet. Sprinkle with sugar and place a second baking tray on top. This will stop the pastry from rising too much, and help it keep a nice, even shape. As soon as you put them in the oven, reduce the heat to 375°F. After 7 minutes, cover the pastry with another baking sheet on top, and leave in the oven for another 10 minutes. Take them out of the oven, remove the paper on top, sprinkle the powdered sugar over them all, and put back in the oven for 5 minutes. Take out of the oven and let them cool down.

3. In a medium bowl, gently fold the *Crème Chantilly* into the *Crème Pâtissière*, until the two are mixed.

4. Very carefully cut each cooked pastry rectangle into 3 equal pieces. Lay a first piece on a serving dessert plate. Spread a nice layer of cream on it. Add another piece of puffed pastry, spread cream on it, and top with a last piece of puff pastry. Repeat for the 5 other *Millefeuilles* and sprinkle powdered sugar on top of all.

5. Serve immediately.

Gâteau d'Ananas (Pineapple Cake)

An easy pineapple cake with a nice pineapple sugar syrup. This is great to make at any time of the year. The recipe calls for canned pineapple, so you don't need pineapple to be in season to make it.

INGREDIENTS | SERVES 6

⅓ cup plus 1 tablespoon butter, divided
2 eggs
½ cup plus 5 tablespoons sugar, divided
¼ teaspoon salt
6 ounces *crème fraîche* or
 whipping cream
1½ cups flour
3 teaspoons baking powder
1 (14-ounce) can sliced pineapple

1. Preheat the oven to 300°F.

2. In a small saucepan over low heat, slowly melt ⅓ cup butter. Remove from heat and let it cool down.

3. Break the eggs into the bowl of a stand mixer. Add ½ cup sugar and the salt, and whisk steadily for 2 minutes, until the mixture whitens. Add the cream and the flour, whisking continuously, and add the melted butter and the baking powder. Stop when the mixture is really smooth and combined.

4. Put a strainer over a medium bowl, and drain the pineapples in it. Reserve the pineapple juice. Butter a 9" round pan, and pour the batter in it. Add the slices of pineapple on top of the batter. Put in the oven and cook for 45 minutes.

5. In a small saucepan, pour the pineapple juice, add 5 tablespoons sugar, stir well, and bring to a boil over medium-high heat. Reduce to about half. When the cake is done, remove from oven and pour the pineapple syrup on it.

6. Unmold and put upside down. Serve cold.

CHAPTER 20

Crèmes, Mousses, et Entremets
(Creams, Mousses, and Desserts)

Crème Renversée (Cream Reversed)

This is a cream that you must serve upside down. As you unmold it, the caramel drips down the top. Kids love it!

INGREDIENTS | SERVES 6

1 vanilla pod
4 cups whole milk
1¾ cups sugar, divided
4 tablespoons water
5 large eggs
3 egg yolks

1. Preheat your oven to 300°F.

2. Slice the top outer layer of the vanilla pod in half lengthwise. In a medium saucepan over medium heat, bring the milk and the vanilla pod to a boil. As soon as the milk boils, stop the heat. Cover and let the vanilla infuse with the milk.

3. In a small saucepan, warm ¾ cup sugar and the water over moderate heat. Stir continuously. When it starts to boil, raise the heat to high until the sugar gets almost golden brown. Pour the caramel into 6 round ramekins or ceramic pots of about 2" in diameter. Tilt them in order to distribute the caramel evenly across the bottom.

4. In a medium bowl, whisk the eggs, the egg yolks, and 1 cup sugar steadily, until the mixture whitens. Take the vanilla pod out of the saucepan, scrape the inside, and put the seeds back in the milk. Pour the milk into the egg and sugar mixture, constantly whisking. Let it cool for 10 minutes. Using a spoon, remove the surface foam. Pour in the ceramic pots.

5. In a large shallow baking pan, pour cold water to a depth of ⅔" high. Place the ramekins in it and bake in the oven for 45 minutes. Take the ramekins out, let them cool, and cover them with plastic wrap. Refrigerate for 12 hours.

6. Eat cold the next day, unmolding each *crème* onto separate dessert plates.

Crème Brûlée

Crème Brûlée is so good that its name is now famous all over the world! But don't be misled by its pompous French name: It's not that difficult to make. It is always a great hit at the dinner table.

INGREDIENTS | SERVES 4

4 egg yolks
½ cup sugar
1 vanilla pod
¾ cup whole milk
1 cup whipping cream
⅓ cup brown sugar

Know When It's Ready

Cooking a *Crème Brûlée* can take a long time, but how long will vary depending on your oven. You will know that the custard is ready if it doesn't shake anymore when you try to move it.

1. Preheat your oven to 225°F.

2. In a large bowl, slightly whisk the egg yolks with ½ cup sugar. Slice the top outer layer of the vanilla pod in half lengthwise. Using a teaspoon, scrape the seeds out and put them in the large bowl. Add the milk. Whisk again to combine everything, then whisk continuously as you slowly pour in the whipping cream.

3. Once the custard is combined and smooth, pour it in 6-ounce ramekins or custard cups. Put in the oven and bake for 1 hour. Take them out of the oven, let them cool down at room temperature, and then put them in the fridge for at least 4 hours.

4. When it is 15 minutes before serving, preheat your oven to broil. Take the custard cups out of the refrigerator and sprinkle brown sugar on each of them. Put them under the broiler for 2 minutes before serving, and take them out as soon as the brown sugar starts to caramelize.

5. Serve immediately.

Pots de Crème au Chocolat (Chocolate Cream Pots)

Petits pots de crème are small pots of custard that you serve at the end of the meal. They make a light dessert, and are perfect after a heavy meal.

INGREDIENTS | SERVES 8

2 cups whole milk
5 egg yolks
⅓ cup sugar
½ pound dark chocolate chips

1. Preheat the oven to 300°F. In a shallow baking dish, pour cold water to a depth of 1" and place it in the oven.

2. In a medium saucepan on medium heat, warm the milk. It should be very warm, but never boil. Stop the heat and cover when it starts to bubble.

3. In the bowl of a stand mixer, whisk the egg yolks and add the sugar. Whisk steadily until the mixture whitens. Pour ⅓ of the warm milk into the bowl, and whisk continuously until well combined. Then pour the whole mixture back in the saucepan containing the rest of the warm milk.

4. Warm the egg and milk mixture over medium-low heat. Using a wooden spoon, stir continuously until the mixture is smooth. Remove from heat and reserve.

5. In a large bowl, put the chocolate chips. Put a colander on top and drain the egg and milk mixture through it. Using a whisk, whisk the contents of the bowl slightly until the chocolate melts. Spoon off the foam at the surface. Ladle the mixture into ramekins, then put the ramekins in the shallow baking dish in the oven. Bake for 30 minutes. Let it cool down at room temperature and then refrigerate for 2 hours before serving.

6. Serve cold.

Petite Crèmes Légères au Thé (Tea-Flavored Custard)

What's better for tea than a pot of delicious tea-flavored cream? This recipe is also better for your waistline: It's trying to be the lowest-fat it can!

INGREDIENTS | SERVES 4

1¾ cups skimmed milk

1 green tea teabag

2 large eggs

1 egg yolk

2 tablespoons raw sugar

Choose Your Tea

You can make this recipe with matcha green tea, but also with different kinds of flavored tea, like Earl Grey or a Christmas spice tea during the holidays.

1. Preheat your oven to 350°F. In a shallow baking dish, pour cold water to a depth of 1" and place it in the oven.

2. In a small saucepan, bring the milk to a boil over medium heat. Once the milk has reached the boiling point, remove from heat and put the teabag in it. Cover and let it infuse for 5 minutes.

3. Put the eggs and the egg yolk in the bowl of a stand mixer. Add the sugar and whisk until the mixture whitens. Take the teabag out of the milk, and slowly pour the milk into the egg and sugar mixture. Whisk continuously until the custard is fluid.

4. Ladle the tea custard into ceramic ramekins. Put them in the shallow baking dish in the oven, making sure the water only comes to halfway up the side of the ramekin (not more). Put in the oven for 20 minutes. Then take them out, leave them at room temperature, and refrigerate at least 2 hours before serving.

5. Serve with *Langues de Chat* or *Petits Sablés* (see recipes in Chapter 18).

Œufs au Lait (Eggs and Milk)

This very simple egg and milk recipe was a favorite of French farmers' wives, who always had milk and eggs at home, and could improvise a last-minute dessert for unexpected guests.

INGREDIENTS | SERVES 6

1 vanilla pod
4 cups whole milk
6 medium eggs
¾ cup sugar

Go Raw

The traditional recipe calls for raw milk, "almost" straight out of the cow. If you are lucky enough to have some, don't forget to boil it once first and skim out the film that will appear when it cools down.

1. Preheat your oven to 350°F.

2. Slice the top outer layer of the vanilla pod in half lengthwise. In a medium saucepan, bring the milk and the vanilla pod to a boil over medium heat. As soon as the milk boils, stop the heat. Cover and let the vanilla infuse the milk.

3. In a large bowl, break the eggs and whisk them steadily with the sugar. Take the vanilla out of the milk saucepan, use a teaspoon to scrape out all the seeds, and put them all back in the milk. Pour the milk slowly in the eggs and sugar, whisking continuously until combined. Pour in a large rectangular baking dish (9" × 13"; a lasagna dish, for example).

4. Put in the oven for 45 minutes. The *Œufs au Lait* are ready when you can dip a knife in it and the blade comes out clean. A slight golden crust should appear.

5. Serve lukewarm or cold.

Flan Parisien (Parisian Flan)

This egg custard pie is also a great snack for kids at quatre-heures, the 4 P.M. traditional snack time.

INGREDIENTS | SERVES 6

1 *Pâte Brisée* crust (see recipe in Chapter 22)

1 vanilla pod

3 cups whole milk

2 large eggs

½ cup sugar

8 tablespoons cornstarch

Prune Flan

You can also make this recipe with ½ pound prunes. Lay them at the bottom of the crust before pouring the custard in.

1. Preheat your oven to 400°F.

2. Roll out your *Pâte Brisée* into a 13" disc. Butter a 12" tart pan, and put the crust on it. Fold overhanging dough under, and crimp the edge of the crust. Reserve in the refrigerator.

3. Slice the top outer layer of the vanilla pod in half lengthwise. In a large saucepan, slowly bring the milk and the vanilla pod to a boil over medium-high heat. When it begins to boil, remove from heat. Using a teaspoon, scrape the inside of the pod, then put the seeds back in the milk. Cover and let vanilla infuse the milk for 10 minutes.

4. In a large bowl, break the eggs and whisk them steadily with the sugar. Add the cornstarch, combine well, then pour ⅓ of the warm milk in the bowl. Whisk continuously until combined, and pour back in the saucepan with the rest of the milk. Whisk continuously over medium-low heat until the first bubbles appear, then immediately take the saucepan off the heat.

5. Pour in the crust and bake for 35 minutes.

6. Let it cool down at room temperature, then refrigerate for 3 hours before serving.

Flognarde aux Poires (Fruit Custard Cake)

Flognarde is a typical fruit and egg custard cake created in the center of France. It can be made all year long, with in-season fruit. Here is a recipe with pears.

INGREDIENTS | SERVES 6

2 tablespoons butter, divided

3 medium pears, peeled, seeded, and thinly sliced

3 eggs

6 tablespoons brown sugar, divided

5 tablespoons flour

½ teaspoon baking powder

2 cups whole milk

Apple *Flognarde*

You can also make this recipe with 3 medium apples. Peel and slice them, then let them marinate in ⅓ cup rum for 1 hour. Lay them at the bottom of the crust before pouring the custard in. Cook as directed in this recipe.

1. Preheat your oven to 400°F.

2. Butter a medium baking dish with 1 tablespoon butter. Lay all the pears at the bottom of the dish.

3. In a large bowl, break the eggs and whisk them steadily with 5 tablespoons sugar. Add the flour and the baking powder. Whisk continuously until combined, then add the milk. Keep whisking until smooth then pour in the baking dish over the pears. Dice 1 tablespoon butter and sprinkle on top of the custard.

4. Put in the oven for 15 minutes, then reduce the heat to 350°F and cook again for 20 minutes. As soon as you take the dish out, sprinkle 1 tablespoon brown sugar all over the top.

5. Serve lukewarm.

Clafoutis aux Framboises (Raspberry Clafoutis)

Clafoutis is a favorite of summer desserts in France. This fruit and custard cake is typical of the Limousin area, and is very easy to make. A great recipe to bake with kids!

INGREDIENTS | SERVES 6

1 vanilla pod
1½ cups whole milk
½ cup plus 1 tablespoon butter, divided
6 large eggs
½ cup plus 1 tablespoon sugar, divided
12 ounces raspberries

All Year Recipe

You can also make this recipe with frozen raspberries, or any frozen berries, which makes it a perfect all-season last-minute dessert. Just add the berries frozen; no need to thaw. Cut in small 1½" squares. It also makes a great dessert for cocktail parties.

1. Preheat your oven to 350°F.

2. Slice the top outer layer of the vanilla pod in half lengthwise. In a medium saucepan, bring the milk and the vanilla pod to a boil over medium heat. As soon as the milk boils, stop the heat.

3. Put ½ cup butter in the saucepan. Take the vanilla pod out, use a teaspoon to scrape out the seeds inside, and put them back in the saucepan. Cover and let the vanilla infuse the milk.

4. In a large bowl, break the eggs and whisk them steadily with ½ cup sugar, until they whiten. Add the flour, and whisk steadily. Slowly add the milk as you whisk continuously.

5. Butter a medium baking dish (about 9") with 1 tablespoon butter. Sprinkle 1 tablespoon sugar at the bottom, and tilt the dish so as to distribute sugar everywhere. Lay the raspberries at the bottom of the dish. Pour in the custard.

6. Put in the oven for 45 minutes.

7. Serve lukewarm or cold.

Clafoutis aux Cerises (Cherry Clafoutis)

Such a simple recipe, and there are tons of different ways to make it. Here is another way to bake clafoutis with the most traditional fruit: cherries. It calls for almond flour, so this is a gluten-free dessert!

INGREDIENTS | SERVES 6

6 large eggs
⅔ cup, plus 1 tablespoon brown sugar
6 tablespoons almond flour
¾ cup whipping cream
1 tablespoon butter
2 tablespoons powdered sugar
2 pounds cherries

The Cherry Pit Controversy

If you want to start a huge debate at the table among your French guests, start talking about cherries in the *clafoutis*! Some will swear cherries have to be pitted, others that the pit adds all the flavor. If you have kids, don't even debate it: no pits.

1. Preheat your oven to 400°F.

2. In a large bowl, break the eggs and whisk them steadily with the brown sugar until they whiten (you can also use a stand mixer, but just with the hand whisk is fine). Add the almond flour, and whisk steadily. Slowly add the whipping cream as you whisk continuously. Stop whisking when the mixture is combined.

3. Butter a medium baking dish (9", for example). Sprinkle 1 tablespoon brown sugar at the bottom, and tilt the dish so as to distribute sugar everywhere. Lay the cherries at the bottom of the dish. Pour in the custard.

4. Put in the oven for 25 minutes. As soon as you take it out of the oven, sift a bit of powdered sugar on top. Let it cool down.

5. Serve lukewarm or cold.

Œufs à la Neige (Eggs in Snow)

The name of this recipe means "eggs in snow," because it features egg whites prepared as if they were snowballs or fluffy white clouds, bathed in Crème Anglaise.

INGREDIENTS | SERVES 4

3 egg whites

¼ teaspoon salt

1 cup sugar, divided

2 cups *Crème Anglaise* (see recipe in Chapter 22)

3 tablespoons water

No Waste Recipe

This recipe is a good way to use the egg whites that have not been used in the *Crème Anglaise* recipe in Chapter 22.

1. In the bowl of a stand mixer, whisk the egg whites and ¼ teaspoon salt. Start whisking slowly, then increase the speed as the egg whites start to get firmer. Slowly add ⅓ cup sugar, continuously whisking. Stop when the egg whites are very firm (you can test by putting a teaspoon in it; it should not fall).

2. Pour the *Crème Anglaise* in a large serving bowl. Prepare two clean cloths next to your burner.

3. Fill a large saucepan with water, and bring to a boil over high heat. When the water starts to boil, reduce the heat to medium. Scoop up 1 tablespoon of fluffy egg whites, and lay it on the simmering water. After a few seconds, turn the egg white over, then take it out of the pan and lay on the clean cloth to drain. Then put the egg white "snow" on the bowl of *Crème Anglaise*. Repeat until all the egg whites have been cooked.

4. In a small saucepan, preferably with a thick bottom, pour ⅔ cup sugar and add 3 tablespoons water, and place over moderate heat. Stir with a wooden spoon from time to time, until the sugar bubbles and turns golden. Pour the caramel immediately on the egg whites, in the bowl.

5. Serve cold.

Mousse au Chocolat (Chocolate Mousse)

Chocolate mousse is a French classic that is now beloved all over the world. Does it mean that only very skilled pastry chefs can make it? Not at all. It's one of the easiest French recipes there is.

INGREDIENTS | SERVES 4

7 ounces dark chocolate (if possible, more than 66% cocoa)

6 large eggs, yolks and egg whites separated

⅛ cup very strong coffee (espresso is best)

¼ teaspoon salt

Spice It Up

Instead of coffee, you can also add a tablespoon of Espelette pepper or paprika. It will add *picante* to the mousse, and you will taste the dark chocolate even better.

1. In a small saucepan, put the dark chocolate (chopped in small pieces, if it's not in chips already). Fill a larger saucepan with water, put the smaller one with the chocolate on top, and warm slowly over moderate heat. Using a wooden spoon, stir the chocolate until it's melted. Remove saucepan from heat.

2. Pour the melted chocolate into a large bowl. Add the 6 egg yolks and stir very quickly. When the mixture is smooth, add the coffee, and stir continuously until smooth again.

3. Put the egg whites and the salt in the bowl of a stand mixer. First whisk moderately for the first minute, then increase the speed as the whites get firmer. Stop when the whites are extra firm. Take ¼ of the egg whites and gently fold them into the chocolate using a wooden spatula, until combined. Then fold in another ¼, and so on until all egg whites are slowly combined into the chocolate.

4. Cover with plastic wrap and put in the fridge for at least 4 hours.

5. Serve cold.

Mousse au Citron (Lemon Mousse)

This lemon mousse is perfect to end a summer meal. Try to use organic lemons so you can use the lemon peel safely.

INGREDIENTS | SERVES 4

3 large eggs, yolks and egg whites separated
¼ teaspoon salt
¾ cup sugar
2 tablespoons cornstarch
¾ cup water
2 lemons, divided
1 tablespoon butter

1. Put the egg yolks in a small saucepan.

2. Put the egg whites in the bowl of a stand mixer, with the salt. First whisk moderately for 1 minute, then increase the speed as the whites get firmer. Stop when the whites are extra firm.

3. In the small saucepan with egg yolks, add the sugar, cornstarch, and the water. Using a box grater, grate the peel of one lemon over the saucepan. Then cut the lemon in two and squeeze it. Squeeze the second lemon, and put the juices of both lemons in the saucepan.

4. Put the saucepan over low heat, and stir continuously until it starts to simmer. Remove from heat once it starts to simmer (it should not boil at all), and add the butter. Stir and let it cool down.

5. Pour the lemon custard in a large serving bowl. When it has cooled down, slowly add the egg whites to the preparation, folding ¼ of the egg whites into the lemon custard at a time, until they are all perfectly combined. Put in the refrigerator for 2 hours.

6. Serve cold.

Riz au Lait (Rice in Milk)

Rice in milk has been treasured by mothers and grandmothers for generations.

INGREDIENTS | SERVES 4

¼ teaspoon salt
½ cup short grain round rice
1 vanilla pod
3 cups whole milk
⅓ cup sugar

Add Pecans

Riz au lait is very soft, creamy, and smooth, but you can add crunch to it by serving with caramelized pecans. Put a nonstick skillet over high heat. When the skillet is very hot, pour 1 cup of halved pecans, stir, and brown them for 3 minutes. Stir continuously, then reduce the heat to low and pour 2 tablespoons sugar on them, stir well, then stop the heat and pour in a bowl. Serve on the side.

1. Fill a large saucepan with water, add the salt, and bring to a boil over high heat. Wash the rice under clean water, drain it, then put it in the boiling water. After 3 minutes, drain the rice and dry it.

2. Slice the top outer layer of the vanilla pod in half lengthwise. In a medium saucepan, bring the milk and the vanilla pod to a boil over medium heat. When the milk starts to boil, add the sugar, and reduce the heat to very low. Take out the vanilla pod, and use a teaspoon to scrape the seeds out. Put the vanilla seeds back in the milk.

3. Add the rice to the warm milk, stir with a wooden tablespoon, and simmer for 40 minutes. Pour in a serving bowl.

4. Serve lukewarm.

Gâteau de Riz (Rice and Caramel Cake)

This very simple rice and caramel cake is always dramatic, with the caramel dripping from the top. French home cooks also love the fact that it is very cheap.

INGREDIENTS | SERVES 8

¼ teaspoon salt
1 cup short grain round rice
1 vanilla pod
4 cups whole milk
½ cup plus ⅔ cup sugar, divided
3 tablespoons water
2 large eggs
2 egg yolks

1. Preheat the oven to 350°F. In a baking dish, pour cold water to a depth of 1½" and place it in the oven.

2. Fill a large saucepan with water, add the salt, and bring to a boil over high heat. Wash the rice under clean water, drain it, then put it in the boiling water. After 3 minutes, drain the rice.

3. Slice the top outer layer of the vanilla pod in half lengthwise. In a medium saucepan, bring the milk and the vanilla pod to a boil over medium heat. When the milk starts to boil, reduce the heat to very low, take out the vanilla pod, and use a spoon to scrape the seeds out. Put the vanilla seeds back in the milk.

4. Prepare a bundt cake mold. In a small saucepan, preferably with a thick bottom, pour ⅔ cup sugar and add 3 tablespoons water, and place over medium heat. Stir with a wooden spoon from time to time, until the sugar bubbles and turns golden (about 2 minutes). Pour immediately in the bundt cake, and tilt the mold until the caramel is distributed everywhere on the mold.

5. In a bowl, whisk the eggs, the yolks, and the remaining sugar until white. Add the rice to the warm milk, stir with a wooden tablespoon, then add the egg and sugar. Whisk continuously until smooth, and pour the mixture in the mold. Put in the oven and cook for 35 minutes.

6. Wait 15 minutes before unmolding. Serve immediately.

CHAPTER 21

Fruit Tarts and Fruit Desserts

Tarte aux Pommes (French Apple Pie)

French apple pie is as easy to make as it is to prepare, especially if you use ready-made applesauce.

INGREDIENTS | SERVES 6

1 *Pâte Brisée* dough (see recipe in Chapter 22)

2 pounds apples, plus 2 apples for the applesauce

2 tablespoons butter, divided

1 teaspoon cinnamon

1 clove

½ cup water

2 tablespoons brown sugar

Easy Applesauce

You can also use 5 tablespoons of ready-made applesauce. Try to use a baby applesauce like Gerber's; it has less sugar and is tastier!

1. Preheat your oven to 350°F.

2. Roll out the dough to a 13" round, and put it on a sheet of parchment paper. Take a 12" tart pan and put the dough and the parchment paper on it. Fold overhanging dough under, and crimp the edge of the crust. Cut away any extra parchment paper. Then, with a fork, make small holes all over the pie dough. Put in the refrigerator.

3. If you're making the applesauce from scratch, peel two apples, core them, and dice them. In a small saucepan, melt 1 tablespoon butter over medium heat, add the diced apples, brown them slowly in butter for about 3 minutes, and add the cinnamon and the clove. Add ½ cup water, stir with a wooden spoon, reduce the heat to low, and simmer until the apples are soft, about 20 minutes. Then mash with a fork and reserve.

4. Put a piece of aluminum foil over the pie dough, then place some dry macaroni or pie weights on it to prevent the crust from bubbling up as it bakes. Put it in the oven for 10 minutes. Peel 2 pounds apples, core them, and cut them in thin slices.

5. Take the pie crust out of the oven, spread the applesauce at the bottom, and arrange the apple slices in an overlapping spiral pattern. Sprinkle 2 tablespoons sugar on top of the fruit. Dice 1 tablespoon butter finely and sprinkle it over the apples well. Bake for 30 minutes.

6. Serve warm, lukewarm, or cold!

Tarte aux Prunes (Plum Pie)

Plum pie is a great summer delight! Add semolina at the bottom to soak up their juices.

INGREDIENTS | SERVES 6

1 *Pâte Brisée* dough (see recipe in Chapter 22)
2 tablespoons semolina
2 pounds plums
2 tablespoons brown sugar
1 tablespoon butter

1. Preheat your oven to 400°F.

2. Roll out the dough to a 13" round, and put it on a sheet of parchment paper. Take a 12" tart pan and put the dough and the parchment paper on it. Fold overhanging dough under, and crimp the edge of the crust. Cut away extra parchment paper. Then, with a fork, make small holes all over the pie dough. Sprinkle semolina all over the bottom.

3. Cut the plums in 4, and arrange them in the crust in a spiral pattern. Sprinkle 2 tablespoons sugar on top. Dice 1 tablespoon butter finely and sprinkle as well. Cook for 35 minutes total, starting on the top rack for about 15 minutes, then baking for the remainder of the time on the lower rack.

4. Serve warm.

Poires au Vin (Pears Poached in Wine)

Pears poached in wine are a great way to finish a meal on a lighter note.

INGREDIENTS | SERVES 4

1 (25-ounce) bottle of red wine
1 vanilla pod
3 cloves
2 star anise pods
3 tablespoons honey
4 pears, peeled

1. In a medium saucepan, bring the wine to a boil over medium-high heat. Slice the top outer layer of the vanilla pod and add it to the wine with the cloves and the star anise pods. Add the honey and stir with a wooden spoon.

2. Using a slotted spoon, put each pear in the boiling wine. Reduce the heat to low and simmer for 25 minutes. Transfer the pears and the cooking liquid into a serving bowl. Take the vanilla pod out, use a teaspoon to scrap the seeds out, and put them back in the wine. Put in the refrigerator 2 hours before serving.

3. Serve the pears in individual bowls, with a ladleful of sweet boiled wine.

Tarte aux Fraises (Strawberry Pie)

This strawberry pie is a classic. You can also make it with fresh raspberries, with Crème Pâtissière (see recipe in Chapter 22) at the bottom, instead of Crème Chantilly.

INGREDIENTS | SERVES 6

1 *Pâte Sablée* dough (see recipe in Chapter 22)

1 cup *Crème Chantilly* (see recipe in Chapter 22)

1 pound strawberries, halved

1. Preheat your oven to 350°F.

2. Roll out the dough to a 13" round, and put it on a sheet of parchment paper. Take a 12" tart pan and put the dough and the parchment paper on it. Fold overhanging dough under, and crimp the edge of the crust. Cut away any extra parchment paper. Then, with a fork, make small holes all over the pie dough. Put a sheet of aluminum foil on it, add dry macaroni or pie weights on it to prevent the crust from bubbling up as it bakes, and put in the oven for 25 minutes.

3. Let the cooked pie crust cool down. Prepare the *Crème Chantilly*. When the crust is cold, spread *Crème Chantilly* on the bottom, then arrange the strawberries in a spiral. Put in the refrigerator for 3 hours.

4. Serve cold.

Tarte Tatin aux Pommes (Upside-Down Apple Pie)

The other classic French apple pie: a baked upside-down apple pie that kids love.

INGREDIENTS | SERVES 6

1¼ cups sugar, divided

3 tablespoons water

3 pounds apples, peeled, cored, and sliced

3 tablespoons butter, diced

1 *Pâte Brisée* dough (see recipe in Chapter 22)

A Great Accident

Tarte Tatin was invented by the Tatin sisters, who owned a small restaurant in the Loire Valley, at the end of the nineteenth century. Legend has it that one sister was so stressed that she didn't see that she put the apples first in the pie dish, and then the dough. They served it to the customers, who instantly loved it.

1. Preheat your oven to 425°F.

2. In a small saucepan bring ¾ cup sugar and 3 tablespoons water slowly to a caramel-like consistency over medium heat. As soon as it gets golden, pour it in a 12" tart pan. Tilt to let the caramel spread.

3. Stick apple slices in the caramel. Sprinkle ½ cup sugar on them, then the butter.

4. Roll out the dough to a 13" round, and lay it over the apples. Using a knife, trim off any dough that is more than 1" beyond the edge of the pan. Tuck the dough in around the edges of the pan.

5. Put in the oven for 10 minutes at 425°F, then reduce to 400°F and cook for another 30 minutes. As soon as you take it out of the oven, put a large plate on the pie, and turn it over. The crust will be on the bottom and the caramelized apples on top.

6. Serve warm, lukewarm, or cold.

Tarte Tatin aux Abricots (Apricot Upside-Down Pie)

This apricot upside-down pie is also delicious, especially with a touch of rosemary.

INGREDIENTS | SERVES 6

1¼ cups sugar, divided
3 tablespoons water
18 apricots, cored
3 tablespoons butter, diced
2 rosemary sprigs, 1 chopped, 1 whole
1 *Pâte Brisée* dough (see recipe in Chapter 22)

1. Preheat your oven to 400°F.

2. In a small saucepan, bring ¾ cup sugar and 3 tablespoons water slowly to a caramel-like consistency over medium heat. As soon as it gets golden, pour it in a 12" tart pan. Put the apricots in the caramel. Sprinkle ½ cup sugar and the butter on them. Add the chopped rosemary, and place the whole sprig in the middle.

3. Roll out the dough to a 13" round, and lay it over the apricots. Trim any dough that extends more than 1" past the edge of the pan, then tuck it in around the edges of the pan. Cook for 35 minutes. As soon as you take it out of the oven, put a large plate on the pie, and turn it over.

4. Serve lukewarm.

Tarte Tatin aux Mangues (Mango Tart)

This mango tart is sweet and sour all at once.

INGREDIENTS | SERVES 6

1¼ cups sugar, divided
3 tablespoons water
3 mangoes, peeled and sliced
3 tablespoons butter, diced
1 *Pâte Brisée* dough (see recipe in Chapter 22)

1. Preheat your oven to 400°F.

2. In a small saucepan, bring ¾ cup sugar and 3 tablespoons water slowly to a caramel-like consistency over medium heat. As soon as it gets golden, pour it in a 12" tart pan. Put mangoes in the caramel. Sprinkle ½ cup sugar and the butter on them.

3. Roll out the dough to a 13" round, and lay it on the mangoes. Trim excess dough, and tuck it in around the edges of the pan. Cook for 35 minutes. As soon as you take it out of the oven, put a large plate on the pie, and turn it over.

4. Serve lukewarm or cold.

Tarte aux Pruneaux (Prune Pie)

Prune pie is a traditional recipe from the southwest of France, where prunes have been grown for centuries now. The original recipe calls for Armagnac (a brandy from the same region), but this one is alcohol free, so it's good for kids!

INGREDIENTS | SERVES 6

1 *Pâte Feuilletée* (see recipe in Chapter 22)
1 vanilla pod
1 cup water
½ cup sugar
1 organic orange, thinly sliced
1 pound prunes, pitted

1. Preheat your oven at 400°F.

2. Roll out the dough to a 13" round, and put it on a sheet of parchment paper. Take a 12" tart pan and put the dough and the parchment paper on it. Fold overhanging dough under, and crimp the edge of the crust. Cut away any extra parchment paper. Then, with a fork, make small holes all over the pie dough. Put in the refrigerator.

3. Slice the top outer layer of the vanilla pod in half lengthwise. Fill a small saucepan with 1 cup of water. Add the sugar, the vanilla pod, and the orange slices. Bring to a boil over medium heat, and simmer for 10 minutes. Add the pitted prunes, and reduce the heat to low. Simmer for 30 minutes.

4. Using a slotted spoon, take the prunes out of the saucepan and layer them in the pie crust in a spiral pattern. Put in the oven for 10 minutes at 400°F, then reduce the heat to 350°F and cook for another 20 minutes.

5. Bring the orange slices and the sugar in a saucepan to a boil over high heat, and reduce to half. Use a strainer to drain the syrup into a small bowl, and pour on the pie as soon as it's out of the oven.

6. Serve immediately.

Fraises au Vin (Strawberries in Wine)

This strawberries in wine cold soup was very common in rural France before WWII. Very refreshing!

INGREDIENTS | SERVES 4

2 cups red wine
1 vanilla pod
2 cloves
2 star anise pods
1 teaspoon ground ginger
¼ cup sugar
1 pound strawberries, hulled and halved
Juice of 1 lemon

1. In a medium saucepan, bring the wine to a boil over medium-high heat. Slice the top outer layer of the vanilla pod and add it to the wine with the cloves, star anises, and ginger. Add the sugar and stir with a wooden spoon. As soon as it begins to boil, reduce to low and simmer for 15 minutes. Pour in a large serving bowl and let it cool down to room temperature.

2. Take the vanilla pod out, scratch the seeds out with a teaspoon and put them back in the wine. Over a large bowl, cut the strawberries in half and sprinkle the lemon juice on them. Add them to the wine when it's cold. Put in the refrigerator for 3 hours.

3. Serve cold in individual bowls, with the cooking liquid.

Pommes au Four (Baked Apples)

Apples just baked in the oven make a simple yet delightful family dessert.

INGREDIENTS | SERVES 4

4 organic apples
4 tablespoons honey
4 tablespoons raisins
1 teaspoon ground ginger
2 tablespoons butter, cut in 4
 equal parts

1. Preheat the oven at 350°F. Using a paring knife, remove cores to ½" of the bottom of each apple. Use a spoon to dig out the seeds.

2. In a small bowl, combine the honey, raisins, and ginger. Using a spoon, stuff each apple with the mixture. Top with half a tablespoon of butter. Place apples in a baking pan, pour cold water into the pan to a depth of 1", and bake for 40 minutes.

3. Serve warm.

Poires Belle-Hélène

This classic recipe of poached pears in chocolate sauce was invented in the nineteenth century and named after a famous operetta. It used to be served with crystallized violets, but you can use sliced almonds.

INGREDIENTS | SERVES 4

4 cups cold water

2 cups sugar

Juice of 1 lemon

1 vanilla pod

4 pears, peeled

4.5 ounces dark chocolate, at least 66% cocoa

½ cup *crème fraîche* or whipping cream

4 tablespoons sliced almonds

1. Fill a large saucepan with 4 cups of cold water. Add the sugar and lemon juice. Slice the vanilla pod lengthwise, and add it to the saucepan. Bring to a boil over medium-high heat.

2. Add pears to the boiling water, then reduce the heat to low and simmer for 25 minutes. When the pears have cooled down, take them out with a slotted spoon and reserve. Increase the heat under the saucepan to high, and boil until the sweetened water has reduced by ¾. Then take the vanilla pod out, use a teaspoon to scrape the seeds out, put the seeds back in the saucepan, and discard the pod.

3. Chop the dark chocolate into small pieces if it's not chocolate chips. Put in the saucepan containing the reduced sugar syrup, and lower the heat to medium-low. Stir continuously as you add the *crème fraîche*, until the chocolate mixture is combined.

4. Serve in individual bowls. First put the pear in the bowl, then pour warm chocolate sauce over it, and sprinkle sliced almonds on top.

Pêches Grillées (Roasted Peaches)

Roasted peaches are the perfect dessert in summer after an intense barbecue day. Add a little thyme and salted butter to make these sweet and sour, or you can just make them plain with justunsalted butter and sugar. You can also use nectarines.

INGREDIENTS | SERVES 4

4 peaches

2 tablespoons salted butter, cut in 4 equal parts

4 thyme sprigs

4 tablespoons brown sugar

1. Preheat the oven to 350°F. Cut the peaches in half and discard the kernel.

2. Lay them in a baking dish. Put ½ tablespoon butter where the kernel used to be on each half. Add a small thyme sprig, and sprinkle sugar on top of each. Put in the oven for 20 minutes.

3. Serve warm, with a scoop of vanilla ice cream.

Pêches Melba

Another classic fruit dessert, Peach Melba (peaches with raspberry purée and vanilla ice cream) was invented by the great chef Auguste Escoffier at the end of the nineteenth century. This recipe tries to be closer to the basic ingredients: no fancy syrup, it's all about the fresh fruits.

INGREDIENTS | SERVES 4

4 cups cold water

2 cups sugar

1 vanilla pod

4 organic peaches

1 pound raspberries

5 fresh mint leaves

2 cups vanilla ice cream

Organic Skin

Each time you cook with an unpeeled fruit, or use the peel, try to buy it organic. You don't want any strange chemicals on the fruit you cook with.

1. Fill a large saucepan with 4 cups of cold water. Add the sugar. Slice the vanilla pod lengthwise, and add it to the saucepan. Bring to a boil over medium-high heat, and boil for 5 minutes. Using a slotted spoon, take the vanilla pod out, scrape the inside with a teaspoon to take out the seeds, and put the seeds back in the still boiling saucepan. Discard the pod.

2. Add the peaches to the boiling water, then reduce the heat to medium-low and simmer for 10 minutes. Stop the heat and let the fruit and the syrup cool down at room temperature for 20 minutes.

3. Put the raspberries and the mint in a blender, and purée them together. Pour in a small bowl. When the peaches are cold enough, peel them and cut them in half. Discard the kernels.

4. Serve in individual bowls. First put 1 scoop of vanilla ice cream at the bottom, then two peach halves, then top with the raspberries and mint purée.

CHAPTER 22

Basic Sauces and Doughs

French Mayonnaise

This French egg sauce is part of many recipes and a great condiment.
Of course, you should always make it from scratch.

INGREDIENTS | YIELDS 4 CUPS

6 egg yolks

1 teaspoon salt

1 teaspoon ground black pepper

2 tablespoons red wine vinegar (or cider vinegar, or lemon juice), divided

4 cups sunflower or canola oil

3 tablespoons boiling water

Room Temperature First!

The secret to a good mayonnaise is to never use the eggs straight out of the refrigerator. Leave them at room temperature for one hour, and you'll see the difference.

1. Fill a small saucepan with water and bring to a boil over high heat.

2. In a bowl, using a whisk (or in a stand mixer), whisk the egg yolks with the salt, pepper, and 1 tablespoon vinegar.

3. Add the oil, at first drop by drop, and go on whisking. After a couple of minutes, pour the oil more steadily, but slowly, still whisking firmly.

4. Add the rest of the vinegar as you go on whisking.

5. When the sauce is thick enough, add the tablespoons of boiling water: It will help the sauce stay thick.

6. Put in the refrigerator and store for no more than 48 hours.

Aioli Sauce

This Aioli Sauce comes from the south of France. It's part of the great fish aioli tradition, but can also be used as a great dip. Lots of garlic!

INGREDIENTS | YIELDS ½ CUP

6 garlic cloves, peeled and crushed

1 teaspoon salt

2 egg yolks

1 teaspoon ground black pepper

⅓ cup olive oil

1. When you've peeled the garlic, use one clove to rub on the surface of the bowl you're going to make the aioli in. Put the others in a mortar with a teaspoon of salt. Crush them with the pestle.

2. Put the crushed garlic cloves in the serving bowl. Add the egg yolks and the pepper, and whisk the mixture steadily. Pour the olive oil in little by little, whisking without stopping, until the sauce is thick.

3. Cover and put in the refrigerator to chill before you use it. The aioli must be very cold!

Béarnaise Sauce

Invented for good King Henri IV, who came from the Bearn region in the southwest of France, this sauce is perfect with grilled meat or grilled fish.

INGREDIENTS | YIELDS 3 CUPS

5 tablespoons tarragon leaves, minced

4 small shallots, peeled and minced

1 teaspoon salt

2 teaspoons ground black pepper

½ cup red vinegar

5 egg yolks

2 cups butter, melted and clarified

1. In a small saucepan, combine the tarragon leaves, the shallots, salt, pepper, and the vinegar over medium-high heat. Reduce to a simmer and cook for around 10 minutes. Let it cool.

2. Melt the butter in another saucepan, over very low heat. Spoon out the foam that appears on the surface.

3. Put the vinegar pan in a *bain-marie*: Place it over another larger saucepan, over medium heat. Add the egg yolks and whisk firmly. When the sauce starts to thicken, stop the heat and add the melted clarified butter little by little, still whisking.

4. Pour in a sauceboat and serve lukewarm.

Vinaigrette (Vinaigrette Dressing)

French dressing is nothing like the sauce you can buy in American grocery stores. This recipe can be made with all combinations of oils and vinegars. The most common is red wine vinegar and sunflower oil.

INGREDIENTS | SERVES 4 (MAKES ¼ CUP)

1 tablespoon vinegar
½ teaspoon salt
1 teaspoon ground black pepper
1 teaspoon Dijon mustard (optional)
3 tablespoons oil

Choose Quality

The secret to any good dressing is the ingredients you use: Choose oil and vinegar of high quality, and the whole salad will taste better.

1. In a small bowl, or in the large bowl you to use toss the salad, combine the vinegar with salt and stir well with a wooden spoon. (Salt doesn't dissolve in oil, so it has to be done before.) Add the pepper, and the mustard if you want to spice it more. Stir until totally mixed.

2. Add a first tablespoon of oil and stir. Slowly add the other tablespoons of oil, stirring continuously.

3. Add the salad ingredients and toss, or store the dressing in an airtight container in the fridge. You can keep it for a week, just whisk it well before using.

Vinaigrette à l'Echalotte (Vinaigrette Dressing with Shallots)

The recipe works with any kind of fresh herbs. To make any vinaigrette in larger quantities, always remember the golden rule: 1 measure of vinegar for 3 measures of oil.

INGREDIENTS | SERVES 4 (MAKES ¼ CUP)

1 medium shallot, peeled and minced (or 1 tablespoon fresh herbs, such as parsley, basil, mint)
1 tablespoon red wine vinegar
½ teaspoon salt
1 teaspoon ground black pepper
3 tablespoons oil

1. Put shallot (or fresh herbs) in a large salad bowl.

2. Add the red wine vinegar and the salt and stir well using a wooden spoon. Add the pepper. Stir until totally mixed. Stir in 1 tablespoon of oil, then slowly add the other tablespoons, stirring continuously.

3. Use immediately.

Béchamel

*This warm sauce is one of the "mother sauces" of French cuisine. It is
used in many recipes, and is a great base for other sauces.*

**INGREDIENTS | SERVES 4 (MAKES
4½ CUPS)**

4 cups whole milk
⅓ cup butter
½ cup flour
1 teaspoon ground nutmeg

1. In a medium saucepan over medium-low heat, bring the milk to a boil. Remove it from the heat as soon as it starts boiling.

2. In another medium saucepan, melt the butter over medium-low heat. It should not get brown. Take the saucepan off of heat, pour in the flour, and whisk immediately. Put back on medium-low heat until the mixture thickens slightly. Take the saucepan off of the heat, pour in the hot milk, and whisk until combined. Put back over low heat, and whisk continuously until the sauce is thick.

3. Add the ground nutmeg and use immediately.

Hollandaise Sauce

*This warm sauce is often served with fish. Although its name means "Dutch sauce," it was
invented in France in the seventeenth century, and named after the war with Holland.*

**INGREDIENTS | SERVES 4 (MAKES
1¼ CUPS)**

1 cup butter, diced
3 egg yolks
1 tablespoon water
Juice of ½ lemon

1. In a small saucepan, melt the butter over low heat.

2. In a medium saucepan, put the egg yolks, the water, and the juice of half a lemon. Whisk until the mixture is combined. Put over medium-low heat, and whisk continuously (be careful not to let the egg yolks cook). Whisk until you get a kind of mousse, then pour the butter in it and whisk again.

3. Serve immediately.

Confit de Canard (Preserved Duck)

Confit de canard, preserved duck, is a classic of southwest of France cuisine. Preserving in duck fat is not only a great way to store a great meat for a long time, it also adds incredible flavor to the duck flesh. Try to choose the fattest duck you can!

INGREDIENTS | SERVES 4

½ cup kosher salt
4 garlic cloves, peeled
2 tablespoons thyme
4 fat duck legs
1½ cups duck fat

1. In a small bowl, mix the kosher salt, the garlic cloves, and the thyme. Put the duck legs in a large dish, and pour the salt mixture over them. Rub all over legs; the skin has to be covered on all sides. Cover the dish in plastic wrap and put in the refrigerator for 24 hours.

2. Preheat the oven to 320°F. Rinse the legs under fresh water, then dry them with a paper towel. In a medium saucepan, slowly melt the duck fat over medium heat. Ready a French oven, or any baking dish with a cover that fits the 4 duck legs all lying in the bottom close to each other. Put the duck legs in the dish, and pour in the melted duck fat. Then cover and put in the oven for 2 hours. Remove from oven and let everything cool down at room temperature.

3. Using a slotted spoon, remove duck legs and put them at the bottom of an airtight container. Put a strainer on top of the box and pour the fat through it. Close the container, and put in the refrigerator.

4. You can keep the preserved duck for 1 month in the refrigerator in glass jars, and for over one year if you sterilize the jars.

Pâte Brisée (Shortcrust Pastry)

Pâte Brisée is the crust most often used in daily French cuisine, for quiches, savory tarts, and sweet pies. You don't need to add sugar for a dessert pie. Try to use the best quality of butter, it makes all the difference.

INGREDIENTS | MAKES 1 CRUST

2 cups flour

½ cup butter, diced, and at room temperature

1 large egg

⅛ cup water

½ teaspoon salt

1. Sift the flour into a large bowl. Create a well at the center of the mixture, like a volcano crater. Add the diced butter to the center of the crater. Use your hands to mix the butter and the flour together, pressing the butter into the flour with the palm of your hands.

2. Create a hole at the center of the mixture again. In a small bowl, beat the egg and the water together. Pour into the center of the crater, add the salt, and mix all elements with a pastry spatula. Once it starts to really combine, squeeze it together with your hands until you can create a large ball. Cover it with plastic wrap and put in the refrigerator for 1 hour.

3. To roll it out, use 2 parchment paper sheets. Place dough on top of one sheet, and then put another sheet on top of the ball of dough. Roll your pin over the second parchment paper sheet. This will allow you to roll a thinner crust without the dough sticking to the rolling pin.

4. Use for quiches or tarts.

Pâte Sablée (Sweet Pastry)

Pâte Sablée means "sandy" crust, because of the way it is made: Crumbling together butter and flour makes the mixture look like sand.

INGREDIENTS | MAKES ENOUGH FOR 1 CRUST

2 cups flour

½ cup butter, diced, and at room temperature

1 large egg

1 cup granulated sugar

½ teaspoon salt

Fruit Lover

This crust is used a lot for fruit tarts, like the Strawberry Pie in Chapter 21. It doesn't need to be precooked to be used, and is sometimes cooked alone, the fruits being added fresh on top.

1. In a large bowl, combine the flour and the diced butter. Use the tips of your fingers to pinch the butter into the flour, as you would crumble sand on the beach. Pinch and crumble for 5 minutes, or until all pieces of butter are coated in flour, and the mixture looks like sand.

2. Create a large well at the center of the mixture, like a volcano crater. In a small bowl, beat the egg and the sugar until it whitens. Pour in the center of the crater, add the salt, and mix all elements very quickly, always with your fingers. Be careful not to work the dough too much. As soon as you can, try creating a ball by pressing the mixture gently into your palms. You can press the dough against the table with the palm of your hands, and finally create a large compact ball.

3. Let it rest for 1 hour in the refrigerator, wrapped in plastic wraps before using.

Pâte Feuilletée (Puff Pastry)

This is the Holy Grail of all French pastry apprentices! Puff pastry is easy to buy already frozen, but there's nothing like making your own.

INGREDIENTS | MAKES ENOUGH FOR 1 BATCH OF *MILLEFEUILLE*

2 cups flour

2 tablespoons butter plus ¾ cup, at room temperature

½ cup cold water

½ teaspoon salt

1. Sift the flour into a large bowl. Create a large well at the center of the mixture, like a volcano crater. In a small saucepan, slowly melt 2 tablespoons butter and pour the butter in the hole in the flour. Add the water and the salt. Using a wooden spatula, stir quickly, and then combine with your hands. This whole process should be done in seconds; do not overwork the dough. Using the palms of your hands, flatten the dough (this particular part is called the *détrempe*) and cover it with plastic wrap. Put in the refrigerator for 2 hours.

2. After 2 hours, put ¾ cup butter on a parchment paper sheet, then lay another parchment sheet on top. With a rolling pin roll it out until you have a ½"-thick square. Reserve. Sprinkle some flour on your work surface, and put the *détrempe* on it. Roll it out until it's a ⅞"-thick square. Place the square of butter in the center of the dough. Fold each corner of the dough in and over the butter, as if it was an envelope.

3. Roll the squared envelope into a rectangle. Fold it in three, to create a square. Give a ¼ turn to the dough, and roll it into a rectangle again. Fold in three. Wrap in plastic and put in the refrigerator for 30 minutes.

4. After 30 minutes, roll the dough into a rectangle again, fold in three, turn, roll, and fold again. Wrap in plastic and put in the refrigerator for 30 minutes, and then repeat rolling and folding one more time.

5. You can use it at once or freeze it flat. Never shape it into a ball.

Crème Pâtissière (Pastry Cream)

A great basic in French pastry, Crème Pâtissière is used in a lot of cakes.

INGREDIENTS | MAKES APPROXIMATELY 2 CUPS

1 vanilla pod
2 cups whole milk
6 egg yolks
½ cup sugar
¼ cup flour

1. Slice the vanilla pod lengthwise. Put in a small saucepan with the milk. Bring to a boil over low heat.

2. In the bowl of a stand mixer, whisk the egg yolks and the sugar until the mixture whitens. Add the flour and stir rapidly, using a wooden spoon.

3. Take the vanilla pod out of the milk, scrape out the seeds with a teaspoon, and put them back in the milk. Slowly pour the milk into the egg mixture, stirring continuously.

4. Put mixture back in the saucepan, on very low heat. Stir continuously and stop as soon as the first bubbles appear.

5. Pour in bowl and reserve. It can be stored 48 hours in the refrigerator.

Crème Chantilly (Chantilly Cream)

Who invented the wonderful Crème Chantilly in France in the eighteenth century? Historians are still debating it, but food lovers all over the world all agree: Whipped cream is just too good to be true.

INGREDIENTS | MAKES APPROXIMATELY 3–4 CUPS

2 cups whipping cream
⅔ cup powdered sugar

1. An hour ahead, make sure that your whipping cream is in the refrigerator, and put the bowl of the stand mixer in the refrigerator too. You can also put the bowl in the freezer for 20 minutes.

2. Put the whipping cream in the chilled bowl of a stand mixer. Start whisking slowly, then more firmly after 20 seconds. When the cream starts to get thick, pour in the powdered sugar. Keep whisking until the cream is fluffy. Be careful not to overbeat it; it will turn to butter!

3. Keep in the refrigerator for 2 hours before serving.

Crème Anglaise (Custard Cream)

This custard cream is used to serve with a piece of cake, for example.

INGREDIENTS | MAKES APPROXIMATELY 2 CUPS

1 vanilla pod
2 cups whole milk
5 egg yolks
½ cup sugar
1 teaspoon cornstarch

1. Slice the vanilla pod lengthwise. Put in a small saucepan with the milk. Bring to a boil over low heat. Take the vanilla pod out when the boiling starts. Scrape the vanilla seeds out using a spoon, and put back in the milk.

2. In the bowl of a stand mixer, whisk the egg yolks, sugar, and cornstarch until the mixture whitens. Pour ⅓ of the hot milk in the bowl, stirring rapidly with a wooden spoon. Pour the mixture into the rest of the milk in the saucepan. Stir continuously, over very low heat. You know that the cream is ready when it is thick enough that if you slide your finger along the stirring spoon, the custard doesn't flow back to cover the track.

3. Pour in a large bowl and immediately put in the refrigerator for 2 hours.

Crème Anglaise à la Menthe (Mint Custard Cream)

This fresh mint-flavored Crème Anglaise is amazing with a chocolate cake.

1. In a small saucepan, pour the milk and add the mint leaves. Bring to a boil over low heat. As soon as the boiling starts, remove from the heat, cover, and let the mint infuse the milk for 15 minutes. Then use a spoon to take the mint leaves out, and put the milk back on a medium-high heat.

2. In the bowl of a stand mixer, whisk the egg yolks, sugar, and the cornstarch until the mixture whitens. Pour ⅓ of the milk over the mixture and stir rapidly, using a wooden spoon. Pour the mixture into the rest of the milk in the saucepan. Set the heat to very low, and stir continuously with the wooden spoon. You know that the cream is ready when it is thick enough that if you slide your finger along the stirring spoon, the custard doesn't flow back to cover the track.

3. Pour in an airtight container and put in the refrigerator immediately. Refrigerate 2 hours before serving.

Appendix A: French Cooking Glossary

Bain-marie

Often used to cook delicate foods, this is similar to a "double boiler" in America. For instance, you would put a small saucepan over a larger saucepan filled with water and boil.

Bien cuisine

The French way of saying "cooking well." It is eating something that tastes good, but that is also good for you and is well balanced.

Bien manger

The French way of saying "eating well."

Bouquet garni

A bundle of herbs, usually tied together with a string. It may contain bay leaf, thyme, and parsley, but it can also contain rosemary, chervil, or tarragon.

Charcuterie

Various prepared meats that are often served with cheese or bread.

Cornichons

Very small pickles, also known as gherkins. They are only about one to two inches long.

Crème fraîche

A soured, thick cream used for cooking.

Crêpes

Paper-thin pancakes usually cooked in a crêpe pan. Sweet crêpes are generally made with wheat flour while savory crêpes are made with nonwheat flours such as buckwheat. They are then stuffed with either savory or sweet fillings.

Crudités

A more traditional French appetizer that consists of whole or sliced raw vegetables, sometimes served with a dipping sauce.

Entrées

In France, *entrée* means "appetizer," unlike in America where *entrée* usually refers to the main course of a meal.

Espelette pepper

A mild red chili pepper that is grown in the southwest of France.

Foie gras

A prepared food made from the liver of a specially fattened duck. It is often eaten spread on bread.

Fromage

The French word for "cheese." Popular French cheeses include Brie, Camembert, Boursin, and Roquefort.

Huile de colza
Canola oil.

Huile de noix
Walnut oil.

Huile de tournesol
Sunflower oil.

La gourmandize
The French way of saying "the love of good food."

Le Goûter
Literally translates to "snack." In France, kids will snack at *quatre-heures*, or 4 P.M.

Le siècle d'or de la Gastronomie
"The golden century of gastronomy."

Nouvelle cuisine
Literally translates to "the new cuisine." This signifies a change in how French chefs prepared food, switching from heavy sauces to reduced stocks. It also emphasized the flavor and pleasure of fresh ingredients.

Œufs
Eggs.

Petit Déjeuner
"Breakfast" in French. This usually consists of bread, croissant, or brioche with butter and jam.

Petit je ne sais quoi
That little thing that will suddenly change everything. It's a touch of spice, a dash of orange blossom water, or just the best meat in town.

Plats Mijotés
The French term for "slow-cooked main dishes."

Poisson
The French word for "fish."

Pommes de Terre
The French term for "potatoes."

Quatre-heures
This refers to the 4 P.M. hour when snacks are served for French children.

Roux
A mixture created by cooking flour and some sort of fat, like butter. This acts as a thickening agent for the final dish.

Viandes
The French word for "meat."

Appendix B: Website Resources

www.frenchandparfait.com
Author Cécile Delarue's website has recipes, blog posts, and photos showing visitors how to cook delicious French food right at home.

www.france.fr/en/gastronomy/ regional-specialities.html
This site was made by the French government to promote French gastronomy to English readers. You will find regional specialty recipes and useful tips such as how to choose cheese and how to eat *foie gras*.

www.kqed.org/food/jacquespepin
Jacques Pépin is a legendary French chef, television personality, and author. His website has recipes for treats like Chocolate Soufflè Cake with Raspberry Sauce and Cream Puff Potatoes. He also offers a techniques slideshow for things like cutting up a duck, stuffing a turkey, and shucking a clam.

www.hertzmann.com
Have a question about French food or culture? This French-focused website has videos, articles, recipes, and a blog.

www.french-at-a-touch.com/Gourmet/ gourmet.htm
With tons of recipes as well as information on famous French restaurants and other goodies like pairing wine with cheese, this site has it all.

www.frenchcookingfordummies.com
This site has a ton of everyday French recipes for anything from appetizers to main dishes and dessert. Each recipe comes from blog editor Véro, who lives and works in Paris.

www.saveur.com/cuisine/French
Saveur has information on food from around the world, as well as tips and techniques for cooking, the best wine and drinks, and kitchen gadgets and tools.

www.foodnetwork.com/topics/french .html
The Food Network has tons of French recipes from a variety of famous chefs including Ina Gerten, Paula Deen, and Anne Burrell.

Index

Note: Page numbers in **bold** indicate recipe category lists.